THE CASE FOR
ENLARGEMENT THEOLOGY

THE CASE FOR ENLARGEMENT THEOLOGY

Alex Jacob

Glory to Glory Publications

First published in 2010 in Great Britain by
Glory to Glory Publications, an imprint of Buy Research Ltd.

This revised edition published in 2011.

Glory to Glory Publications
PO Box 212 SAFFRON WALDEN CB10 2UU

Cover design by Roger Judd

ISBN 978-0-9567831-1-0

Printed in Great Britain by
CPI Books (Croydon) CR0 4DT

Contents

ACKNOWLEDGEMENTS

A book drawing upon significant research in the areas of Jewish-Christian relations and Biblical Theology would not be possible without the help, wisdom and encouragement of numerous teachers, theologians and fellow students over many years. However I would particularly like to acknowledge the support from Northern College (Manchester), Westminster College (Cambridge) and St John's College (Nottingham). I would also like to thank members of Linton URC and the trustees and staff of The Church's Ministry among Jewish People (CMJ), without whose help, kindness and prayers this book would have simply remained as 'a good idea'.

On a specific personal note I acknowledge with thankfulness the creative thinking and good scholarship of my academic supervisors, John Kelly, Ian Paul and Richard Harvey. I also would like to acknowledge the important contributions to this publication by Peter Sammons, John Proctor and the team at Terranova books.

Finally, my immediate family, Mandy, Luke, Emily and Ben, your company, love and support has kept me going through the struggles of part-time academic study, research work and writing — Thank you!

If I stand Lord let me stand on the promise that you
will pull me through —
and if I can't
let me fall on the grace that first brought me to you.

FOREWORD
by David Pawson

I doubt if this will ever be a popular book. It looks and reads like a thesis for a higher degree and probably was. 'My academic supervisors' in the Acknowledgements, over 500 footnotes and a bibliography of over 200 authors confirm this impression. It is clearly written for the theologically literate.

Nevertheless, I enjoyed reading it and, more importantly, regard it as a fresh, stimulating and necessary contribution to the contemporary debate on Jewish/Christian relations. For one thing it takes seriously the increasing number of Messianic Jews and their communities, a new feature on the landscape which embarrasses both sides of the dialogue.

To appreciate the author's courage and conviction we need to look at a wider context. Our Bible is made up of three quarters of Jewish scriptures and one quarter Christian scriptures. The most fundamental issue in interpreting and applying the whole is how these two parts (Old and New Testaments) relate to each other. To put it another way – is there continuity or discontinuity between them? Or a mixture of both and, if so, in what proportion?

At one extreme of discontinuity is Marcionite theology, named after the heretic who taught two different Gods, the harsh and cruel one of the Old Testament against the gentle and kind one of the New. (He also had problems with parts of the New, particularly the Book of Revelation, with over 300 allusions to the Old). There appears to be an incipient revival of this today, both in the general neglect of the Old Testament by many Christians and the emphasis on God's 'unconditional' love.

Towards the opposite end of the spectrum is Reformed theology, believing in 'one covenant of grace' running straight through both Testaments. Israel can be called the Church and the Church can be called Israel (citing Acts 7:38 and Galatians 6:16 as 'proof texts'). Direct lines of equivalence are drawn (for example, between circumcision and infant baptism, sabbath and Sunday). However, advocates are right to emphasise that the Holy One of Israel and the Father of Jesus are one and the same God; and that Abraham and Paul were both justified by faith.

It is against this backcloth that we can assess Alex Jacob's proposition. Positively, it is a plea for a biblical theology of more continuity, for which he has coined the label 'Enlarged'. Negatively, it is a direct challenge to current theologies with too much discontinuity, two in particular.

On the one hand is 'Replacement theology', favoured in evangelical circles, which believes that God has changed his agency on earth from the ethnic Jewish nation to the international Christian Church. Promises made to the former have been transferred to the latter, albeit adapted to a metaphorical and spiritual fulfilment rather than a literal and physical one.

On the other hand, favoured in liberal circles, is the 'Two Covenant' theology, teaching salvation comes to Jews and Christians differently, each through their own relationship with God. It is therefore wrong for either to 'convert' the other. Mutual respect and tolerance are the right attitude, expressed in dialogue rather than evangelism.

There could, and perhaps should have been, a third major target: 'Dispensational' theology, which keeps Israel and the Church in even greater isolation from each other and holds a double replacement view: the Church having replaced Israel as a temporary 'interim', only until it is 'raptured' out of the world so that Israel can regain her primary role. Alex Jacob does deal with this, almost as an aside, perhaps because it is far more prominent in the USA than the UK, where it is profoundly linked with Christian Zionism. Superficially, this seems inconsistent until it is realised that the return of the Jews to their promised land is seen as a sign of the imminent escape of Christians, leaving Jews to cope with the 'Big Trouble'.

Over against these two major and one minor targets of his polemic, all stressing discontinuity, the author presents his case for continuity, particularly in God's chosen people on earth. Not surprisingly, he focuses on Romans chapters 9-11, the only New Testament passage to major on relations between Christians (especially Gentiles) and Jews (believing and unbelieving) and therefore between Israel and the Church. He rightly criticises those who dismiss this part of Paul's letter as a parenthesis, an excursus or an appendix, instead of viewing it as an 'integral' portion of the whole.

I would go further and see it as the climax, revealing the pastoral purpose of the epistle: to reconcile arrogant Gentile believers with returning Jewish believers after Emperor Claudius' eviction (Acts 18:2).

The exegesis of this crucial passage occupies eight out of thirteen chapters in the book. And these are so full of quotations from other writers, from Karl Barth to Rowan Williams, Archbishop of Canterbury, that the author's own views are somewhat overshadowed (a degree candidate must impress examiners with wide reading!).

But the heart of it is the olive tree metaphor, from which *some* Jewish branches were pruned and 'wild' Gentile shoots were grafted in *among* those who remained. Ultimately, the 'natural' branches 'as a whole' will be re-grafted into their own tree. It is the 'enlargement' of the whole tree to include the Gentile as well as the Jew which is the essence of 'Enlargement Theology'.

Another essential element is that 'God's one ultimate purpose is being worked out within three contradictory communities' (I would prefer to say that they are 'complementary'), namely the

Church, Israel and Messianic Jewish assemblies. Personally, I see them as two overlapping circles rather than three separate spheres, with Messianic Jews as the overlap, belonging to both Church and Israel, rather than neither. Whatever, the growth in this group in our day means that they must be taken into account. The tensions they raise will only be resolved in an eschatalogical context when the two circles finally merge into the 'one new man/humanity' which was God's intention all along.

I have indicated some of the strengths in the case for 'Enlargement Theology' presented here but I must also draw attention to a serious weakness. Restoring the biblical continuity of God's people must be balanced by the biblical discontinuity between the 'old' and 'new' covenants. But which is the 'old'? (There is no argument about which is the 'new'.) Many have been misled by the labels 'Old' and 'New' *Testaments*, a synonym for 'covenant'. So they lump together all the covenants in the Old Testament into one between God and Israel, making no differentiation between them. Alex Jacob has fallen into this trap. Throughout the book he refers to '*the* covenant' of God with Israel, as if there were only one, preferring the adjective 'covenantal' to the noun. He does acknowledge the plural noun 'covenants' in Paul's list of Israel's privileges (in Romans 9:4), even listing them, but quickly returns to the singular.

It is only the Mosaic covenant established on Sinai that is treated as 'old' and therefore rendered obsolete by the 'new' Messianic covenant established on Golgotha (Hebrews 10:15-18, quoting Jeremiah 31:33-34). The Abrahamic and Davidic covenants, both of which had international components, are continued into the 'new' relationship (see, for example, Hebrews 6:13-20).

Gentile believers are certainly freed from Mosaic laws, hence Paul's opposition to circumcision (Galatians 5:2-4; cf. Romans 7:4). Whether Jewish believers should keep them as a matter of human culture or divine command, is debated among

Messianic Jews today, and is as yet unresolved. One thing is clear: their salvation does not depend on it.

In spite of this reservation, I urge clergy, ministers, pastors and elders to purchase and study this volume. Whether the label 'Enlargement' catches on or not, here is a vital contribution to the 'continuity-discontinuity' debate which can help to release the 'impasse' in Jewish-Christian relations.

INTRODUCTION TO
THE REVISED EDITION

I am very pleased to present this revised edition of *The Case for Enlargement Theology*. The original paperback edition came out in April 2010 and was generally well received.

Since April 2010, I have shared in many personal conversations and much correspondence with a range of Church and Rabbinical leaders, theologians, students and ministry colleagues who have read the book. As a result of this, I have been able to correct a number of typo errors and clarify some sentences. I have also added to the Bibliography and included a new section about the Marranos in regards to the teaching about the development of Two Covenant Theology in Chapter 3.

I do hope this new edition will be helpful and the learning process of *'Iron sharpening Iron'* (Proverbs 27:17) will continue as we explore God's redemptive purposes within the context of Enlargement Theology.

Enlargement Theology is a response to the impasse within contemporary Jewish-Christian relations, arising from the inherent weaknesses and mutual incompatibility of Replacement Theology and Two Covenant Theology in the light of Romans 9-11.

This thesis sets out in thirteen chapters my case for a new theological approach in the field of Jewish-Christian relations which I am naming Enlargement Theology. Enlargement Theology is not a complete theological system, but it is a way of focusing on the church's relationship with Israel, Jewish people and the emerging contemporary Messianic Jewish movement.

Enlargement Theology draws from a faithful study of biblical texts and a largely sympathetic engagement with the emerging contemporary Messianic Jewish movement. At the heart of Enlargement Theology are the following five core tenets:

- God's covenantal relationship with the Jewish people is eternal. Yet this relationship is not static.

- Gentiles are brought fully into God's covenantal relationship through the enlargement of covenant relationship, and not its replacement. This enlargement is through the person and work of Jesus.

- This enlarged covenant needs to be entered into by all people, both Jews and Gentiles. This is done by responding in faith/trust to the person and work of Jesus. Therefore, it is vital that the message of Jesus is shared to both Jew and Gentile (Romans 1:16).

- The ongoing purposes of God are being worked out through three different yet mutually inter-connected communities of God's people.

- God is faithfully expressed within Trinitarian models and this has a creative link to the three different yet mutually inter-connected communities of God's people.

In this work it is noted that Replacement Theology and Two Covenant Theology are not the only theological options and many Christians would not perceive themselves as following either of these approaches within the field of Jewish-Christian relations. However, in presenting Enlargement Theology as a new and alternative theological approach it is hoped that all theological approaches not just Replacement and Two Covenant theologies will engage with this new approach and in so doing reflect and refine their own various and nuanced positions.

The thesis is developed on the basis of study firstly exploring the development of Replacement Theology and Two Covenant Theology. This is then followed by a study of the key biblical text on the basis of a particular hermeneutic. This leads to the promotion of five key understandings of the text. From this study the argument is presented for a rejection of both Replacement Theology and Two Covenant Theology, alongside a promotion of Enlargement Theology. This promotion of Enlargement Theology is seen as a significant contribution to moving beyond the current impasse and then on towards a hoped for new paradigm in the field of contemporary Jewish-Christian relations.

Chapter One

An Initial Historical and Theological Overview of Jewish-Christian Relations

'Butterflies, Caterpillars, Trees and Branches'

1.1 Setting the Scene

There has been and there continues to be a significant relation-ship between Jews[1] and Christians.[2] How could anything else be the case when one considers the historical, sociological and theological roots of Christianity? Developing from these roots there has been nearly two thousand years of ongoing and evolving 'contacts' between Jews and Christians. Such contacts have ranged from genuine dialogue encounters, mutual support, shared community and vocation, to fierce polemic and forced 'conversions', outright hostility and shameful violent conflict. Both Judaism and Christianity have been shaped, and continue to be shaped, by such far-ranging contacts.

For some these contacts have been largely beneficial, as Michael Hilton states:

> To recognise that there has been for two thousand years a symbiotic relationship between twin faiths has profound implications for Jewish-Christian relations today.[3]

For others, however, such contacts cannot be viewed as symbiotic, but rather such contacts have been seen as largely destructive, having been driven by unhelpful polemic which often resulted in the promotion of crude stereotypes. Such stereotypes have resulted in the creation of mutually demeaning and polarized positions.[4] Such positions have diminished both faith communities.

Marcel Simon, in his epic work *Verus Israel*[5] gives a detailed outline of this interplay between the emerging Christian faith communities and the Jewish people within the Roman Empire (135-425 CE). He argues that the key areas of conflict between Christians (including Jewish believers in Jesus) and Jews can be seen in terms of Christology and in terms of attitudes to the Jewish Law. A similar assessment is made by Hans Schoeps in his book, *The Jewish Christian Argument*.[6]

Schoeps outlines four specific areas of theological and pastoral conflict in this 'embryonic period': namely the Messianic claims of Jesus and his followers, the election of Israel, the nature of 'Law' versus 'faith' and the implications of the destruction of the Jerusalem Temple (70 CE).

N T Wright in commenting on the implications of the destruction of the Temple in the context of the development of first century Judaism states:

> The covenant god did nothing. It was a very different Judaism that then reconstructed itself, with grief and pain and a sense not only of crushing disaster but of belief overturned and hope dashed.[7]

Such conflict and interplay led Jews and Christians to define their emerging identity over and against each other. Such defining themes can be seen clearly in the second century work undertaken by Justin and Trypho[8] and in later polemic encounters between Timothy and Aquila[9] and Athanasius and Sacceus.[10] The growth and development of Rabbinic Judaism and Christianity would have been very different if such growth and development had taken place in mutual isolation. Yet, clearly, no such isolation could or did exist,[11] for there is as already stated a clear common history. Marcel Simon therefore concludes *Verus Israel* with this very point:

> Judaism's withdrawal stemmed from the very acknowledgement of its own powerlessness. But the structure of Christianity, which was progressively taking shape, would doubtless have been different

if there had been no struggle. By defending itself so fiercely, Judaism has helped to make her rival, in Justin Martyr's phrase into 'another Israel'.[12]

The key to so many of these encounters rests on the theological nature of the chosen mission and meaning of 'Israel' and the issue of discontinuity versus continuity within Jewish/Christian encounters. This is a theme which will be visited a number of times as this thesis develops. As A Roy Eckardt states:

> One specific way to express the central issue that has stayed with us, not only in recent years but through the centuries, is to ask whether the relation between the Church and Israel is one of discontinuity or one of continuity. The theory of discontinuity focuses on elements that separate Christians and Jews, the theory of continuity upon things that unite them.[13]

This point about discontinuity versus continuity opens up debate about the nature of discontinuity and continuity. This is drawn out helpfully by James Dunn who sees (in contrast with the position advanced, for example, by E P Sanders)[14] that in Paul's thinking there is no discontinuity between his experience as a Jew and his experience of the saving work of Christ. Dunn states (while commentating on Romans 9:6):

> After all there can be a continuity by transformation, where the caterpillar becomes a butterfly, and the empty skin of the caterpillar is all that is left behind of the old stage of existence. Is Paul arguing for that kind of continuity and fulfillment? Has God's purpose for Israel as such failed because Israel as such is now only an empty skin of the earlier of God's purpose? But there is also continuity by development and extension, as when a tree grows substantial new branches, or new branches are grafted in, where the new stage does not require the abandonment of the old, but new and old are parts of the larger whole.[15]

In the early period of Christian history, certainly prior to the destruction of the Jerusalem Temple, the 'demarcation lines' between Rabbinic Judaism and 'Christianity' seemed very fluid. At one level, initial encounters could be viewed as 'in house' encounters within the first century developing Jewish communities.

The first believers in Jesus were Jewish. They were a mixture of people[16] who were convinced that through his teaching, atoning death, resurrection, ascension and the outpouring of the Holy Spirit, God had made this Jesus the Lord and Messiah of Israel. This declaration is the fundamental truth which Peter proclaimed during his address, recorded in Acts 2, to the crowds in Jerusalem at the Jewish festival of Pentecost. This Jesus is the fulfilment of the hopes and longings of their Jewish Covenant promises and the Jewish prophetic witness. This faith in this Jesus could only be fully understood within the wider Jewish worldview. However, this faith in this Jesus also challenged and sought to redefine and renew the prevailing Jewish worldviews and associated Jewish practices. This 'in-house' Jewish encounter, however, could not remain 'in-house':

> The single most striking thing about early Christianity is its speed of growth. In A.D 25 there is no such thing as Christianity; merely a young hermit in the Judean wilderness and his somewhat younger cousin who dreams dreams and sees visions. By A.D 125 the Roman Empire has established an official policy in relation to the punishment of Christians; Polycarp has already been a Christian in Symryna for half a century; Aristides (if we accept the earlier date) is confronting the emperor Hadrian with the news that there are four races in the world, Barbarians, Greeks, Jews and Christians; and a young pagan called Justin is beginning the philosophical quest which will take him through the greatest of the pagan thinkers and lead him, still unsatisfied, to Christ.[17]

This rapid Christian growth, outlined in part within the book of Acts, was growth shaped by a missionary vocation. The early Christians understood that the faith they had in and the truth they had received through Jesus the Messiah was not a private or relativist truth, but a faith and truth that must be shared as widely as possible. For this faith and this truth had universal relevance and pressing eschatological significance. Such an understanding fueled the missionary growth of the early Christian communities.

This missionary vocation contained in key texts such as Matthew 28:19, led the early Jewish believers in Jesus into the wider Gentile/Pagan world. At first some conflict over this move out from the prevailing Jewish context existed within the community of Jewish believers in Jesus. Yet this conflict was largely overcome when the reality of the subsequent Gentile faith, marked by the outpouring of the Holy Spirit, became evident. This is first proclaimed by Peter in Acts 10:47, when he declares that the Gentiles: 'have received the Holy Spirit just as we (Jewish believers in Jesus) have'. This statement is one of the defining moments of early Christian theology and pastoral practice. From this point on, the normative initiation process [18] and the defining experience of Christian identity outlined in the book of Acts of repentance, faith, baptism in water and baptism in the Holy Spirit was fully available to Gentiles without their prior 'conversion' to Judaism. The issue then for the church was how to encourage and facilitate this Gentile response to the gospel and to unite both Jewish and Gentile believers within this new and growing faith community. This issue of finding, safeguarding and celebrating such unity became one of the major teaching themes within the writings of the New Testament.[19] Such teachings flowed in part from the decisions of the Council of Jerusalem, as outlined in Acts 15, and the ongoing development of missionary and pastoral practice.

In terms of contemporary Jewish-Christian relations, one sees an element of rich irony within this issue of Gentile inclusion. The irony being that in Acts 10 some of the Jewish believers in Jesus were amazed that Gentiles like Cornelius could become fully part of the body of believers without first becoming fully Jewish. Today the situation for many is the opposite:

. . . . many Gentile Christians are amazed at a movement of

Messianic Jews that claims Jews can accept the Jewish Messiah, Yeshua, without taking on the lifestyle of Gentiles. The more things change, the more things stay the same! In both cases it is the expectations of the 'in-group' that God overturns.[20]

The Christian community was largely successful in encouraging and facilitating evangelism amongst and the inclusion into the faith community of the wider Gentile communities. The result of this was that the church communities became increasingly more 'Gentile' in terms of numbers and ethos. Many Jewish believers in Jesus found their position was becoming increasingly more difficult. They were being 'squeezed' from both within the church community, with its increasingly prevailing Gentile ethos and from the various Rabbinic Jewish communities.

In terms of the Rabbinic Jewish synagogue communities, this 'squeeze' became unbearable with the insertion of the eighteenth benediction or curse (the Birkat-Ha-Minim of the Shmoneh-Esreh) into the daily Jewish prayer liturgy. This addition took place about twenty years after the destruction of the Temple/first Jewish revolt and stated: "May the Nosrim [Jewish believers in Jesus] and the Minim [other Jewish heretics?][21] perish suddenly, may they be blotted out of the book of life, not to be recorded with the righteous." In addition to this forced separation from the Rabbinic synagogue community, additional separation took place between Jewish believers in Jesus and the wider Jewish community as a result of the Bar-Cochba Revolt (132-135 CE).

This increasing isolation of Jewish believers in Jesus contributed to some of them evolving what the 'main stream' Christian community would understand as heretical ideas and practices. Such ideas and practices were embraced and promoted by both Ebionite[22] and Elkesaism[23] sects. Arnold Fruchtenbaum comments on the decline of Jewish believers in Jesus (which he identifies as the Hebrew-Christian movement) and states:

By the end of the fourth century, the Hebrew-Christian movement had largely ceased to exist and with its demise ended the quest for a Messianic theology. By then, it showed an inability to defend itself from both Gentile Christianity and Rabbinic Judaism.[24]

From the point in history which witnessed this demise of a distinct movement or group of Jewish believers in Jesus, the dominant theological position which shaped Christian attitudes to Jews was Replacement Theology.[25] This theological position created a hostile climate for wider relationships between Rabbinic Judaism and Christianity. Such hostility can be traced in terms of much anti-Semitic polemic and practice.

Although, over the centuries, Jewish people continued to come to a personal faith in Jesus, by and large they were assimilated into the largely Gentile church community. This level of assimilation led to the new 'convert' or at least his or her children losing touch with their Jewish identity because of the largely Gentile ethos and the prevailing Replacement Theology of the church community. Such loss of identity gave very little room for the exploration or the nurture of an individual's Jewish heritage, or identity and, as a consequence, restricted many creative avenues for possible Jewish-Christian encounters.

1.2 Contemporary Jewish-Christian relations

In terms of the more modern era, there has been a moving away in the Christian community from the dominant position of Replacement Theology. This has, along with many other factors, resulted in a new climate for Jewish-Christian relations. These new relations between Jews and Christians have been shaped by contributions by a number of key individuals, such as Franz Rosenzweig[26] and Martin Buber.[27] Also into this area of contemporary encounters, one can add additional historical realities such as the rise of Zionism, the Holocaust, the creation of the State of Israel and the growth of Messianic Judaism.[28] All of these historical realities contributed to a greater or lesser extent to this new and evolving climate within Jewish-Christian relations.

There has also been in this contemporary period a new awareness of the Jewish roots of the Christian faith. This important work has been advanced both by Christian and Jewish scholars. From the Jewish perspective Oskar Skarsaune in the Mishkan article comments:

> Since Klausner, Jewish scholars have been involved in re-search on the life of Jesus, and consistently emphasized his Jewishness; partly in polemic to Christian interpret-ations of Jesus and partly in polemic against the Christ-dogma of the Church. Not only was Jesus a Jew, he was also strictly observant of the Law and a pious Jew who never broke the Torah nor taught his disciples to do so. This Jewishness of Jesus and his positive relation to the Torah have been the basic condition to what has been called the Jewish 'bringing home' of Jesus.[29]

This work has also contributed to related areas of theological reflection; for example, the work relating to the 'New perspective on Paul'.[30] Also within this period there has been the growth of many formal gatherings for dialogue and reflection between Jews and Christians,[31] and the production of many official church statements and documents.[32] However, the key defining event which has shaped contemporary Jewish-Christian relations is the Holocaust. As Torleif Elgvin states in his editorial within the Mishkan Journal:

> The Nazi atrocities against the Jewish people changed the picture. Christians understood that anti-Judaic traditions within the church through the centuries belonged to the background of modern anti-Semitism. A rethinking of the relation between the church and Israel followed. Western churches have tried to put an end to church triumphalism and supersessionist theology. For many thinkers the Holocaust has been made a hermeneutical key for rethinking theology. Christianity and ecclesiology were understood anew, albeit in a less absolutist way. Some make the Holocaust a revelatory event that reveals to the church not only the sad truth

about the past, but also new knowledge about Israel, the church and salvation.[33]

In terms therefore of much of the contemporary Christian involvement in Jewish-Christian dialogue there has been, as stated earlier, a moving away from the traditional Replacement Theology model with its supersessionist outlook and an embracing of a Two Covenant Theology[34] model. This model has become the prevailing theological map for many Christians involved in Jewish-Christian relations.[35] This has been a significant shift. David Ford comments on this significant shift:

> Supersessionism is intrinsic to the Christian pathology in relating to Jews. Moreover, if supersessionism is replaced by a better theology then the implications ramify far beyond the core matter of relations between Christianity and Judaism. [36]

Undoubtedly for many committed to the pursuit of creative Jewish-Christian dialogue this 'better theology' has been provided by a Two Covenant approach. However, some commentators sense that much of this contemporary dialogue has not led to real encounters between Jews and Christians. This view is presented by Torleif Elgvin writing in the Mishkan Journal:

> To a large extent modern Christian-Jewish dialogue has been a street with one-way traffic. Christians have continued to express guilt and shame, continuing to walk the second mile with their opponents. But did it come to a real dialogue, as the one Rosenzweig was involved in? Was this a broken record, playing the same tune over and over again? After 40 years the tune may appear boring.[37]

In addition to the dominance of the Two Covenant model, another prevailing trend in contemporary Jewish-Christian dialogue is the apparent lack of any significant engagement with Messianic Jews and the emerging contemporary Messianic Jewish movement. Why has this been the case? I will explore issues around this key question in my presentation of the case for the development of Enlargement Theology within this thesis.

'Enlargement Theology' is my own term which I have chosen. I am not aware of this term having been used by others, yet the term Olive Tree Theology is used by David Stern[38] and the term Promise Theology is promoted by Walter Kaiser.[39] Both these terms are seeking to convey and explore teaching and core values similar to Enlargement Theology. I have also come across in general conversation within contemporary Messianic Jewish circles terms such as Fulfilment Theology and Completion Theology, however both these terms imply a degree of closure which may well be unhelpful. This is partly why I have advocated the term Enlargement Theology because it has within it a degree of fluidity, which I see as essential in terms of engaging with the ongoing outworking of God's purposes. I will seek to present the case that an Enlargement Theology which sympathetically connects with a Messianic Jewish perspective may provide the 'new tune' to enable a 'new dance' to begin within the crucial area of Jewish-Christian relations. Maybe this move will be as significant as the move away from Replacement Theology and the associated rejection of the anti-Semitism which lurked at the heart of much of Replacement Theology[40] and subsequent church teaching and aspects of missionary and pastoral practice?

If this is to be the case we will be moving towards a new paradigm. This new paradigm will hopefully create a renewed relationship between the 'elder and younger brother' which, in the words of A Roy Eckardt,[41] will result in the bringing together of history and theology as elder and younger brothers face the reality that "the inner mystery of the people of God remains a mystery of faith. It lives within the greater mystery of the hidden God and his story." It is to the ongoing unfolding of this story that we now turn.

Chapter Two

The Development of Replacement Theology

'Severing the roots'

2.1 Introduction

As outlined in chapter 1, the rapidly growing early church moved out into the wider 'Gentile' world and became, with the large numbers of Gentile converts, gradually less 'Jewish'. Jewish believers in Jesus continued within the life and faith of the church. However, increasingly they found themselves as a diminishing minority within an increasingly Gentile church:

> Jews who came in were the exception, not the rule; the conversion of the Jews en masse remained, at least in most periods of history, a Christian aspiration, not a reality.[1]

The rapidly growing, now increasingly Gentile church needed in part to define herself against the continuing Jewish groups who had not become followers of Jesus.

Such Jewish groups developed ongoing religious commitment and identity which adapted to the demands of the expansion of the Christian community, the destruction of the Temple, the failure of the Jewish resistance to Roman domination as the result of the failure of the Bar Kochba revolt (133-135 CE) and the subsequent exile. From the Christian perspective, such events as the destruction of the Jerusalem Temple and Jewish exile tended to be seen as confirming signs of God's judgment and rejection of the Jewish people who had not responded to the person and work of Jesus. This point is developed powerfully by Rabbi Jonathan Sacks:

Far from being a challenge to Christianity the Jews dispersed and, powerless as they were, were its living proof.[2]

2.2 Defining Terms

Replacement Theology[3] is the belief that the New Covenant replaces or supersedes the Old Covenant[4] given to the Jews. The church replaces Israel within God's purposes. The promises given to Israel are either now dead or transferred to the church. Such an understanding severs the church from her Jewish roots; consequently greater emphasis is placed on issues of discontinuity which the ministry of Jesus brings in relation to the Jewish biblical narrative, rather than with issues of continuity.

2.3 The Birth of Replacement Theology

The birth of Replacement Theology took place when the emerging church community began to see her own identity in terms of being the successor of the covenant promises given to the Jewish people. This identity flowed from holding a triumphalist stance toward the Jewish people. The church had replaced Israel and had become the 'True Israel', the 'New Israel' and the 'Only Israel of God'.[5] Christian leaders frequently affirmed a complete discontinuity between the church community and the Jewish community. The promises made in the scriptures to Israel were now fulfilled or would be fulfilled solely by the church. God therefore had no purposes for the Jewish people; they had become disinherited. Even the formerly good elements within Jewish faith and practice had become of no value since the coming of the faith and practice of the church.

As Replacement Theology developed, nuances within the theology emerged. R Kendall Soulen identifies three main forms of Replacement Theology — economic supersessionism, punitive supersessionism and structural supersessionism:

I distinguish three kinds of supersessionism in the standard canonical narrative; economic, punitive and structural. The first two designate explicit doctrinal perspectives, i.e. that carnal Israel's history is providentially ordered from the outset to be taken up into the spiritual church (economic supersessionism), and that God has rejected carnal Israel on account of its failure to join the church (punitive supersessionism). Structural supersessionism, in contrast, refers not to an explicit doctrinal perspective but rather to a formal feature of the standard canonical narrative as a whole. Structural supersessionism refers to the narrative logic of the standard model whereby it renders the Hebrew Scriptures largely indecisive for shaping Christian convictions about how God's works as Consummator and as Redeemer engage humankind in universal and enduring ways.[6]

2.4 The Initial Failings and Subsequent Development of Replacement Theology

Replacement Theology, especially in its more punitive models, created an atmosphere in which the Jewish people were often seen as the 'curse bearers' or 'Christ killers'.[7] The polemic, which began initially in an internal Jewish[8] context, became gradually more defined as conflict increased between a largely Gentile church and a remaining/developing Rabbinic Jewish community. The historian Jules Isaac sums up this Christian polemic with his phrase, 'the teaching of contempt'.[9]

The growing church, with its progressively more dominant Gentile identity and accompanying mindset, began to wrestle with important issues of identity. This can be seen for example in regard to the issue of the nature of the church's foundation in the scriptures. 'What does it mean for Gentile believers to be grafted in as wild branches?' (Romans 11:17-24). 'What does the nature of covenant mean, if the promises and call of God are not irrevocable?'(Rom 11:29). And, 'On what foundation does the church rest, if not upon the eternal promises to the Jewish people?' The church Fathers responded to these and similar questions by an ongoing process of fostering and developing aspects of an emerging Replacement Theology.

In part, this developing of a Replacement Theology was drawing from what could well appear to be seen as an interpretation of Paul, other New Testament writers and the emerging historical and social realities of numerous Christian communities within the context of the wider Jewish and Roman worlds. For example, Paul states that not all who are descended from Israel are Israel (Rom 9:6) and that there is a division between a 'physical Jew' and a 'spiritual Jew' (Rom 2:28-29). Paul clearly sees that certain Jewish people in terms of their rejection of the gospel and the persecution of Christians are to be considered as 'enemies'(Rom 11:28). Paul in proclaiming the fullness of the power of the gospel clearly redefines, or starts the process of redefining aspects of Jewish identity (Gal 3:29, 6:15-16 and Col 3:10-11).[10] Such redefining could be understood in terms of an enlarging, fulfilling or as a replacing of God's purposes. Alongside these views, texts such as Acts 3:23 together with the clear teaching in the Book of Hebrews (which deals in part with the reality of Jewish believers in Jesus reverting away from Jesus and back into certain aspects of Jewish practice) stress the all-sufficiency of the New Covenant which is superior to the Old Covenant[11] (Heb 8:6) which is obsolete and will soon disappear (Heb 8:13).

This theology, focusing primarily on replacement, created a 'distorting mirror' from which the church community drew from what they saw. This led to an increased anti-Jewish polemic and consequently led to an undermining of the position of many Jewish believers in Jesus.

The following statements are three examples of such anti-Jewish polemic, which is a key component of Replacement Theology. Such theology fanned the flames of later anti-Semitic teaching and Church pastoral practice:

> We may thus assert in utter confidence that the Jews will not return to their earlier situation, for they have committed the most abominable of crimes in forming this conspiracy against the Saviour of the human race. Hence the city where Jesus suffered

was necessarily destroyed. The Jewish nation was driven from its country and another people was called the blessed election. Not only was Jerusalem destroyed and Israel sent into exile for crimes, but the divine election was revoked; they were destined to stand in perpetual opposition to God.[12]

Before the law was given the Jews were possessed of an unclean devil, which the law drove out, but which returned immediately after their rejection of Christ.[13]

The Jews do not worship God but devils, so that all their feasts are unclean. God hates them and indeed has always hated them. But since their murder of Jesus, he allows them no time for repentance. It was for this set purpose that He concentrated all their worship in Jerusalem that he might more easily destroy it. What is clear is that God hates them; it is the duty of Christians to hate them too.[14]

The promotion of Replacement Theology tore out the essential Jewish roots from the church. This had implications both in terms of the church losing a Hebraic worldview, a clear historical context[15] for the Gospel narrative and in the reading and application of scripture. For example, there is a link between Replacement Theology and the extensive use of allegory as a hermeneutical tool. When allegory is used to interpret the promises to Israel and the Jewish people, the literal and direct meaning of the biblical text is often lost. The term 'Israel' is seen to refer to different realities at different times. This allegorical or symbolic method of scriptural interpretation can lead to an inability to see and understand legitimate Rabbinic Jewish interpretations of such texts. For example, the tendency by some Christian commentators to see references to Jerusalem as referring to 'heavenly eternal Zion', rather than as referring to a literal city with 'earthly' hopes of restoration and on-going struggles for peace and prosperity.

In addition to issues of worldview and the interpretation of scripture, the loss of the Jewish roots of the Christian faith also had cultural and pastoral implications for an emerging

Christianity. One can see how some of the five rulings outlined below undermined the position of Jewish believers in Jesus and created a growing wedge between such believers and the wider Jewish community.

The position of being Jewish and a follower of Jesus became increasingly more difficult. Many Jewish believers in Jesus faced intolerable choices regarding identity and legitimate cultural belonging following various rulings of both the church and the wider Rabbinic Jewish community.

In terms of rulings from the church, the following five rulings give a useful overview. Firstly, Christians may not enter a synagogue.[16] Secondly, Christians may not eat Passover with Jews.[17] Thirdly, Jews may not appear in public during the celebrations of Holy Week.[18] Fourthly, no member of the clergy who is free to marry must ever marry a Jew.[19] Fifthly, any Jew, prior to being baptized, must denounce the whole of his or her Jewish identity and heritage by making the following statement:

> I renounce all customs, rites, legalisms, unleavened breads and sacrifices of lambs of the Hebrews and all other feasts of the Hebrews, sacrifices, prayers, aspersions, purifications, sanctifications and fasts, and new moons, and Sabbaths, and superstitions, and hymns and chants and observances and Synagogues, and the food and drink of the Hebrews. In one word, I renounce absolutely everything Jewish, every law, rite, and custom, and above all I renounce Antichrist, whom all the Jews await in the figure and form of Christ; and I join myself to the true Christ and God.[20]

Replacement Theology remained dominant throughout the centuries of church development and theological formation. However, dissenting voices began to be heard. From the Reformation period many Puritan and Pietistic groups following from the teaching line of Calvin[21] rather than Luther[22] began to question if the scriptures presented a view in line with the prevailing model of Replacement Theology. Many, such as James Bicheno,[23] argued that it did not and they perceived in scripture clear promises that Israel had not been 'written off' by God, but rather Israel as a nation would be restored and renewed. Such restoration and 'end times' prophecies, especially from the prophet Daniel and the Book of Revelation, were interpreted within the context of present world events, especially the event of the French Revolution. Such interpreters also argued against allegorical methods of interpreting Scripture and promoted the view that the term 'Israel'[24] always referred to the Jews, and not Jews and Gentiles and certainly not Gentiles replacing Jews. They also understood that the land of Israel had been given to the 'People of Israel' as an everlasting possession and that God would restore them to their ancestral land and renew them as a people. This view of restoration and renewal was linked in with an eschatological model nearly always pre-Millennial in tone.[25]

Such views were embraced further by the Evangelical revival of the early nineteenth century:

> A number of evangelicals had been influenced by the writings of the Puritans and others, including the Frenchman Pierre Jerieu, about the fulfillment of the prophecies in the later days and in particular the restoration of Israel to her land. Jurieu, for instance, wrote in 1687 of a future great revolution in France, the result being that the Jewish people 'shall be gathered together in their own land.'[26]

From this Evangelical revival many Christian groups[27] focused on specific outreach to Jews and sought to foster and nurture Jewish believers in Jesus. The emergence of Christian missionary groups reaching out to Jewish people and the subsequent higher profile of Jewish believers within the church community[28] bore eloquent witness to living Jewish roots and, by so doing, undermined many assumptions of a rigidly applied Replacement Theology.

In the twentieth century further undermining or re-thinking of the validity of Replacement Theology can be traced to the soul-searching of many Christians in the light of the horror of the Holocaust and the perceived links between the events leading up to the Holocaust and the long history of 'Christian anti-Semitism'. Such soul-searching led many Christians[29] to attempt to find new theological models which would create space for meaningful dialogue with Rabbinic Judaism and would act as a catalyst for new avenues of exploration within Jewish-Christian relations. This searching led to many, as I will outline in the next chapter, embracing a new theological model, namely Two Covenant Theology. This theological position is now probably the prevailing theological model for the majority of contemporary encounters in the field of Jewish-Christian relations. It is to this theological model which we now turn.

Chapter Three

The Development of
Two Covenant Theology

'Telling a different story'

3.1 Defining Terms

Two Covenant Theology[1] is the belief that God deals with Jews and Gentiles in different ways. Jewish people are in a 'right relationship' with God through their election, marked by the covenant implemented through Abraham and Moses. This covenantal relationship has not and never will be revoked, superseded or replaced. Gentiles, however, are not in this covenantal relationship, but a new covenantal relationship is 'opened up' for Gentiles through the person and work of Jesus Christ. These two covenantal relationships work alongside each other within the purposes of God.

3.2 The Birth of Two Covenant Theology

The first building block of Two Covenant Theology can be traced back on the Rabbinic 'Jewish side' to the understanding that the covenant relationship between the Jewish people and God is, in the words of Rabbi Jonathan Sacks, 'Inherently pluralist':

> It (the covenant) does not negate the possibility of other covenants, nor does the existence of many faiths relativise them all. To do so confuses absoluteness with universality.[2]

Additional building blocks in the development of Two Covenant Theology can be traced from two other lines of Jewish thinking and experience. Firstly, the Marranos[3] Jews developed (as a result of severe persecution resulting from the

Spanish Inquisition) a view on personal salvation as flowing directly from observing the Law of Moses. They spoke of Moses as their personal Saviour in ways which show a fusion between traditional Jewish and Roman Catholic elements. This emerging fusion has some echoes with Two Covenant Theology as later developed by Rosenzweig. Secondly, Rabbinical Judaism with, as already stated, its inherently pluralist mindset (unlike the exclusivist mindset of Orthodox/ Evangelical Christianity), assumed that a Gentile could have in some sense a right relationship with God and have a share in the life to come without converting to Judaism.[4] This 'right relationship' according to much Rabbinic thought was initiated by God-fearing Gentiles keeping the Noachide laws.[5] The prophetic words of Micah have often been used as a pivotal point for such an understanding:

> Each person will sit under his vine and fig tree, with no one to upset him, for the mouth of the Lord Almighty has spoken. For all the people will walk, each in the name of its god; but we will walk in the name of the Lord our God forever and ever.[6]

This understanding of a distinctive Jewish Covenant way alongside a way or ways for Gentiles flowed from the understanding of the Noachide laws and from the Rabbinic teaching of Shittuf[7](Idolatry). This understanding of a shared 'partnership' in rejecting idolatry was developed by the Jewish philosopher Maimonides who argued that God has given a special purpose to the Christians (and adherents of Islam). This special purpose and partnership was in terms of presenting monotheism and the knowledge of the Jewish scriptures to the wider world and by so doing preparing the world in part for the coming Messianic age. Such an approach allowed the Jewish minority to be respectful and placating of the dominant religious culture,[8] while clearly hoping for some level of reciprocal treatment based on mutual tolerance.

These building blocks were then elaborated on and refined by Franz Rosenzweig. Rosenzweig was the pioneering advocate of Two Covenant Theology to both the Rabbinic Jewish and Christian communities. He was born in 1886 in Cassel, Germany, into a largely assimilated and affluent Jewish family. His education [9] as a Jew was mainly secular rather than religious. It was his great uncle Adam Rosenzweig who is regarded as giving to him an understanding and appreciation of his religious Jewish heritage. At the heart of his conviction is the understanding that God's covenant with Israel is special and unique. As Maurice Bowler states:

> . . . God's covenant with Israel is seen to be of a different nature from that with the rest of the world. Whereas one is a 'way' involving movement into a covenant relationship with the Father, the other is a 'Life' which is, itself, a relationship with God and in Rosenzweig's view, exempts the Jew from any recourse to the mediation of Jesus. [10]

The essence of his work is outlined in his book, *The Star of Redemption*. [11] This major philosophical work is more than theological analysis and speculation, for it contains the clear marks of a personal and passionate spiritual search. The work is divided into three main parts, the elements, the path and the form.

This spiritual search began with Rosenzweig entering into deep discussion with Eugene Rosenstock-Huessy about the nature of Judaism and Christianity. These discussions led Rosenzweig to consider his own identity and his relationship with God. The step of becoming a Christian and being baptized appeared close at hand. However, in preparing for the step of baptism, Rosenzweig was determined to enter the church like the first followers of Jesus as a Jew and not as a Gentile converting from a pagan tradition. Yet, following from what can only be described in mystical terms as a 'spiritual encounter' while attending the Yom Kippur services at the Orthodox synagogue in Berlin, his position changed radically. From that of someone seriously considering Christian baptism (and in his understanding leaving Judaism) he became one of the most staunch and creative defenders of Rabbinic Judaism.

At the heart of Rosenzweig's defense of Judaism is the conviction that as a Jew he is fundamentally secure in his own calling and identity. Nahum Glatzer, in his Foreword to *The Star of Redemption*, states:

> . . . in Rosenzweig's view the Church is historically justified in her conversion efforts, yet the Jew must live his own role in God's world. 'Shall I become converted, I who have been chosen?'[12]

Rosenzweig, throughout his writings, emphasised this sense of calling. In a letter to his cousin Rudolph Hans Ehrenberg (who had become a Christian) he acknowledged that for a Christian the only way to enter into the Fatherhood of God is through Jesus, but for himself, a Jew, he asserted:

> After prolonged and, I believe thorough, self examination, I have reversed my decision. It no longer seems necessary to me and therefore, being what I am, no longer possible. I will remain a Jew.[13]

For Rosenzweig, Rabbinic Judaism and Christianity are equally valid yet different perceptions of reality:

> The truth, the whole truth thus belongs neither to them nor to us. For we too, though we bear it within us must for that very reason first immerse our glance into our own interior if we would see it, and there for a while we see the stars, we do not see the rays. The whole truth would demand not only seeing its light but also what is illuminated by it. They (the Christians) however, are in any event already destined for all time to see what is illuminated and not the light. Thus we both have but a part of the whole truth.[14]

Rosenzweig understood that Jews and Christians have a shared mission in terms of being faithful to God. Jews have a special place or rather a special 'life' within the eternal purposes of God. While however, Christians have entered into a special way to God through a new covenant established by the person and work of Jesus. This way involves movement and transformation (conversion) from a pagan past. This way is for all who are not yet with God the Father. Christians have a God-given imperative to share the news of the way and by so doing help prepare all the Gentiles for the coming of the Messianic age.

In the thinking of Rosenzweig, each Jew has a unique life as a result of Abraham's response to God and through their adherence to the Mosaic covenant. Every descendant of Abraham through the line of Isaac and Jacob is born a Jew. The Jewish person never needs to choose to become a Jew at some point of decision. A Jew is born, not made by subsequent choices. It is God who has brought the Jewish people into an eternal relationship with himself and God will sustain that relationship in this age and into the Messianic age to come.

The position for a Christian is very different from that of a Jew in Rosenzweig's understanding within an emerging Two Covenant perspective. As stated earlier, the Christian enters the way from a pagan past which involves spiritual rebirth. This rebirth breaks the hold of the past and makes a new and right relationship with God possible for that individual. This relationship is not necessary or appropriate for a Jew because as Rosenzweig argues, a Jew has for all time an ongoing and corporate role within the eternally elect 'people of God'.

The implications of Rosenzweig's position have been taken up by other modern Jewish thinkers, such as Herberg,[15] Schwartzchild,[16] Dorff,[17] Cohen,[18] Buber[19] and Berger.[20]

This Two Covenant approach, as stated earlier, has become the dominant theological map for exploring contemporary Jewish-Christian relations. This has led to a greater appreciation of Christianity in Jewish terms and has helped to draw new lines of encounter and enquiry in a largely post-missionary environment. This approach shields Jewish people from Christian missionary agendas and, it is argued, creates a genuine safe place of mutual respect from which creative encounters, meaningful partnerships and ongoing dialogue can flourish.

From the Christian side this Two Covenant approach has many advocates such as Cracknell,[21] Parkes,[22] Van Buren,[23] and Brearley.[24] Brearley, for example outlines powerfully three reasons why she believes as a Christian any attempt to convert Jewish people goes against God's eternal purposes:

> First, theological; early Christianity was clearly not designed to replace Judaism. There is a continuing covenant with the Jewish people. Paul, Peter and other Jewish believers remained orthodox Jews worshipping in the Temple and observing the Law. Jesus affirmed the Law (Mt 5:17) as did Paul for Jews though not for Gentiles. (Rom 3:1-3, Acts 21:20-26)

> If Christians knew Orthodox Judaism better, they would judge it more humbly. The Holy Spirit has been widely taught and experienced in the Synagogue and the Word of God loved, cherished and lived in countless Jewish homes since Rabbinic times. The exiled Jewish people have been faithful to the covenant, sensing God's forgiveness, love and blessing being renewed each Shabbat and festival, sustaining them in the task of tikkum olam (mending the world).

> Second, historical; the church has preached the love of Jesus to the Jews but practised hatred; it is time to change. Until the Gentile Church, the prodigal son, repents of its past in humility and remorse, true brotherhood with our Jewish elder brother cannot be re-established.

> Thirdly, strategic; the New Age movement[25] today stands opposed to the Judeo-Christian tradition and seeks to destroy biblical monotheism and all orthodox worship of the God of Abraham, Isaac and Jacob. Christians and Jews must stand together against this common threat.[26]

Christian advocates for this Two Covenant approach come from different positions. Some like Brearley, hold to some form of Christian-Zionist agenda, others come from a more 'liberal' pluralist position such as Cracknell. While for others the prime motivation appears to be some form of emotional response to the horrors of the Holocaust and a determination to move away from any implicit anti-Semitism.

The more liberal pluralist position is affirmed by much of

what could be generally perceived as a prevailing 'post-modern' and 'post missionary' climate which is largely resistant to any exclusivist truth claims and rejects a singular religious meta-narrative. Such claims and narratives are seen as the assertion to know the truth over and against others as simply a declaration of misplaced power. Sadly the history of Christian mission towards the Jewish people (and other groups) has at times shown clear elements of such misuse of power. The emotional post-Holocaust response is expressed clearly by Arnulf Baumann:

> The terrible facts of the Holocaust and of the contribution of the Christian teaching of contempt gradually dawned on Christians in Germany and other countries. It can be well understood how such Christians began seeking a new way of relating to Jews and Judaism, a way which would exclude any sort of contempt, hatred or triumphalism on the Christian side. It seemed to be a fascinating idea to understand Christianity and Judaism as two separate entities, emerging from the same root but now neatly separated: one belonging to the world of many nations with the task of leading all nations to the true God through Jesus Christ, the other belonging to the one elect people, with the task of leading the scattered remnants of this people to covenant faithfulness in the ancient way of Israel. If the relationship between Christian and Jews was seen in this light there would be no room for interference with each other any more. [27]

Whatever the motivation for embracing a Two Covenant approach (which like Replacement Theology has within it many different nuances), Two Covenant Theology became formally endorsed by some church groups. Groups such as the American Presbyterians who in 1987 abandoned the supersessionist model of Replacement Theology and stated:

> Christians have not replaced Jews. Jews are already in a covenantal relationship with God, and remain with Christians as partners in waiting. [28]

The following year the World Council of Churches issued a statement which clearly has all the marks of a Two Covenant position, both in tone and substance:

> We see not one covenant displacing another but two communities of faith, each called into existence by God, each holding its respective gifts from God and each accountable to God. There is one way for Gentiles which leads to the Father through the Son, and there is another way for the Jews who are with the Father since His covenant with them on Mount Sinai.[29]

3.3 The Initial Failings and Subsequent Development of Two Covenant Theology

While Two Covenant Theology has become the dominant theological position within much contemporary Jewish-Christian dialogue, there are however some strong challenges to Two Covenant Theology from both the Rabbinic Jewish positions and from Christian positions, including key input from Messianic Jews.

From the Rabbinic Jewish position there is the conviction expressed by Jacob Taubes in his article "Argument and doctrine" namely that Rosenzweig has arranged:

> . . . a rapprochement between Christians and Jews somewhat too neatly.[30]

There is the shared concern of many Jewish leaders such as Emil Fackenheim and Arthur Cohen that Rosenzweig's esteemed view of the church and Christianity creates a corresponding lowering of the status of the synagogue and Judaism. They would also argue that at times Jewish Theology must contend vigorously against Christian Theology, yet this is not in keeping with the overall emphasis of the Two Covenant approach.

Other Jewish concerns about Rosenzweig's approach tend to focus on five main areas. Firstly, his strong emphasis on the racial definition of Judaism. Secondly, his understanding of the sacramental understanding of Mitzvah. Thirdly, and more generally Rosenzweig's perception of history, (coming from his European diaspora setting and seeing the church in terms of triumphant Constantinian Christendom) is simply out of step with the historical realities of today's world and today's church some three generations later. Fourthly, the question is posed that as a pluralistic openness exists within many aspects of Judaism to 'faithful' Gentiles, "Why is there then a need for the establishment of a second universal way or covenant for Gentiles?" From such a pluralist or universalistic position any insistence on a second way can be seen as simply superfluous. Fifthly, there is the conviction that the biblical material does not give credence to a Two Covenant position. This fifth point is taken up by Richard Robinson:

> There is evidence that the Two Covenant theory is designed for export to the Christian community rather than for internal consumption. Alan Segal is no friend to Jewish evangelism and interprets Romans 11v29 to suggest that no mission to Jews is needed; yet he cannot find a two- covenant theory in Paul.[31]

Robinson continues to quote from Segal,[32] and introduces what, from Robinson's perspective, is a stunning admission made by Segal:

> As a believing Jew and a twentieth-century humanist, I could have hoped for a different outcome of Paul's interpretation of these passages. The theology outlined by Stendahl, Gaston and Gager (that Paul teaches two ways of salvation) makes more sense today than does Paul's actual conclusion. It would have been easier for today's Christianity had Paul embraced cultural pluralism more fully.[33]

From the Christian side those who reject Two Covenant Theology do so primarily because a Two Covenant Theology fails to take seriously the absolute centrality of the person and work of Jesus Christ. This point is made by David Torrance:

> There is no such thing as being elect apart from Jesus Christ. There

is no elect community, Jewish or gentile apart from the election of Jesus Christ. All alike are elect when, by union with him through the Spirit and by grace they share in His one election. Christ is the ground and source of all other elections. Therefore, there are not and cannot be two covenants, one for Jews and one for gentiles; there is only the one covenant of grace in which all alike share through union in the Spirit with Jesus Christ.[34]

In addition to opposition based on the absolute centrality of the person and work of Jesus Christ, the Two Covenant approach is opposed on two other main fronts. Firstly, the Two Covenant approach is unable to engage with the existence and vibrant witness of the current Messianic Jewish movement. By so doing it fails to understand the nature of the Jewish covenant promise. As Mitch Glaser (a contemporary Messianic Jewish leader) states:

> The salvation paradigm which has the Jew going through Moses and gentiles through Jesus is untenable, as it confuses the great intent of the great Old Testament covenants. The Mosaic covenant was never intended to provide personal salvation for the Jewish people; its purpose was to point toward the New Covenant. Paul says the Law was a schoolmaster to teach us the way of salvation in Christ (Gal 3:34). It would be the height of irony if we Jews were barred from graduating from the school of our own Law! For according to the Apostle, Christ is the very fulfillment of the Torah (Rom 10:4).[35]

Secondly, it is argued that the Two Covenant approach is totally out of step with the historical reality of the early church which began with Jews telling Jews about the significance of Jesus with special reference to his atoning death and victorious resurrection. It would be inconceivable to the early Jewish church leaders such as Peter, James and Paul that there was no need for them to proclaim the way of salvation in and through Jesus Christ to their fellow Jews. This they did proclaim often at great cost. This Jewish proclamation of Jesus as Lord and Messiah to their fellow Jews was considered vital. In fact it was this very proclamation which was the bedrock for the rest of the church's missionary thrust out into the largely Gentile world.

Arnulf Baumann concludes in his article, "The Two Ways/ Two Covenant Theory" with these words which capture the essence of much Christian opposition to the Two Covenant approach:

> The two ways (two covenants) theory, fascinating as it may appear at first glance, does not fit into the realities of New Testament or present times. In finding fault with this theory we should not, however, turn away from the goal of a new relationship between Christian and Jews. It may appear difficult to achieve this goal if there are not two neatly separated entities on their way to ultimate fulfillment. It may appear easier to strive for that goal without the interference of Jewish Christians, but this is the reality. By the will of God, Christians and Jews can never be neatly separated.[36]

In terms now of exploring the 'will of God', which as Arnulf Baumann stated does not allow for the neat separation of Christian and Jews, we turn to the key New Testament Text in regard to Jewish-Christian relations, namely Romans 9-11.

Chapter Four

Exploring the Key Text: Romans 9–11

'Paul, Apostle of the Church and Prophet to Israel'

4.1 Why Romans 9-11?

In establishing a biblical framework for a Christian position with regard to contemporary Jewish-Christian relations the key text is Romans 9-11. It is within these chapters that one encounters the deepest questions of Paul's own journey of faith and one glimpses into the sovereign purposes of God. Thomas Merton, the Roman Catholic monk and mystic, catches the essence of Romans 9-11 when he states:

> I am more and more convinced that Romans 9-11 (the chapters on the election of Israel) are the key to everything today. This is the point where we have to press and search and listen to the word. From here we enter the understanding of scripture, the wholeness of revelation and of the church.[1]

In addition to the above personal affirmation about Romans 9-11, the overall significance of the Romans 9-11 text is also clearly shown from the following analysis of the unabridged collection of Christian documents, compiled by Helga Croner, titled, *Stepping Stones to Further Jewish-Christian Relations*.[2] Within these documents 83 direct references are made to New Testament texts,[3] of which 30 are taken from Romans 9-11.

It is not only the frequency of the references to Romans 9-11 but also the weight given to this text which is of note throughout many of these documents and within wider areas of discussion and dialogue. For example, the statement on Catholic-Jewish relations by the U.S. National Conference of Catholic Bishops

(1975) states (in reference to Romans 9-11):

> We find in these rediscovered, precious chapters Paul's love for
> his kinsmen and a firm basis for Christian reverence for the Jewish
> people. Admittedly, Paul's theology of Judaism has its more
> negative aspects; they have been adequately emphasized over the
> centuries in Catholic teaching. It would be well today to explore
> and emphasize the positive elements of Paul's thought that have
> received inadequate attention.[4]

This line of argument then continues:

> In effect, we find in the Epistle to the Romans (9-11) long-
> neglected passages which help us to construct a new and positive
> attitude toward the Jewish people. There is here a task incumbent
> on theologians, as yet hardly begun, to explore the continuing
> relationship of the Jewish people with God and their spiritual bonds
> with the New Covenant and the fulfillment of God's plan for both
> Church and Synagogue.[5]

A similar statement made in 1969 by the Roman Catholic
Diocesan Synod of Vienna clearly affirms the centrality of
Romans 9-11 for engagement in the field of Jewish-Christian
relations. The statement declares:

> We firmly believe that the New Covenant in Christ did not abrogate
> the promises of the old, as the Apostle said in chapter 11 of his
> letter to the Romans (particularly verses 1, 26, 28). All other New
> Testament passages relating to the Jews must be suitably interpreted
> in the light of that text.[6]

4.2 Bibliographical Overview

The vast majority of contemporary Christian biblical commentators would see Romans 9-11 not as a distraction from the
main thrust of Paul's thought outlined in Romans, but rather
would see Romans 9-11 as an integral part of his thought.

Within this thesis I have drawn from the following commentators.[7] The first four names have specific insights relating to
the emerging Messianic Jewish movement; namely David H

Stern, Mark Kinzer, and Joseph Shulman with Hilary Le Cornu. The following 23 commentators, while far from in any sense being an exhaustive list, nevertheless I believe contribute to a coherent, balanced and detailed corpus of study material: Robert Badenas, Karl Barth, Richard Bell, James M Boice, F F Bruce, C E B Cranfield, C H Dodd, J W Drane, James Dunn, Robert Jewett, John Lodge, Paul Minear, Anthony J Guerra, Ernst Käsemann, Douglas Moo, M D Nanos, A Headlam and W Sanday, K Stendahl, S Stowers, N T Wright and John Ziesler.

For many commentators Romans 9-11 is celebrated as the apex of Paul's theological reflections as he explores key issues of God's call, human response, faith identity and future hope:

> Chapters 9-11 of the book of Romans contain the New Testament's most important and complete discussion of the Jewish people. In them God promises that "all Israel will be saved"(11:26) and commands that Gentile Christians show the Jews God's mercy (11:31). In the face of what these chapters teach, every form of Christian anti-Semitism stands condemned; and every claim, whether by Jews or Christians, that the Gospel is not for Jews must collapse. [8]

4.3 Paul's Dual Role

I understand that Paul is writing both as an apostle of the church and also as a prophet to Israel. Paul's critique of Israel is a critique from within the community of Israel. This sense of having in part an 'insider's' perspective is a key building block within the development of Jewish-Christian relations and this point is commented upon helpfully by John Lodge:

> What is clear is that Paul's personal pathos stems from his sense of membership among God's people. He speaks from inside Israel as such. Even if Paul prays for something which he knows to be impossible, there is no doubt that he has demonstrated his unshakable solidarity with his people. [9]

For Paul it is in this 'insider's' role as a Jewish man steeped in Torah combined with and complemented by his 'outsider's' calling to a ministry primarily amongst the Gentiles that results in creating this dual role. This dual role helps to give to Paul's teaching a particular dynamic and resonance to contemporary engagements within the field of Jewish-Christian relations and especially in areas of contemporary Messianic Judaism. For Messianic Judaism could be understood as having within itself this dual role as it does not sit comfortably and is in some ways discontinuous with the classic Christian frame of reference. While equally, Messianic Judaism challenges many aspects including identity issues and core values within the wide ranging area of contemporary Rabbinic Judaism.

This understanding of this dual role of Paul is in part the fruit of the biblical insights which flow from the field of study generally referred to as the 'New Perspective on Paul'.

This new perspective affirms both Paul's Rabbinic mindset and seeks to reappraise first century Judaism. Such reappraisal flows largely from the work of E P Sanders.[10] This reappraisal undermines the paradigm of Pauline interpretation promoted by mainly Protestant theologians who tend to see Paul (and elements of first-century Judaism) from the mindset and context of Reformation history/theology.

In my exploration of Romans 9-11, I will attempt to focus upon issues relating to contemporary Jewish-Christian relations and the establishing of a biblical mandate for such encounters from an evangelical Christian position. I will attempt to draw from insights both from the 'New Perspective on Paul' and from contemporary Messianic Judaism, which I believe will both shed new light upon Romans 9-11 and will consequently open up new lines of interpretation and understanding. In doing this I will firstly outline my hermeneutical method in exploring Romans 9-11 and then I will outline six introductory points.

4.4 My Hermeneutical Values and Methodology in Exploring Chapters 9-11

My overarching hermeneutical value in terms of an understanding of the Bible is to affirm the infallible inspiration and authority of the Bible.[11] This is linked to my conviction that God is sovereign in the process of revelation to people. Such sovereignty is well expressed in the words of Cornelius Van Til:

> God could not be sovereign in his disposition of rational human beings if he were not also sovereign in his revelation of himself to them. If God is sovereign in the realm of being, he is surely also sovereign in the realm of knowledge. Scripture is a factor in the redeeming work of God, a component part of the series of his redeeming acts, without which that series would be incomplete and so far inoperative for its main end.[12]

Such an understanding of God's sovereignty in his self-disclosure to people clearly presupposes in people the capacity to respond appropriately to God's revelatory initiatives. Such initiatives have been placed in certain groupings such as natural revelation,[13] historical revelation and personal revelation. In terms of the general hermeneutical method used to respond to God's self-disclosure/revelation in the Bible, I would primarily identify with the Grammatico-Historical approach[14] in regard to encountering, interpreting and applying the text. In terms of a full and coherent presentation of this hermeneutical approach, I have found the work of B B Warfield to be of great value. Warfield carefully outlines this approach in his book, *The Inspiration and Authority of the Bible*.[15] In addition to and in order to complement Warfield's approach I would also affirm the hermeneutical principles and practices laid out in the 25 articles of the Chicago statement on biblical hermeneutics.[16]

The Bible is in my hermeneutical method synonymous with the content of revelation/the word of God. This view of the Bible makes the Bible in the words of W Randolph Tate:

> The standard for the Christian's faith and practice.[17]

A similar view to that expressed by W Randolph Tate is that of Grant R Osborne who entreats the reader to:

Let God's Word be the final arbiter of truth.[18]

In the light of this 'high view' of the Bible,[19] I would hold to a range of convictions which clearly impact upon my interpretation of Romans 9-11. Let me outline two examples, which develop within my thesis.

Firstly, I understand that within the Bible we are given a full and complete revelation of God's redemptive purposes. Therefore, any event claiming to be a new revelatory act must be rejected. Therefore, when some proponents of a Two Covenant approach declare that one must reinterpret Romans 9-11 in the light of the 'new revelation' that the Holocaust brings,[20] my position would reject such a declaration. Clearly, the Holocaust does bring into reality a new climate for Jewish-Christian relations, there is also unquestionably and appropriately new emotional contexts, however, these do not amount to 'new revelation' on the same level in terms of authority as that of scriptural revelation.

Secondly, I understand that there is an inherent perspicuity[21] and consistency within scripture.[22] This does not mean that there are not different principles and methods of arrangement of material within scripture. For example, in John's Gospel it seems probable that the cleansing of the Temple narrative (John 2:13-22) is deliberately placed for 'theological reasons'[23] at the commencement of the public ministry of Jesus. However, the Synoptic Gospels place the same event[24] within the historical setting of the final week of the public ministry of Jesus.

There can also be different details in various accounts of the same event. For example, Paul's own account of coming to Jerusalem recorded in Galatians 1:13-20 is a much fuller and personal account that that given of the same event by Luke in Acts 8:25-30. However, my understanding of the inherent consistency of scripture does not allow for the line of interpretive reasoning presented, for example, by Richard

Bell. Bell presents the view[25] that Paul's view of Israel both in terms of election and salvation is in Romans substantially different to that given in Galatians and 1 Thessalonians. Bell sees clear substitution models in Paul's teaching in Galatians and a very negative view of the Jewish law. I would agree fully with Bell that there are differences between Galatians and Romans, but such differences are not discrepancies, based on Paul's inconsistency,[26] but rather should be explained in terms of the vastly different contexts Paul is addressing in Galatians and Romans.[27] For example, in Galatians Paul is largely opposing Jewish teachers (Judaizers) who are insisting that Torah observance is the key to salvation for Gentiles. While in Romans, the context is very different, namely Paul in part is addressing Gentile teachers who are seeking to undermine the Torah. Such undermining is sourced by a 'replacement agenda' and Gentile arrogance. When one fully appreciates the differing contexts faced by Paul, an alternative to Bell's approach can be endorsed, namely Paul is consistent in his view (outlined in scripture) of Israel, election and Torah.

Following on from my overarching hermeneutical value relating to the inspiration and authority of scripture emerges the intent to allow the revealed text to speak for itself. With this in mind every effort must be made to find as closely as possible the original meaning each text had at the time it was written. In this sense, I share the goal expressed by Grant R Osborne[28] to get back to the meaning the ancient author intended to convey. Later Osborne defines meaning as the original intended meaning of the text[29] and for Osborne the final determiner of a specific word meaning is context.[30] I believe this approach by Osborne is helpful in that it attempts to allow the text (author's original and inspired intent) to speak for itself, rather than reading one's own ideas and insights into the revealed text. I realise that seeking to find the true understanding of a text is dependent on, to use Manfred Oeming's phrase,[31] "the risky business" of grasping the author's intent. However, it is a risky business worth investing in and pursuing, if the alternative is to embrace a basic post-modern hermeneutic in which the intent of the author is of no interest[32] and a single text may legitimately bring forth differing and even contradictory meanings.[33]

With this conviction in mind the text of Romans 9-11 is given priority and prominence within the flow of discussion and the development of my thesis. Therefore, each biblical section begins with the text (and not with my theological understandings or systems of belief) and from the study of that text, (with a particular commitment to explore Paul's original intended meaning) flows the theological understandings and epistemic convictions which then allow me to present a case for Enlargement Theology. Such a theology, I hope, will be based on an inductive[34] encounter with the text.

In seeking to allow the author's intent within the text to speak for itself I am aware that all who study the text come with some presuppositions/insights which will be shaped by specific personal understandings, experiences and historical contexts. In terms of my exploration of Paul's teaching in Romans 9-11, I bring in addition to my overarching hermeneutical values, two specific insights, which I hope will help in carefully exploring Paul's intended meaning. Firstly, I bring the understanding that Paul is teaching out of a dual role as both an apostle of the church and also as a prophet to Israel.[35] Secondly, I bring insights from encounters with the contemporary Messianic Jewish community. I believe as a result of their reading of scripture and the reality of their identity[36] and current experiences, Jewish believers in Jesus bring to the ongoing hermeneutical debate, many important questions and deep convictions. In the light of my hermeneutical values and these specific insights, I offer the following four basic steps in my exegetical method in order to try to discover the author's intended meaning of the text and also to then apply this meaning appropriately.

Step one. It is important to assess the grammatical, historical and textual context. A text should be interpreted by its most plain meaning (literal interpretation). A text may have many helpful applications but it can have only one meaning based on the author's intent. I understand that this literal or normal sense is the grammatical-historical sense, that is the original meaning or meanings which the writer expressed.[37] However, this approach takes into account and values literary genres[38] and figures of speech, therefore symbolism, allegory, poetry and typology should be recognised and evaluated. Within this approach there is a corresponding rejection of any method of interpretation of a text which attributes a key meaning which is not supported by the literal sense.

In terms of prophetic texts it should be noted that a prophecy may have an immediate historical context, a later historical context or a future application. Also a prophecy may be conditional or unconditional, general or specific.

In terms of specific words it is important to recognise that words can have a number of meanings but only one interpretation in each case in terms of the author's intent. Words should be interpreted consistently in the same context. When a word appears out of context, the word should be probably seen figuratively.[39] The first time a word or idea appears (the principle of first use) will bring about some specific information which should guide in the future understanding of other usage. Correct grammar must precede theological interpretation.

Step two. It is important to assess the historical context. Key questions such as the background of the author (including the hermeneutical methods used by the author),[40] the date, and prime purpose of the text and to whom was the text written must be explored. In the six introductory points which follow within this chapter, I address some of these issues drawing from insights of my listed commentators. I also specifically affirm my understanding of Paul's dual role as both an apostle of the church and as a prophet to Israel. I continue to address the grammatical and historical context in both the general comments and within the specific text comments in each section of the text.

Step three. In following on from steps one and two, I attempt to establish, based on the insights of many commentators and my own study, what the author's original intent was. It seems to me that you can place suggestions in a scale ranging from shades of the impossible, through to the possible, the probable and on towards the definite. This process is helped by seeing how a particular idea or teaching fits in with other sections of the text or other texts written by the author (the principle of correlation). In this way scripture interprets scripture, or to put it another way, Paul interprets Paul by moving from the 'clear' to the 'less clear' passages.[41]

Step four. Following on from attempting to address what the author's intent was, I go on to explore how other theologians, biblical commentators and practitioners within Jewish-Christian relations have understood and continue to understand, apply and reflect upon the text. In terms of this thesis, the area of understanding, application and reflection is primarily focused upon Jewish-Christian relations with a particular emphasis on the development of Enlargement Theology and the contemporary Messianic Jewish movement.

As I reflect upon my overarching hermeneutical values as I explore Romans 9-11, I am aware that at one level there is a four-way discourse emerging.[42] Firstly, I in faith submit to the inspired text. Secondly, I bring to that text all the exegetical tools at my disposal in order to discover the author's inspired intent. Thirdly, I attempt to share this discovery as appropriately as possible in my own context as I deal with specific questions and try to develop a coherent biblical and theological mindset. Fourthly, I reflect upon the reactions of those with whom I share and who share with me (especially in this context within the field of Jewish-Christian relations) in order to reengage with the text in faithful, reflective and effective ways.

4.5 Six Introductory Points with a Focus on the Historical Context of Romans 9-11

In terms of my general understanding of Romans I would affirm the following introductory points. I also want within these introductory points to draw out some initial insights relating to the envisaged historical context of Romans 9-11.

Firstly, Paul is the author.[43]

Secondly, Paul is probably writing from Corinth around 57 CE. Paul is not the founding apostle of the 'Christian community'[44] in Rome, yet both the way Paul appears to address specific questions from within the community in Rome and the extensive greetings and pastoral concern shown in chapter 16 assumes that Paul knew reasonably well at least elements within this emerging community. In terms of referring to a community it may be more helpful to speak of emerging communities or congregations. This point is made by William L Lane:

> Ignatius and Herrmas provide evidence that even in the first decades of the second century Rome was not centrally organized under the administrative authority of a single bishop. In six of his seven letters, Ignatius insists on the importance of the office of bishop. His silence in regard to this pastoral concern in the Letter to the Romans (ca.110 CE) is explained best by the absence of a monarchical bishop in Rome. Herrmas refers only to "the elders who preside over the church" (Herm. Vis. 2.43; 3.9.7). The existence of several house churches only loosely connected with one another throughout Rome suggests why diversity, disunity and a tendency toward independence were persistent problems in the early history of the Christian communities in Rome.[45]

Issues around the formation, identity and the context[46] of the Christian community in Rome is an area of much debate,[47] yet clearly a Christian community or communities had been established, probably through the witness of Jewish believers in Jesus who travelled to Rome or who were part of the established Jewish diaspora community in Rome. There is no record of specific missionary activity directed to Rome, apart from that undertaken by Paul. The size of this community is difficult to estimate with figures ranging from as high as fifty thousand to as low as fifteen thousand at the time of Nero.[48]

Paul is hoping to visit the Christian community in Rome (1:11-12), after fulfilling his immediate responsibility of bringing the collection from the largely Gentile churches to the church in Jerusalem/Judea. This collection is more than a practical act of support — it reflects part of the 'spiritual partnership' of Jew and Gentile in the Messiah which is a core truth of Paul's proclamation. After this, Paul hopes to use Rome as a base and a catalyst for further mission work in Spain (15:24).

Thirdly, Paul is proclaiming the "gospel of God" (1:1). Paul seeks to instruct and encourage the Christians (both Jew[49] and Gentile) in Rome. Paul has this opportunity to present in depth the 'heart of the gospel' message which he has proclaimed throughout his apostolic ministry. Also probably, Paul is seeking to address some misunderstandings which may have arisen from his previous letters (such as the letter to the Galatians) which may have been misinterpreted by some (mainly Gentile) Christians in Rome and taken by them to legitimise an anti-Jewish stance in their thinking and doing. Such a stance may have been enhanced for some by the expulsion of the Jewish community from Rome.[50]

Fourthly, Paul is involved in an exposition of scripture[51] within the letter. Anthony Guerra in commenting on Paul's uses of scripture in Romans 9-11 states:

> . . . 39 percent of Romans 9-11 consists of Scriptural quotations. This frequency of quotations is striking and is approached nowhere else in the Pauline corpus. [52]

Paul clearly bases much of his argument upon the 'Old Testament' texts and his methods of presentation and interpretation seem to draw from well-known paths of Jewish midrash[53] which would clearly be of help to some Jewish members of the Roman congregation(s).

Fifthly, Paul is proclaiming the 'gospel of God' (Rom 1:1) not in an abstract way but in order to both promote his own mission agenda, especially in terms of his impending journey to Jerusalem,[54] and to address specific issues/questions from within the Christian community of Rome. Romans is therefore not best read as a systematic summary of doctrine (although clearly the letter contains detailed doctrinal teaching) but as a pastoral and theological letter. This point is affirmed by Douglas Moo who states:

> It is not a systematic theology but a letter, written in specific circumstances and with specific purposes. The message of Romans is, indeed, timeless; but to understand its message aright, we must appreciate the specific context out of which Romans was written.[55]

Sixthly and finally, Romans 9-11 is an integral part of Romans:

> It is important to realize that these chapters are not an excursus, or an appendix to an argument already complete in itself.[56]

We now turn in the next chapters to an exploration of Romans 9-11 with sections focusing on firstly general comments, secondly, specific textual comments and thirdly comments especially relevant for the developing of Enlargement Theology.

Chapter Five

Romans 9:1–5

Commentary on Romans 9:1–5

> [1] *I speak the truth in Christ — I am not lying, my conscience confirms it in the Holy Spirit —* [2] *I have great sorrow and unceasing anguish in my heart.* [3] *For I could wish that I myself were cursed and cut off from Christ for the sake of my brothers, those of my own race,* [4] *the people of Israel. Theirs is the adoption as sons; theirs the divine glory, the covenants, the receiving of the law, the temple worship and the promises.* [5] *Theirs are the patriarchs, and from them is traced the human ancestry of Christ, who is God over all, for ever praised! Amen.*

Romans 9:1-5 (NIV)

5.1 General Comments

The personal and solemn tone of these opening verses described as a "lamentation" by Moo,[1] is in stark contrast to the note of triumph and praise which concludes the previous section (8:28-39). This section makes it clear that Paul has a great and deep love for the people of Israel. This love hurts. There is real anguish in what Paul is experiencing as he reflects upon and wrestles with the plight and privileges of Israel. Dunn states:

> Paul wants his audience to be in no doubt of the depth of his identity with and concern for his own people.[2]

Paul is and will always be a Jew. The Jewish people are his people and his faith in Jesus and his subsequent apostolic ministry has not, despite what may have been suggested by some of his opponents, undermined his love and loyalty for the people of Israel, nor his own clear identity with them.

This love, loyalty and identity is passionate and would lead him (if it were possible),[3] to be cut off from Christ if in some way this would help his own Jewish people. This willingness to be cursed and cut off has echoes with Moses[4] (Exodus 32:30-32) and, on a different level, has links with Jesus, who was cut off and cursed (becoming sin) through his atoning death.[5]

Paul also states here the great heritage and present advantages of being Jewish. This list of 'privileges' which draws from the earlier (and at this stage incomplete) statement in Romans 3:2, is perhaps given here to address some of his Gentile audience who have developed some form of arrogance towards the diverse Jewish communities in Rome. This arrogance may well have been fuelled to some degree by the perceived failure of Peter's mission to the Jewish communities in Judea or in Rome.[6]

This list of 'privileges' may well have echoes for Paul with the midrash based on Genesis 1:4,[7] which teaches that six things,[8] were created or contemplated before the creation of the world. Within this list is the receiving of the Law (Torah) which is obviously seen here by Paul in a very positive light. This positive understanding of the Law as part of the outworking of the covenant relationship (covenantal faithfulness) is an important theme of Paul's teaching in this segment of Romans.

The place of the Law must not be misinterpreted as has been the case in terms of seeing the Law as an integral part of a failed scheme of 'works righteousness.' The climax or culmination of these 'privileges' is indeed the Christ.

5.2 Specific Text Comments

Verses 1-2. The opening rhetoric of Paul in using both the positive "I speak the truth" and the negative "I am not lying" and then linking both to his relationship "in Christ" clearly adds a note of solemnity. This linking by Paul to his relationship "in Christ" not only adds solemnity but also authority. This point is made by Robert Jewett:

> To question Paul's truthfulness in this circumstance is to question the truth of Christ, for as he says in 2 Cor 11:10, "the truth of Christ is in me." Skepticism about Paul's truthfulness would also contradict the belief that believers share this mystical union with Christ, as stated in 2 Cor 1:21, "it is God who establishes us with you in Christ."[9]

Dunn[10] suggests that in regard to this rhetoric Paul may be using an oath which is repeated in 1 Tim 2:7. In Rabbinic teaching style it is noted by Pryor[11] that the term "I speak the truth" points to that which follows will be something of weight and authority. If this is a Rabbinic teaching device, then in the later part of this verse the reference to 'conscience' and the Holy Spirit may well be seen as providing the two witnesses, along with Paul's own testimony, which the Torah[12] requires for confirmation of important matters.

Verse 3. The Davidic reference here, as in Romans 1:3,[13] is essential for Paul in showing the continuity of the ministry of Christ to God's past actions in terms of his covenant with Israel. This would be of great assurance to those Jewish believers in Jesus who were perhaps being challenged by groups[14] within the Roman congregations who wanted to stress the 'discontinuity' with Jewish history in order to promote the 'newness' of the kingdom/community of faith which Jesus established.

Verse 4 (a). The focus here is upon the term 'the people of Israel'. The term 'Israel' which Paul uses here opens up one of the core issues in Romans 9-11. I would understand that here

Paul is using the term to refer to all Jewish people. For Paul here all the Jews are Israelites. In this context, Paul is speaking from within his own people's ethnic self definition of themselves as God's covenant people rooted in God's promises to Abraham which are continued and renewed through Isaac.[15] However, Stern in his Jewish New Testament commentary differs from my understanding:

> Sha'ul is not speaking of all Jews but only those who have not come to trust in Yeshua.[16]

How commentators interpret and define the term 'Israel' will affect greatly the understanding of the text. Stern clearly defines Israel in this context as 'unbelieving Israel'. However, I see Israel here referring to the ethnic Jewish people, made up of both believers in Jesus (messianic Jews/faithful remnant) and non-believers in Jesus. The term 'Israel' appears eleven times (9:4, :6 (x2) :27, :31, 10:19, :21, 11:1, :2, :7 and :25) within Romans 9-11, and as Dunn states:

> If any name characterized Jewish self understanding it was 'Israel'.[17]

Dunn's position is affirmed by Jewett:

> Dunn is correct in concluding the term "Israel" and "Israelite" which occur twelve times in chaps 9-11 in contrast to "Jews" in the earlier chapters are "therefore deliberately chosen by Paul to evoke his people's sense of being God's elect, the covenant people of the one God."[18]

Should the name Israel be interpreted in the same way in each context? Or does Paul redefine the name/term? Is Ziesler right in his commentary when he states:

> Certainly the meaning given to 'Israel' varies from place to place within 9-11.[19]

Ziesler goes on to state:

> The real problem is the place of 'all Israel' in the purpose of God:

does it, or only a smaller group within it serve as the focus of the divine plan?[20]

Is it possible to find resolution to the use of the term, or is there a discrepancy within Paul's own thinking and use of the term 'Israel'? Moo in commenting on issues relating to the use of the term 'Israel' in this verse states:

Paul's selection of the term "Israelites" to head this list is significant. For in contrast to the colourless, politically and nationally orientated title "Jew", "Israelite" connotes the special religious position of the members of the Jewish people. It is therefore no accident that Paul in Rom 9-11 generally abandons the word "Jew" which has figured so prominently in chaps 1-8, in favour of the terms "Israelites" and "Israel". Paul is no longer looking at the Jews from the perspective of the Gentiles and in their relationship to the Gentiles but from the perspective of salvation history and in their relationship to God and his promises to them. The appellation "Israelites" then is no mere political or nationalistic designation but a religiously significant and honorific title. And despite the refusal of most of the Israelites to accept God's gift of salvation in Christ, this title has not been revoked. Here is set up the tension that Paul seeks to resolve in these chapters.[21]

Verse 4 (b). The term 'covenants' is the main focus point in this part of the verse. This is the third 'privilege' of Jewish heritage in the list of eight. The plural term 'covenants' is somewhat unusual with the singular term being much more in use in both the Old Testament and New Testament. The plural use here probably points to the range of the biblical covenants[22] which includes the covenant with Noah, Abraham, Moses and David, and includes the New Covenant promised by Jeremiah (Jer 31:30-36) to the house of Israel and the house of Judah and inaugurated in Paul's understanding through the person and work of Jesus (Mt 26:28). The key point which Paul is probably making here is that the New Covenant is the fulfilment and continuation of God's ongoing purposes. The New Covenant, as with the previous covenants beginning with Abraham, are all made with Israel, yet the New Covenant extends the covenantal blessing and covenantal status to believing Gentiles. By this extension the origin intention/promise of the covenant with Abraham finds the promised fulfilment (Gen 12:3-4).

Verse 5. This great list of blessings climaxing with the gift of the Messiah leads Paul into an outpouring of praise. This pattern of a doxology concluding a segment of teaching is often found in Paul's writing.[23] For Paul, all theology finds its ultimate destination in praise and awesome contemplation.

In this doxology there is a debate over the interpretation of the words which the New International Version text renders; ". . . of Christ, who is God over all, for ever praised! Amen." The difficulty is raised partly because Paul writing in Greek used no (or very little) punctuation. How translators choose to punctuate the text clearly will guide the meaning, or rather translators will decide on which of the two main meanings is most appropriate and then insert the relevant punctuation. The various options with many nuances are outlined at some length in the various commentaries.[24]

The way in which verse 5 is stated clearly has significant Christological implications. If one follows the punctuation outlined in the New International Version, New Revised Standard Version, King James and the Jerusalem Bible, one is presented with a direct identification of Christ with God. This interpretation was the overwhelming interpretation of the early Patristic tradition. This identification would stand alongside other such New Testament texts, for example; John 1:1, 1:14, 10:30, 20:28, Rom 10:13, Col 1:19, Titus 2:13 and Heb 1:3 where it appears that references to the Word, Lord and Christ are directly affirming of divine status. However, if one follows the punctuation outlined in the Revised Standard Version, New English Bible and the Complete Jewish Bible, one is presented with a separation of the statement about the Messiah from the ascription of praise to God which follows.

In relation to the core commentators I have referred to, both

Pryor and Moo, for example, affirm that this verse is making a direct identification of Christ with God. The Greek text is not ambiguous and the grammar allows for and probably promotes a direct identification of Christ with God. Moo makes this very clear when he concludes his comments:

> Connecting "God" to "Christ" is therefore exegetically preferable, theologically unobjectionable, and contextually appropriate. Paul here calls the Messiah Jesus, "God," attributing to him full divine status.[25]

Moo also refers here to the identification of Messiah Jesus with God as being not only grammatical appropriate, but also, and probably more controversially, he states that such identification is also appropriate in terms of the missionary and pastoral context in which Paul is writing:

> The argument from context is that it would be inconceivable for Paul to describe Christ as God in a passage where he is trying to create common ground with his unbelieving "kindred". However, as we noted, Paul's shift in construction when introducing the Messiah implies a certain "distance" between unbelieving Jews and the reality of Jesus the Messiah. And this fits naturally into Paul's overall perspective, accepting his grief at Jewish unbelief by highlighting the divine status of the Messiah whom his fellow Jews have rejected.[26]

Moo therefore disagrees with Stern over the issue of contextual appropriateness. Stern's position is as follows:

> One can understand the desire of Christians to find Scriptural support for affirming Yeshua's divinity. But although such a strong and surprising theological statement—especially shocking to Jews—would enhance Sha'ul's argument, it craves more than simple expression without any explanation whatsoever; for any Jewish hearer of the letter would immediately have so many questions that he would be unable to concentrate on Sha'ul's following discussion. Furthermore, it makes the "Amen" irrelevant, since it no longer is a congregational response to a b'rakkah.[27]

Stern goes on to outline his own position which is reflected in the Complete Jewish Bible text:

> . . . the phrase first speaks of the Messiah as being over all. After this, God is to be blessed forever for having chosen a people for himself and given them these many advantages, crowned with the advantage of having the Messiah, who is in charge of everything, be one of their number.[28]

Ziesler in his commentary helpfully outlines the options and concludes that:

> The whole point is decidedly moot . . . .[29]

Dunn affirms the translation, "God who is over all, may he be blessed for ever. Amen." Dunn concludes his comments:

> Again, while Paul was already well used to associating Christ with God and attributing divine functions to Christ (1:7; 1 Cor 8:6), it is less likely that he would have intended Christ to be hailed as "God over all." (contrast 1 Cor 15:24-28) Just as likely is it that the juxtaposition of references to the Messiah of Israel and "God over all" would be read as an identity; the more conscious of his readers were of the continuity between Israel's faith and Paul's gospel the less likely they would be to read the ambiguous phrasing as the abrupt departure from Israel's monotheism which the more straightforward syntax would apply. In fact it is probably Paul's desire to stress the universality of God's embrace, Gentile as well as Jew, which results in the unusual phrasing. Just as in 3:29-30 he used Jewish monotheism to make the same basic point, so here rather than the more regular form of the doxology to the one God ("Blessed be God...") he chooses to stress that the God he adores is God over all: "he who is God over all, may he be blessed for ever, Amen."[30]

5.3 Comments relating to the Development of Enlargement Theology

These opening five verses raise a range of material which exposes the weaknesses inherent within Replacement Theology and Two Covenant Theology. I will outline the following four which I will argue contribute to the development of the core tenets of Enlargement Theology.

We have in this segment Paul's passionate identification with his fellow Jews and his sense of deep concern for their future. This raises, I suggest, two fundamental points in regard to establishing an overall theological perspective. Firstly, if one is going to present a Two Covenant approach which states that there is 'a Jewish way' to an on-going covenant relationship with God which is separate from the way of Messiah Jesus, then how can one account for Paul's heart-rending anguish? For Paul clearly believes that the way of Messiah Jesus is the only way for both Jews and Gentiles to be in this on-going full covenant relationship with God. Paul is not promoting a specific religious insight or some separate Gentile message, but rather he is promoting what he understands to be nothing less than the "gospel of God" (1:1) for the salvation of the Jew first (chiefly or especially for the Jew) and also (equally) for the Gentile (1:16).

For Paul the salvation of the Jew first or chiefly[31] is the outworking of the covenant with Abraham. The saving purposes of God are tied in with the promise to Abraham. God could not righteously bring salvation to anyone if it bypassed the promises to Abraham. This covenant to Abraham and his seed is the source for Paul of the hope for all who believe in the saving power of Jesus. If one is to be an advocate for a Two Covenant approach one must look elsewhere for support for such a position. A Two Covenant approach would result in by-passing Paul's passionate concern and rejecting his line of teaching outlined here in Romans.

Secondly, linked to this first point is that Paul's passionate concern for his fellow Jewish people is also a reminder that when a Jew (like Paul) embraces faith in Messiah he or she does not, as is sometimes assumed, cease to have a clear Jewish identity or an active love for Jewish people or concern for Jewish issues. For a Jewish person to become a follower of Jesus does not make that person any less a Jew. This was certainly Paul's personal conviction, experience and theological expression. It is also the conviction, experience and core theological expression today of Messianic Jewish believers. Messianic Jewish believers would understand that it was through coming to faith in Messiah Jesus that their love for and loyalty to their fellow Jews became enhanced and renewed.[32] Such renewal often includes new and 'deeper levels' of Torah observance.[33]

The point in regard to future dialogue and genuine encounters is that the experience of Messianic Jewish believers should be heard and not simply rejected as is often the case. It is often impossible for Messianic Jewish believers to go beyond being seen either as simple deceivers of or traitors to the wider Jewish community. This is clearly a huge issue which we will return to on a number of occasions within this thesis as we focus on the development of Enlargement Theology and how it connects to the church's relationship with Israel, Jewish people and especially the emerging contemporary Messianic Jewish movement. However, at this point the following quote from Walter Riggans, is I believe extremely helpful in marking out the current situation of Messianic Jews within the wider field of Jewish-Christian relations:

It is without doubt hopelessly naive for Messianic Jews to ever imagine that they could act as a bridge between the Church and the Synagogue, but on the other hand it is surely tragically immature and self serving of both the Church and Synagogue to refuse Messianic Jews any participation at all in the modern movement to build bridges among religious communities. If it is decided that Messianic Jews can not be considered to be authentic members of the body of the Messiah, or that they do not qualify as authentically

Jewish, then let that point emerge from a genuine meeting of minds and spirits.[34]

Thirdly, Paul lists the 'privileges' of Jewish heritage. These privileges are not relegated to the past or transferred to the church as Replacement Theology would teach. These advantages are proclaimed by Paul as present day realities. In the light of these 'privileges' rooted in God's sovereign choice there is no space for the position of Gentile arrogance and triumphalism which would attempt to deny the reality of Jewish blessing. Such a position is often linked to a prevailing Replacement Theological perspective which attempts to undermine the Jewish foundation of Christian faith and create a gulf of discontinuity between the Old and New covenants. Dunn helpfully comments:

> To break the link between old and new covenant is not to liberate the gospel but to destroy it, for the gospel is nothing if it is not the continuation and fulfillment of all that God intended for and through his chosen people.[35]

Fourthly and finally, the issues raised by the debates over the interpretation of the doxology are of interest. Of special note is the issue over what would be, to use Moo's phrase, "contextually appropriate" for Paul. This issue of what is contextually appropriate has huge repercussions not just in the study of Paul but within wider Jewish-Christian relations. I will simply focus here on the one area of the divinity of Christ which directly flows from the text. However, the issue of contextually appropriate use of religious symbols, language and religious practice is also a core issue at the heart of Jewish-Christian relations, especially as they interact with the emerging contemporary Messianic Jewish movement.[36]

Firstly, linking in with the doxology is the issue of the divinity of Christ. Messianic Jewish Theology would fully endorse belief in the triune nature of God and thereby endorse the full divinity of Christ.[37] Yet Messianic Jewish Theology is attempting in part, in regard to the divinity of Jesus, to reformulate the traditional (Nicea) trinitarian formula in order to communicate effectively and faithfully to the contemporary Jewish mind. Richard Harvey in his Mishkan article refers to David Stern's arguments in terms of the contextual use of religious language and theological models and states:

> In the Jewish New Testament and Jewish New Testament commentary Stern addresses such questions as "Is Yeshua God?" and "Is God a Trinity?" but tries to push past the reflex responses of "Absolutely" (Christian) and "Absolutely not" (Jewish) in order to discuss the substance of the matter- what positive and negative answers might mean, and whether both Christian and Jewish contexts might admit of "less confrontational formulations without compromising the scriptural data."[38]

In addition to this approach by David Stern, Dwight Pryor, writing in the same Mishkan edition as Richard Harvey, explores further the Hebrew term 'Ehad', and presents the following argument:

> . . . when Israel affirms the Shema it acknowledges the indivisible unity of YHWH. The Hebrew word ehad speaks of unity not singularity. The one and only God is a unity of all that he is-was-will be, of all his attributes, actions and appearances. Though he has many names, there are not many gods. The plural noun, Elohim, always takes a singular verb in the Hebrew, when referring to the God of Israel. [39]

Pryor then continues this line of argument:

> I am simply noting that the severe monotheism of Islam differs from the unified monotheism of Judaism and Christianity in a way parallel to the differences between yahid (singular "one") and ehad ("one" of unity). The God of the Bible has an inner harmony and indivisible unity of all that he does and is. In his oneness there is plurality-in-unity, a unity that must not be broken, a plurality that must not be diminished. Unlike the uniformity of monism, biblical monotheism is irreducibly relational and characterized at its core by love.[40]

This work by Stern, Pryor and others seems to me to have within it some very helpful elements for ongoing Jewish-Christian dialogue and theological reflection. The experiences of Messianic Jewish worshiping and witnessing communities may be key places for helping to re-contextualise traditional Christian doctrine. Such a re-contextualising is at the heart of a developing Enlargement Theology. It is my hope that this theological development could lead to a real theological and pastoral engagement with contemporary religious Jewish communities. Clearly, there are dangers in aspects of re-contextualising as Pryor himself identifies, namely that in doing this work old heresies such as Modalism and Adoptionism may reappear simply disguised in contemporary Messianic Jewish theological clothing.

Chapter Six

Romans 9:6–29

Commentary on Romans 9:6 – 29

⁶It is not as though God's word had failed. For not all who are descended from Israel are Israel. ⁷Nor because they are his descendants are they all Abraham's children. On the contrary, "It is through Isaac that your offspring will be reckoned." ⁸In other words, it is not the natural children who are God's children, but it is the children of the promise who are regarded as Abraham's offspring. ⁹For this was how the promise was stated: "At the appointed time I will return and Sarah will have a son."

¹⁰Not only that, but Rebekah's children had one and the same father, our father Isaac. ¹¹Yet before the twins were born or had done anything good or bad—in order that God's purpose in election might stand: ¹²not by works but by him who calls—she was told, "The older will serve the younger." ¹³Just as it is written: "Jacob I loved, but Esau I hated."

¹⁴What then shall we say? Is God unjust? Not at all! ¹⁵For he says to Moses,

"I will have mercy on whom I have mercy, and I will have mercy, and I will have compassion on whom I have compassion."

¹⁶It does not, therefore depend on man's desire or effort, but on God's mercy. ¹⁷For the Scripture says to Pharaoh: "I raised you up for this very purpose, that I may display my power in you and that my name might be proclaimed in all the earth." ¹⁸Therefore God has mercy on whom he wants to have mercy, and he hardens whom he wants to harden.

[19]One of you will say to me: "Then why does God still blame us? For who resists his will?" [20]But who are you, O man, to talk back to God? "Shall what is formed say to him who formed it, 'Why did you make me like this?'" [21]Does not the potter have the right to make out of the same lump of clay some pottery for noble purposes and some for common use?

[22]What if God, choosing to show his wrath and make his power known, bore with great patience the objects of his wrath- prepared for destruction? [23]What if he did this to make the riches of his glory known to the objects of his mercy, whom he prepared in advance for glory — [24]even us, whom he called, not only from the Jews but also from the Gentiles? [25]As he says in Hosea:

"I will call them 'my people' who are not my people;
and I will call her 'my loved one' who is not my loved one,"

[26]and,

"It will happen then in the very place where it was said to them,
'You are not my people', they will be called 'sons of the living
God'."

[27]Isaiah cries out concerning Israel:

"Though the number of Israelites be like the sand by the sea,
only the remnant will be saved.
[28]For the Lord will carry out his sentence on earth with speed
and finality."

[29]It is just as Isaiah said previously:

"Unless the Lord Almighty had left us descendants, we would have
become like Sodom, we would have been like Gomorrah."

Romans 9:6-29 (NIV)

6.1 General Comments

Paul in this section wrestles with the issue which flows from his deep love for his fellow Jewish people and the fact that so many of them are currently rejecting the "gospel of God"(1:1). This current act of rejection is in marked contrast to the fact that so many Gentiles are responding to the gospel and by God's grace and call are now in Paul's understanding having full covenantal status as members of 'God's people' (without firstly seeking to become Jewish). This fact sits uncomfortably to say the least with the prevailing Rabbinic Jewish understanding of the nature and purpose of election and raises many fundamental questions for Paul. These are the questions which are to be worked out both in terms of Paul's ongoing theological reflection and his missionary practice.

Something unexpected has taken place and the result of this is a profound questioning of God's promises. Does what has happened undermine God's ability to fulfil the promises of his word? Has in some senses the word of God failed? In engaging with such key questions, Stern states:

> This is the logical place to start, for it was the questioning of God's ability to fulfill his promises that raised the issue. The passage establishes on the unshakable ground of God's sovereignty (vv.19-23), justice and mercy (vv.14-18) not only that the promise apply to but a limited "seed"(vv.6-13) or "remnant" of Israel, but also that at least some of them apply to certain Gentiles who never were part of Israel (vv.22-26).[1]

Moo makes a similar point to Stern:

> If the OT teaches that belonging to physical Israel in itself makes a person a member of God's true spiritual people, then Paul's gospel is in jeopardy. For were this the case, the gospel proclaiming that only those who believe in Jesus Christ can be saved (cf.3:20-26), would contradict the OT and be cut off from its indispensable historical roots. Paul therefore argues in vv.6b-29 that belonging to God's true spiritual people has always been based on God's gracious and sovereign call and not on ethnic identity. Therefore,

God is free to 'narrow' the apparent boundaries of election by choosing only some Jews to be saved (vv.6-13; 27-29). He is also free to "expand" the dimensions of his people by choosing Gentiles (vv.24-26).[2]

The key point stressed by Moo which is fundamental to Paul's argument at this stage is that this unexpected turn in 'salvation history' should not be unexpected to those who rightly understood the prime intent of Abraham's blessing — namely that God's call was and is based on 'grace not race' and 'mercy rather than merit'. This call of God is not unjust (v14) or arbitrary. Neither does it result in a denial of human responsibility (vv19-21).

In this section we come face to face with key core issues such as the nature of God's election, his call, human freedom and sovereign choice. As we do so, there is a need to be aware of the wider context, namely the debate between various Calvinistic and Arminian perspectives[3] and the numerous exegetical positions which are shaped by such perspectives. It is also worth noting that as a modern reader of the text one may be asking some questions here which would be very different from the questions Paul would be pursuing. This point is made helpfully by Anthony Guerra:

> One may wonder how Paul could think that the quotation of Exodus 33:19 sustains his denial of divine arbitrariness. The issue of the justice of God is for him quite different from the accent of modern theodicy. Whereas modern theodicy focuses primarily on the unjust suffering of innocent people, Paul believes all to be sinners and worthy of condemnation (cf. 3:10, :19).Thus for Paul the issue is quite the opposite of modern theodicy, for he is prone to ask: why does a righteous God allow sinners to go unpunished? From this perspective, one begins to understand how the Exodus quotation provides Paul with an answer: it is God's mercy that explains divine restraint toward human iniquity (cf. 3:25). It is not human striving but divine mercy that accounts for all forbearance (9:16).[4]

As one wrestles with such issues, there is a need for humility and caution to be mixed with convictions, namely, that the biblical picture is beyond logical reasoning but is not contrary to such reasoning. In terms of fundamental convictions relating to God's elective purposes, the following two statements by Barth are worthy of note in this initial setting. Firstly, in terms of the orientation of the doctrine:

> We must not seek the ground of this election anywhere but in the love of God, in His free love-otherwise it would not be His—but still in His love. If we seek it elsewhere, then we are no longer talking about this election. We are no longer talking about the decision of the divine will which was fulfilled in Jesus Christ. We are looking beyond these to a supposedly greater depth in God (and that undoubtedly means nothingness, or rather the depth of Satan). What takes place in this election is always that God is for us; for us, and therefore for the world which was created by Him, which is distinct from Him, but which is yet maintained by Him. The election is made with a view to the sending of His Son.[5]

Secondly, in terms of the election of the community:

> The meaning of its (Israel) election is that, in the very act of becoming guilty towards God, it must genuinely magnify His faithfulness.[6]

This spirit of humility and caution mixed with conviction is admirably expressed by Moo:

> I can only reiterate that the introduction into this text of any basis for God's election outside God himself defies both the language and the logic of what Paul has written. The only logical possibility, then, would seem to be to reverse the relationship between God's choosing and faith; as Augustine stated it: "God does not choose us because we believe, but that we may believe." This way of putting the matter seems generally to be justified by this passage and by the teaching of Scripture elsewhere. But it comes perilously close to trivializing human faith, something that many texts in Romans and in the rest of the NT simply will not allow us to do. We need perhaps, to be more cautious in our foundations and to insist on

the absolute causality and meaningfulness of human decision to believe at the same time as we rightly make God's choosing of us ultimately basic. Such a double emphasis may strain the boundaries of logic (it does not I trust break them!) or remain unsatisfyingly complex, but it may have the virtue of reflecting Scripture's own balanced perspective.[7]

6.2 Specific Text Comments

Verse 6. This verse introduces a fundamental argument in Paul's theology. The issue of God's election of Israel and the related promises are ultimately issues about the trustworthiness of God. Paul argues passionately that the heartbreaking rejection of the Gospel by the majority of his fellow Jews in no way undermines God's word or nullifies the covenant promises. This line of argument picks up the theme initially introduced in 3:3.

Verse 7. The key for Paul which is presented in the following verses is that the election of Israel (covenantal promise) through the call to and the response of Abraham was never to be understood simply in terms of physical descent,[8] or human merit (v 1) but rather in terms of God's promise, mercy (v 16) and ongoing sovereign plan. Within this sovereign plan, there stand various pairs of individuals who in contrasting ways testify to God's purposes. For example, the pair Ishmael and Isaac (v 7), Esau and Jacob (vv 11-13) and Pharaoh and Moses (vv 14-17). Yet within this unfolding plan the focus here is on the promised seed of Isaac. This point is made clear by Robert Jewett:

> What Paul denies here is that the covenantal promise extended to all of Abraham's children. It was the child of Sarah (Gen 21:1-3), not the children of Hagar and Keturah (Gen 16:15; 25:2), who would bear the promise of becoming the people of Israel (cf. Gal 4:22-31). The distinction between the broader category "children" and the restricted term "seed" thus corresponds exactly to that between all Israel and the true Israel in v. 6b. That there was a kind of "divine

exclusion process" in Israel's history was developed in Gal 3:16 to prove that Jesus was the single heir, but here Paul takes the more traditional path of Jewish exegesis, claiming that the line of Abraham, Isaac and Jacob received the promised inheritance. His point is that from the beginning of Israel's history, physical descent alone was incapable of guaranteeing inclusion in the promise.[9]

Beyond these individual pairings (and the wider groupings they represent) there stand two additional implicit contrasts for Paul. Firstly, that of the unbelieving Jewish community and the faithful remnant and, secondly, that of the wayward and disobedient synagogue and the church. These contrasts and especially the existence of the wayward and disobedient synagogue community alongside a faithful (elect) group (the church — made of Jews and Gentiles) affirms that for Paul such a remnant reality is not a new thing and such a reality should not in any way undermine the faithfulness of God and his word. Also, I would suggest that it shows that, for Paul, the emerging 'church' is never seen as identical with Israel but the church is a key part of God's redeeming purposes alongside ethnic Israel. This includes both the believing remnant of ethnic Israel within the church and the unbelieving majority of ethnic Israel outside of the church.

The gift of physical descent from Abraham is not in itself a guarantee of future salvation (the 'guarantee' for Paul is to respond in ways which exhibit Abraham's own faithful response).[10] There is in this line of arguing echoes of the teaching of John the Baptist (Matthew 3:7-9) and of Jesus (John 8:31-47) although there are as Paul has already argued (Rom 9:4-5) still many benefits, privileges and responsibilities of being in the physical lineage of the patriarchs.

This sovereign plan is traced through the line of Isaac (the child of promise). It is worth noting here that in Paul's list of God's covenantal gifts to Israel, it was the gift of promise which was placed emphatically at the end of the list of those gifts distinctly for Israel in contrast with the gift of Christ (9:5) which is from Israel. Again, this theme of promise is linked to the word of promise which remains true (9:6). The line is then traced to Jacob (with a quotation from Malachi 1:2-3) and on to the events of the Exodus with reference to Moses and Pharaoh and concludes with the prophetic words of Hosea and Isaiah.

In all of this retelling of the line of promise, Paul is recounting and celebrating the narrative of Israel from Abraham to the present which is marked in part by the calling of the Gentiles (v24) and then on to the future when the Lord will carry out his sentence (v28). In this retelling of the story Paul draws on the biblical metaphor[11] of the potter and the clay (v21). Also within this exploration of sovereign freedom and human response, Paul draws from the wisdom literature with echoes of Job (Job 1:22 and 9:12).

Verse 14. There is debate amongst the commentators as to whether this question (and the other questions within Romans) is simply a method of Paul's own rhetoric or is a genuine question which has been presented to Paul. The important point, however, is that the tone of this question comes from a genuine position of faith and is in keeping with much Jewish discussion on the nature of God's purposes (note the "we" of v13) rather than pure unbelief or cynicism. Paul's response to the question is emphatic (see also 3:4, 11:1 and 11:11).

From this point to verse 29, Paul continues the line of argument seeking to show that God's elective purposes do not undermine the covenant, nor are they arbitrary, but rather that both in mercy and judgment God is sovereign. This sovereign outworking results in both Israel's partial hardening/apostasy and Pharaoh's actions serving God's ultimate purposes, both in terms of the universal proclamation of God's name (v17) and in the closely related issue of the calling of the Gentiles (v24).

Verse 16. The comment by Dunn is helpful here, namely:

> Paul does not disparage "willing" (desire — NIV) or "running" (effort — NIV); willing and running are, of course, part of the human response to God. But they are not factors in election, neither

in the initial choice nor in its maintenance. Paul's concern is not
to debate the issues of predestination and free will with Pharisee
and Essene but to clarify what the covenant means for Israel.[12]

Verses 20-24. Paul is now continuing with what Ziesler terms
"the rhetorical device of the diatribe",[13] and responds to the
question of verse 19 with the question of verse 20. Paul is not
entering into a full debate about determinism/predestination
but is rather seeking to affirm that God is just and his justice is
being worked out throughout the ongoing history of his people.
The emphasis of this working out is that of God's mercy rather
than his judgment, yet as Stern states, this mercy is highlighted
in contexts of judgment:

> . . . God's mercy is more evident and more wonderful, more
> glorious, more "mercy-full" when the background of judgment is
> clearly perceived.[14]

This ongoing history is then clearly brought into focus (v24)
as Paul is no longer dealing with analogies and hypothetical
questions, but is proclaiming that the church is the object of
God's mercy. Also the church, as a community of Jew and
Gentile and as the object of God's mercy, was always part of
the goal of God's redemptive purposes. This is given a context
in the quotations from Hosea 2:23 (v25) and Hosea 1:10 (v26).
This 'widening out' of God's mercy and bringing in of the
Gentiles is not some addendum to God's original purpose in
response to the obstinacy of the majority of Israel.[15]

Verses 25-26. Paul is using these texts not as direct proof texts
but rather as contexts. The term 'call' in the quote from Hosea
(which is probably Paul's own change/addition) is generally
seen to emphasize the point that being or becoming 'God's
people' is brought about exclusively as a result of God's
gracious initiative.

I suggest also there may be here an implicit reference to
the Shema, with its demand for Israel to hear and respond.
In Hosea, the call is to Israel (in this context, the rebellious/

exiled Northern kingdom) not to the Gentiles. However, Paul is using the text[16] to infer the widening of God's mercy to include the ingathering of Gentiles. Joseph Shulam suggests that the Hosea texts:

> ... were possibly adapted from their original reference to Israel in circles influenced by Qumran ideology and applied to the Gentiles, and Paul follows this tradition here.[17]

Dunn concisely concludes:

> It is simply that scripture proves that those who were not God's people can by God's gracious act become his people.[18]

The reference to the 'very place' may refer to Jerusalem.[19] If so, Paul may have in mind the Gentiles flocking to Jerusalem as an eschatological act.[20] Clearly the collection which Paul was determined to take to Jerusalem from the largely Gentile churches seems to have more than simply a practical element but rather has spiritual and perhaps, for Paul, eschatological undertones. Interestingly, the significance of this collection seems to grow in importance[21] for Paul in the later stages of his apostolic mission. This apostolic mission Paul sees as reflecting God's elective purposes, namely not of excluding some but of extending to all peoples the offer of God's redemptive mercy and covenantal purposes.

Verses 27-29. The focus on the remnant for Paul is here something which could be seen either as something consoling or condemning. As John Lodge points out:

> ... the scriptural language about the remnant can be used threateningly (e.g., 2 Kgs 21:14; Isa 14:22, v. 30; Ezek 5:10) or confidently (Gen 45:7, 2 Kgs 19:31; 1 Mac 3:35:). It is not automatically negative. Paul's use of the quote with the term does not indicate in itself whether Paul has salvation or condemnation in mind.... The reader is challenged to find a word of hope for Israel or a word of condemnation. Whichever way a reader decides, the notion of remnant can be made to support his or her reading.[22]

While I agree with the above quote from Lodge that the term 'remnant' can in general be seen as a word of hope or condemnation, I would in this case see that this remnant reference connects back to 9:6 and shows that the faithfulness of some at least of Israel, of which Paul is a representative, is evidence in part that God's word has not (and cannot have) failed. If this is the context then, on balance, I would see that the term 'remnant', although it may sound somewhat limited, leads to the future hope. The hope spoken of in the quote from Isaiah (v29) is in the term 'descendants' (seed). This term can include a limitless number. It can include both Jew and Gentile. It can also, I suggest, allow for future growth and it does not exclude the final restoration/salvation of 'all Israel'. These are themes which Paul will take up in the following sections of this letter. These are clearly themes which have an emphasis on hope and mercy rather than on wrath and condemnation.

6.3 Comments relating to the Development of Enlargement Theology

This section (vv. 6-29), with its tightly argued rhetorical ebb and flow, engages with core questions about the elective purposes of God. Paul is arguing here that God is continuing to shape his people as he did in the period of the patriarchs, through a divine process of choosing, calling, hardening and renewing. Within this there are many issues raised for consideration in the area of contemporary Jewish-Christian relations and especially the development of Enlargement Theology. I will outline the following two.

The first area for consideration and comment is fundamental. Namely, "What does it mean to belong to 'God's people'?" Related to this are numerous questions such as: "What are our experiences of being called by God?" "In what ways, if any, does belonging to the 'New Covenant people' differ from belonging to 'historical/ethnic Israel'?" "On what does our identity and security in God rest?" "Is Paul's redefining of 'Israel' consistent with the witness of the scriptures?" "In what ways can the ministry of Jesus be faithfully seen in terms of a discontinuity as well as a continuum and a climax of the history and destiny of Israel?"

Such questions will be revisited throughout the development of this thesis. However, I will address now those aspects which seem to flow in part from this section of Romans. The first verse (v6) contains two clear statements which are of great importance, namely, that God's word has not failed and that not all who are descended from Israel are Israel. The first statement affirming the reliability and trustworthiness of God's word is crucial for Paul and the development of Enlargement Theology. This is because the line of reasoning which is at the heart of Replacement Theology is that God's word has failed in regard to the promise to Israel, especially in regard to the promise of the land which is explicit within the Abrahamic covenant. This failure has led either to the promises in some way being transferred from ethnic Israel to the Christian community, or that these promises have lapsed because of Israel's failure and have in some way been revived, restored or fulfilled 'spiritually' solely within the church. Either of these options is, I suggest, beyond the scope of Paul's convictions as outlined in Romans 9-11:

> The later Gentile church may have found it possible to make such a transfer, but not Paul.[23]

I would argue that, for the later predominantly Gentile church, it was not only found possible but was highly desirable at times to make such a transfer. If such a transfer was not seen as an option for Paul, then clearly this undermines the position of those who hold to Replacement Theology, who often use parts of Paul's writings as an initial source for the development of their theological position.

The link between Replacement Theology and the trustworthiness of God's word and character is fundamental. If God has in some way forsaken the promises made to ethnic Israel then what guarantee has the church got that, at some arbitrary future point, God will not replace the church and the Gospel with some new group, people, promise and message? This link has a certain logical force to it and it is an important weapon in undermining Replacement Theology, however supporters of a Replacement position often counter this deductive logic with the conviction that the Gospel (ministry of Jesus) is the final and decisive act within God's redemptive purposes, therefore nothing more can be added or changed. Jesus himself as the resurrected and ascended Lord is the final guarantee of God's faithfulness.

Replacement Theology, in tearing the Jewish roots from the church and the reliability of the covenant promises from the Jewish people, ultimately creates a flawed foundation for the church in its identity, security and mission. Such a flawed foundation has made and continues to make creative encounters between Jews and Christians extremely problematic.

The affirmation of the trustworthiness of God's word seems to undermine a classic Replacement Theology with its accompanying secessionist mindset. However, it could be argued from the second part of verse 6, that we are presented with some 'seeds' for the future growth of Replacement Theology — namely, that there is here unquestionably a redefining of Israel taking place.[24] This redefining is within the context of 'historical/ethnic Israel' (up until verse 23) and then this is followed by the affirmation of God's calling of the Gentiles.

Clearly for Paul there is a redefining taking place. This redefining will be affirmed within the development of Enlargement Theology. The first core tenet of Enlargement Theology is that God's covenantal relationship with the Jewish people is eternal, yet this relationship is not static. The eternal nature is rooted in God's unconditional promises made within the Abrahamic covenant to ethnic Israel. In this context, Enlargement Theology upholds a clear distinction between ethnic Israel[25] and the church.[26] This distinction is a core tenet of Dispensational Theology,[27] yet Enlargement

Theology is not necessarily dependent on being placed within a wider dispensational framework.[28] This redefining within Enlargement Theology allows for the inclusion of Gentiles into God's redemptive purpose and this is neither the same as nor comparable to the transferring explicit within Replacement Theology. As Dunn states:

> It is important to note that by the second Israel Paul does not mean believers over against national Israel . . . hence the inadequacy of any talk of transfer of the name and blessings of "Israel" to the church as though Paul saw them as distinct entities.[29]

In the development of Enlargement Theology, there is the upholding of God's promises to ethnic Israel based on the Abrahamic covenant. Yet this faithful continuity of God's word does not restrict the understanding of Israel simply to ethnic Israel. For within the fourth tenet of Enlargement Theology, God's redemptive purposes are being worked out through three different yet interrelated communities of 'God's people'.

These communities of 'God's people' within the presentation of Enlargement Theology consist of ethnic Israel, the church and Jewish believers in Jesus.[30] Each of these communities, in different contexts, can claim (with degrees of legitimacy) part of the defining biblical term 'Israel'. In regard to the legitimacy of the church in claiming the term Israel, the nuance within Enlargement Theology would be on continuity as the church is rooted into and fulfils in part the calling of Israel as the 'true', 'spiritual' and 'historical' 'people of God'. In this sense the church is part of the fulfilling of what, for want of a better term, can be seen as the 'old Israel of God' and not in terms of discontinuity explicit within Replacement Theology which claims that the church is to be understood primarily as the 'new Israel of God'.

The second closely related area for consideration is the issue of the remnant. The teaching about the remnant, introduced in 9:27 with the quote from Isaiah and taken further in 11:5 and 11:25, is an important theme in Paul's teaching. It is a theme which has important echoes for both Rabbinic Jews and Christians. This is especially true for contemporary Jewish believers in Jesus, who would see themselves (and their predecessors) as part of this faithful remnant. In what sense can this claim made by Jewish believers in Jesus be tested and validated?

The identifying of Jewish believers in Jesus as the remnant has already been made within the presentation of the contours of Enlargement Theology. Yet I also understand that this identification is also a core conviction of the contemporary Messianic Jewish movement of the present day. As Stern states in commenting on 9:29:

> God cannot be blamed for the nation of Israel's failure to accept Yeshua as her Messiah. On the contrary, God must be thanked for showing enough mercy to preserve a "seed" or "remnant" of individual Jews who did accept him, namely, the Messianic Jews.[31]

The same connection is made by Harold Moore:

> As Messianic communities they see themselves as the 'natural olive tree grafted back' into the divine roots (Rom 11:24). They regard themselves as God's faithful remnant (Rom 11:5) and wish to remain faithful in maintaining their Jewish identity for the sake of the salvation of other Jews.[32]

The existence of those who would term themselves primarily 'Messianic Jews' is seen by many to be highly significant in regard to ongoing contemporary encounters between Jews and Christians. James Dunn sums up this conviction:

> We need to rediscover the character of the earliest Christian mission as a movement for the renewal within Judaism of the time. The increasing number of Messianic Jews today offers fresh bridging possibilities since the Jew/Christian spectrum is more complex now than at any other time since the early decades when Jewish Christianity was a vital option.[33]

The reality of a Messianic Jewish community today, claiming in some way to be the successors of the Elijah remnant[34] (Rom

11:2-4) must be taken seriously. This serious consideration may in fact lead to a new paradigm in Jewish-Christian relations[35] or it may lead to the other end of the spectrum, namely that engagement with the Messianic Jewish community is at best an unhelpful side issue and at worst a deceptive and dangerous dead end. However, whatever stance one has decided to take within the spectrum with its various nuances, what is clear is that the place one has taken must be based on serious, robust and open consideration of the various claims from all the various groups, of which contemporary Messianic Judaism is one.

Chapter Seven

Romans 9:30 – 10:13

Commentary on Romans 9:30 – 10:13

[30] *What then shall we say? That the Gentiles, who did not pursue righteousness, have obtained it, a righteousness that is by faith:* [31] *but Israel, who pursued a law of righteousness, has not attained it.* [32] *Why not? Because they pursued it not by faith but as if it were by works. They stumbled over the "stumbling stone". As it is written:*

"See, I lay in Zion a stone that causes men to stumble and a rock that makes them fall, and the one who trusts in him will never be put to shame."

[1] *Brothers, my heart's desire and prayer to God for the Israelites is that they may be saved.* [2] *For I can testify about them that they are zealous for God, but their zeal is not based on knowledge.* [3] *Since they did not know the righteousness that comes from God and sought to establish their own, they did not submit to God's righteousness.* [4] *Christ is the end of the law so that there may be righteousness for everyone who believes.*

[5] *Moses describes in this way the righteousness that is by the law: "The man who does these things will live by them."* [6] *But the righteousness that is by faith says: "Do not say in your heart, 'Who will ascend into heaven?'" (that is, to bring Christ down)* [7] *"or 'Who will descend into the deep?'" (that is, to bring Christ up from the dead).* [8] *But what does it say? "The word is near you; it is in your mouth and in your heart," that is the word of faith*

we are proclaiming: [9]That if you confess with your mouth, "Jesus is Lord," and believe in your heart that God raised him from the dead, you will be saved. [10]For it is with your heart that you believe and are justified, and it is with your mouth that you confess and are saved. [11]As the Scriptures says, "Anyone who trusts in him will never be put to shame." [12]For there is no difference between Jew and Gentile - the same Lord is Lord of all and richly blesses all who call on him, [13]for, "Everyone who calls on the name of the Lord will be saved."

Romans 9:30-10:13 (NIV)

7.1 General Comments

This section begins and continues with Paul's rhetorical method.[1] Paul wrestles here with what appears to be, in David Stern's phrase, "a monumental paradox",[2] or as Robert Jewett describes as "the ironic antithesis".[3] Namely that somehow the Gentiles have received a righteousness through faith without pursuing it, while Israel, despite their commitment to a 'Law of Righteousness', have not received such righteousness. Such a monumental paradox has echoes with the previous paradox of God's sovereign choice alongside human freedom and responsibility. This new paradox is in need of an answer, or at least a level of clarification. What this paradox appears to result in is that God's order and purpose has been distorted or changed in some way. This is the very point made by John A T Robinson:

> The order of theology was to the Jew first and also to the Greek (1:16), the order of history has turned out to be 'to the Gentiles first and also to the Jew.'[4]

Throughout this section Paul is focusing on key themes, namely the Law, justification and righteousness. All such terms need careful unpacking and defining. The term 'righteousness' for example is clearly 'a multi-dimensional term' and how this term is understood shapes the subsequent interpretation of the text. John Ziesler, in commenting on the term offers the definition:

> ... seems to mean something like 'life as God's people'.[5]

I find this general open definition by Ziesler to be helpful for it alludes to the understanding that righteousness for Paul can not be reduced to a personal moral category, but rather points to the understanding that God in response to his covenant promises would act uniquely and supremely in the Messiah to bring about redemption and restoration for his people.

In focusing on such terms and introducing directly the person and work of Jesus Christ (10:4, :6, :7, :9, :11 and :13) it seems as if Paul is entering into a significant turning point within his overall argument within this section, namely he firstly seeks to summarise the arguments up until this point. Such arguments in this section have engaged with the identity of 'God's people', especially the nature and status of their calling. Paul then moves to introduce how the ministry of Jesus Christ has brought this calling to a surprising climax. Paul goes on to pursue how this climax has led to a 'renewed righteousness' and a subsequent renewal and extension of the covenantal purposes of God.

This decisive act has been missed by many of Paul's own people, despite, as Paul would argue, that the act that has taken place is in direct fulfilment of the prophecies in the 'Old Testament'. Paul sees that his message is completely in step with God's eternal and consistent purposes. Paul's key assertions are that his fellow Israelites have, despite their zeal for the Law, misunderstood the Law (10:1-4). For Paul the core purpose of the Law is to lead to faith in Jesus Christ (10:5-13). In regard to the debate about the purpose of the Law, Ernst Käsemann offers the significant insight of how the context and content of the debate about the law shifted in the subsequent generations of the increasingly Gentile church:

> Later Gentile Christianity was no longer in the same situation as the apostle. It did not grasp the importance his debate with Judaism had for him and replaced it with an internal debate within the church.

Hence the conflict concerning the Mosaic Torah was ethicized, and survived only in this truncated form. Exhortation thus came to be seen as the hidden word of the law (Asmussen), and ethicizing in the direction of a general moral law was necessarily accompanied by individualizing. The problems of Christian existence and fellowship pressed to the fore in such a way that sight was lost of the profoundly apocalyptic argument of the text which sets Christ and the law (like Christ and Adam in 5:12ff.) in the contrast and contradiction of the old and new aeons.[6]

7.2 Specific Text Comments

Verses 30-33. Paul's use of the term 'Israel'(v31) rather than the term 'Jew'(v24) is of interest. James Dunn comments on the use of the term 'Israel':

> Paul's charge is not against a whole sequence of individual Jews as such; it is against his people's self-understanding of what it means to be the covenant people.[7]

As we explore verse 31 it seems that the New International Version text (as do most other texts, but not the Revised Standard Version or the Complete Jewish Bible) conceals the key point of the text by the phrase 'has not attained it'. The phrase, as rendered in the New International Version, could refer to the 'it' being 'righteousness', while the reference should be to the Law. Steve Motyer, in commenting on this verse, helpfully states:

> He [Paul] is not just claiming that Israel has failed to attain righteousness (in contrast to the Gentiles). He is saying more than that: like a huntsman after his prey, Israel set out to catch the law, but it eluded her grasp. For all her devotion to the law, she has failed to tame it, failed to persuade it to yield up the prize it guards (righteousness), missed its inner purpose and meaning. So her failure to enjoy the righteousness which has been poured out

on the Gentiles is not the essence of the problem, but merely a symptom of a deeper ill— her failure to understand what the law is and to discover the key that unlocks it.[8]

Following on from this, the term 'Law of righteousness' has in Douglas Moo's commentary, ". . . become a storm centre of debate".[9] There seem to be a number of key issues relating to the translation, interpretation and application of the term. Clearly there is the need to define the term 'Law'.[10] Firstly, it has been argued[11] the term 'Law' here means a principle, namely 'righteousness'. Israel failed in finding such a principle because their search did not take place in the context of trust but in works. The main difficulty with such an interpretation seems to be that in the following context in which the term 'Law' appears (Rom 10:4-5) the term 'Law' refers to the Law of Moses (Torah) and not to a more general principle of moral conduct.

How one interprets the term *'nomos'* (law) throughout Romans is crucial and it raises similar issues to the interpretation of the term 'Israel'.[12] It is worth noting that in the New International Version text the term 'law' is consistently presented in the lower case rather than the capital case 'Law', which would be appropriate if the intention is to connect the term with the Law of Moses. Significantly the Complete Jewish Bible text consistently translates *'nomos'* as Torah.

Secondly, the Law is taken to mean the Law of Moses. The Law is seen to point to and confirm the need for God's righteousness. However, this Law does not and can not offer the righteousness to which it bears witness. The difficulty with this approach is if that were Paul's understanding, there would be no need for him to state in verse 32 why and how Israel had failed, for if the Law does not offer the possibility of righteousness there is no need to explain their failure in terms of their method of pursuing the Law.

Thirdly, as in the second case, the term 'Law of righteousness' is taken to refer to the Law of Moses. However, there is the conviction that the Law offers the same 'righteousness' as the

Gentiles have received by faith (v30). The issue here is that the Law, in David Stern's phrase:

stems from, defines, demands and offers God's righteousness; [13]

For Paul, this pursuit of 'righteousness' through the Torah is not misplaced. Paul holds firmly to this typical Jewish understanding of the Law as a worthy goal to be earnestly sought. It is not a futile exercise born to failure and frustration. For the Torah in itself teaches that obedience to the commands must flow from an attitude of faith and trust and not of works. My reading of Paul is that he is able to stand within the prevailing Jewish tradition in seeing that the Law (meaning Torah) defines righteousness, but he would insist that this righteousness can never simply remain for those within the confines of ethnic Israel. The importance of faith and trust in living out the Law is emphasised by Paul's teaching in the following section (10:1-13). Ultimately for Paul the righteousness which the Law both demands and offers is the righteousness of Jesus. This point is made powerfully by Joseph Shulam:

Paul's comparison between Israel and the Gentile believers is not between righteousness as faithfulness and righteousness through the Torah. Most commentators have normally expanded the elliptical phrase "did not arrive at law" in an attempt to describe "what" or "which" law Israel did not "arrive at." However, Paul is actually arguing here that Israel "did not arrive at (the goal of the) Torah" — Yeshua. He draws this claim out in verse 32, where the direct question 'Why?' refers to the reason for Israel's failure to achieve the "goal" of the Torah. He appeals first to the distinction between faithfulness and works (cf. chapter 4). The "goal" of faithfulness, however is Yeshua, and Israel "stumbled" because they were "unfaithful" to God in not accepting His Messiah.[14]

Also in verse 32 Paul affirms that Israel has stumbled over the "stumbling stone". Clearly stumbling has consequences, namely that the Gentiles have in general terms arrived first at receiving 'righteousness through faith'. John Ziesler, in pursuing the racing imagery, simply and starkly states,

The non-starters have won the race.[15]

However, in regard to the wider theological implications, stumbling does not mean terminal failure, which is an axiom of Replacement Theology in regard to Israel. It is indeed possible that one may frequently stumble yet still reach the destination and complete/win the race.

The identification of the stone with the Messiah or the gospel of Jesus rather than with the Torah[16] is affirmed on balance by Dunn, Jewett, Moo, Ziesler, and Stern. This identification is based primarily on the two points, namely that Paul here is using a conflation of Isaiah 28:16 and 8:14. In these texts the stone is spoken of in personal terms. Secondly, in 1 Corinthians 1:23, Paul clearly identifies the Messiah (and his own apostolic preaching of the crucified Messiah) as the stumbling stone. The key issue here as affirmed by Jewett[17] is that the offense is Christological regardless if the intended focus is on the Messiah or the gospel. Other texts which shed light onto the stumbling stone image would include Genesis 49:24, Psalm 118:22, Luke 20:18, 1 Peter 2:6-8 and possibly Exodus 17:6. Dunn, in his commentary, makes the interesting point that Paul is probably drawing from a collection of stone testimonies used by early Christian communities in their outreach and apologetics. Dunn goes on to state:

In this case Paul could be abbreviating a well-established (oral, Käsemann) proof-text collection (Luke 20:17-18 presupposes a similar combination; cf. Barn. 6.2) which he would assume was well enough known among the Roman congregations (it is of relevance to note that both 1 Pet and Mark are most often linked to Rome as the place of their composition).[18]

Dunn also sees that the term translated as 'stumble' has the sense of 'to strike against', as of a foot against a stone. Dunn references Psalm 91:12. I would suggest that for Paul this term may have had echoes of his Damascus Road [19] encounter where he is identified as someone who, in his misplaced zeal, has been 'striking against' the person and work of Jesus Christ.

For Paul, those who do not stumble or strike against the stone/rock but rather trust in him will never be put to shame. Again this could have reflections in Paul's own personal journey of faith for, despite his sufferings,[20] he remains confident and secure[21] in his relationship with Jesus Christ. However, as Dunn, Stern and Ziesler state, the prime context for this 'not being put to shame' is not the circumstances of the present day, but the future final judgment.

10:1. As in 9:1-3 Paul shows his love and solidarity for his fellow Jews in terms which echo the dramatic passion and prayer of 9:1-5, although the term 'brothers' (not used since 8:12) refers here probably to both Jewish believers in Jesus and Gentile believers, while, in the context of 9:3, the term seems to point only to his fellow Jewish believers. In regard to Paul's use of the term 'brothers' with its apparent dual meaning within Romans, there may be here some parallels to the use of the term 'Israel' which has, in my promotion of Enlargement Theology, three differing legitimate degrees of identification.[22]

> For Paul, the source of the desire of such love and solidarity is the desire for Israel to be 'saved'. How this salvation is to be perceived and received becomes a central motif of the verses (v9 and v13) that follow in this section.

Verse 2. As in 9:1, Paul here testifies to a central truth and desire. Such legal terminology points to the solemn nature of this teaching. Also important for Paul is that he is speaking from personal experience in regard to the use and misuse of 'zeal'.[23] However, while throughout the New Testament there is an ambiguity about being 'zealous' with many positive[24] and negative[25] examples of zeal (the key to the validity from my reading of the texts being one of purpose),[26] Paul here is seeing such zeal as good, for it is rooted in a passion and commitment to God and is in line with God's revealed will. For Paul, the zeal of his fellow Israelites, like his previous zeal in persecuting the church, sadly is fundamentally misplaced because it has, in Ziesler's phrase, 'left no room for Christ'.[27]

Such zeal was also misplaced because it tended to be an exclusive Jewish righteousness which left no room for Gentiles. The right place for such zeal for Paul is to be found in a commitment to the person and work of Christ.

Verse 4. How the term "Christ is the end of the law" is understood and applied is of great significance. It is another area of Romans 9-11 which is debated at great length. In one sense, by choosing to translate *'telos'* as 'end', as do the main English translations (New International Version, Jerusalem Bible, Good News Bible, New English Bible, Revised English Bible, Revised Standard Version) rather than 'goal'[28] (Complete Jewish Bible), or possibly 'purpose', 'high point', 'aim' or 'consummation' for example, one has already shaped possible interpretations. David Stern makes this point forcibly:

According to Ardnt and Gingrich's, A Greek-English Lexicon of the New Testament the Greek word 'telos', used 42 times in the New Testament, has to mean "finish, cessation, termination" in four or five places (Mk 3:26, Lk 1:33, 2 C 3:13, MJ 7:3, 1 Ke 4:729). But in the great majority of cases its meaning is either (1) "aim, purpose, goal" toward which a movement is being directed (1 Ti 1:5, 1 Ke 1:9) , or (2) "outcome, result, consummation, last part" of a process not obviously being and which may or may not terminate (6:21-22 above, Mt 26:58, MJ 6:8). These words are reflected in the English word "teleology", the branch of philosophy dealing with goals and purposes. Then why is "telos" regularly regarded as meaning "termination" here? Because theology gets in the way of exegesis, wrong theology that falsely understands the Mosaic Law as not offering God's righteousness through trust, wrong theology that denigrates God's Torah and thereby both the God who gave it and the Jewish People to whom he gave it.[30]

Anthony Guerra also helpfully explores the possible range of meanings for the term *'telos'*:

> The datum hard to evade is that Paul proclaims salvation to the Gentiles without obedience to the Law as a consequence of the Christ event. Paul's view of the Law for Jewish Christians is more complicated, but I see no reason for denying that he allows Jewish Christians to abide by the Law as long as they center themselves in Christ—contra Watson. Sanders also argues that Paul would demand Jewish Christians in community with Gentile Christians to abandon the Law, but Sanders' argument is based on the incorrect assumption that Paul, at least in this matter, is a pragmatist. [31]

It is not, however, simply a matter of how the term *'telos'* is translated and interpreted, for it is also important to decide how to translate and interpret *'nomos'*. In general terms, a number of views have been presented; I will outline the following three.

Firstly, seeing *'nomos'* in terms of legalism, namely the use of the Law in constructing one's own sense of self-righteousness. Clearly, for Paul faith in Christ should put an end to any sense of self-righteousness and legalism. However, there is little support for this view and it seems to me that seeing the Law in terms of legalism is more in keeping with some commentators being influenced by historical issues surrounding the Reformation, namely conflict over Law versus grace and a false spirituality based on 'works' (sale of indulgences, etc.) versus faith, rather than issues which Paul was facing, or how Paul and the early Christians understood and appreciated the Law/Torah.

Secondly, seeing *'nomos'* in terms of setting out the boundary markers of righteousness and defining therefore how to live as God's people. Clearly faith in Christ redefines the boundary markers and in this sense such redefinition could be seen as a termination of the Law. This redefining has led some[32] to argue that Paul understood that, with the coming of the Messiah, a new Messianic Torah would be established for the Messianic age. In this sense, the Torah is terminated in the coming of Messiah, although aspects of fulfilment would also be interwoven into this termination of the old and the establishing of the new. While Paul does speak of the Law of Christ, there is not, in Paul's writings compelling evidence for a new Messianic Torah replacing the Torah which for Paul remains as God's eternal gift.

Thirdly, seeing *'nomos'* in terms of the witness to the forthcoming promise of God (Rom 3:31). For Paul, this promise is wonderfully fulfilled in the person and work of Christ. This view is presented helpfully by Joseph Shulam:

> Paul states in 3:21 that the Torah "witnesses" to the righteousness of God. This "witness" is the "goal" of the Torah; i.e., God's gift of righteousness in the Messiah not only to the people of Israel but also to the Gentiles. Verse 4 therefore sums up Paul's argument from 9.19ff, in which he argues that although Israel have been disobedient they have also transgressed God's word by not accepting His declaration in the Torah and the prophets that He would make the Gentiles part of His people, and through them provoke His own people back to Him through jealousy. Israel have "stumbled" over this goal, because they have not believed in the "stone of stumbling" and not accepted God's righteousness in Yeshua.[33]

A similar point to Shulam is made by Karl Barth, who argues that the end of the Law should be understood in terms of the Rabbinic concept of *'kelal'*.[34] The *'kelal'* is the Messiah. Karl Barth goes on to state:

> It is with him and him alone that the Law is concerned as the order of life under promise. It is He who interprets this order and fulfils it. It is He who guarantees its validity. To live in obedience under this order means to believe in Him. By refusing to do so, Israel transgresses and breaks its own Law. It fails to recognise the kelal of it, and with all its zeal for keeping its individual parts, according to 9:31 it comes short of the whole, the Law as such.[35]

In all these explorations of the possible meanings attributed to the term 'telos', it seems that there is a spectrum of possibilities ranging from a terminal/temporal interpretation to a teleological one, or maybe some possible harmonising between the two.[36] Clearly a terminal interpretation fits in to a prevailing Replacement Theology with its emphasis on discontinuity between the church and the Old Testament Torah. While a teleological approach, with the focus on Christ upholding and honouring Torah[37] and bringing it to its true place of practice, purpose and completion, clearly gives emphasis to strands of continuity. Such strands of continuity would fit in with the general contours of Enlargement Theology.

It is my understanding that a teleological interpretation fits in better with the context of Romans 9-11. For Paul, in Romans 9-11, is giving an overview of salvation history in which the calling, destiny and identity of Israel is to be determined wholly by its encounter with the person and work of the Messiah. This encounter with the Messiah is in keeping with God's word (9:6) and purpose (9:11) declared and demonstrated within the remnant and supremely in the Messiah. The thrust is that of fulfilment with the Messiah as the key to understanding and appropriating the gift of Torah.

Verses 5-8. Paul continues within this line of argument by referring to Moses and quotes from Leviticus 18:5 and thereby adding weight to the 'positive view of the Law'. It is not a Law of works-righteousness but one of faithful trust which offers life. This 'positive' sense of the Law is affirmed by Paul Minear:

> God has not changed the basis of the covenant with Abraham, but has simply enforced it (9:30-10:4). Christ is 'the end of the law' not in the destructive but in the constructive sense that faith in him has become the benchmark of the righteousness to which God has called Israel. The inclusion of Gentiles, far from being the denial of Israel's hope, has become its confirmation.[38]

A similar and complementary point is also made by Robert Badenas:

> Since Paul saw Christ as the end to which the law was directed it may be deduced that Christ took the place of the centrality of the

law in Paul's life, but that Paul's respect for the law remained the same (3:31,7:12, 14). However, Paul's veneration for the law was surpassed by his veneration for Christ. This surpassing of Torah by Christ is what Paul wished to teach Israel and this is what Israel did not accept. As a corollary to Paul's understanding of the law in the light of Christ, it follows that he could not view the law anymore as an end in itself but as a means. Precisely what Paul reproached the Jews for was their looking at the law as a goal in itself (9.31-32); they did not see that it pointed and led to Christ (10.4)[39]

So often the term 'but'(v6) is taken as contradicting or contrasting the position of Torah with the position of faith. However, I understand, based on the teleological interpretation of 10:4 and in part from Paul's own practice glimpsed from the book of Acts,[40] that for Paul his intention is not to contradict or contrast but rather affirm that the position of faithful trust is the very position upheld by the Torah, when the Torah is rightly understood. Paul is using therefore the terms 'Moses' (v5) and 'the righteousness that is by faith' as allies rather than opponents in this line of argument. Hence, the quotations which follow are also from the Torah (Deuteronomy 30). The term 'but' would therefore be better translated as 'moreover'[41] as is the case in the Complete Jewish Bible, or perhaps 'furthermore'.

Also in verse 8 it is worth noting the term "heart" is used (as it is in 10:1) and is repeated again in verse 9 and verse 10. A number of commentators pick up on this. For example, Robert Jewett:

> The threefold reference to the heart in 10:8-10 shows that for Paul faith is more than a set of beliefs, it is related to the condition of the heart. That motivating centre of mind, emotion, experience and purpose.[42]

Verse 9. This is the 'crux of the matter' according to John Ziesler namely that:

> The righteousness based on faith is readily and universally available wherever the preaching of Christ is heard.[43]

This verse (and the following elaboration in vv10-13) is seen as a very clear statement of Christian faith. Here we have Paul presenting what appear to be the two essential elements of faith, namely the Lordship of Jesus and his resurrection. Maybe these two essential elements of faith helped shape the form of an early baptismal confession? Robert Jewett speaks of the statement "Jesus is Lord" as a 'slogan of identification' and an 'attitude of subserviency'.[44] The verse draws in part from Joel 2:32 which is the very verse used so powerfully by Peter in his explanation of the events that took place in Jerusalem on the day of Pentecost (Acts 2:21). For Paul this verse is a defining statement of both the substance of faith and the context of faith. The centrality of this verse has led me to see Romans 10:9 as the New Testament equivalent of the Shema, with Paul contrasting the initial response of Israel in terms of hearing to the new response for all of calling (on the name of the Lord).

In this calling on the name of the Lord, there is for Paul no distinction between the needs of Jews and Gentiles. This sense of there being no distinction or difference has direct echoes of Romans 3:22, which, as John Lodge[45] points out, is the only other place within Romans where Paul uses the term 'no difference'.

7.3 Comments relating to the Development of Enlargement Theology

Once again there are many points of possible engagement within this section of Paul's teaching. However, I will address the following four points, believing them to be the most significant in terms of the development of Enlargement Theology.

Firstly, it is worth reiterating the point made in this segment of comments focusing on 9:1-5, namely that Paul's very obvious and passionate desire for his fellow Jews to be saved which is declared again (10:1) makes any presentation of a Two Covenant Theological approach incongruous to Paul's line of teaching, with its clear desire to see Jewish people coming to a saving faith in and through the person and work of the Messiah. However, if a Two Covenant Theological approach is incongruous then so is a strict punitive Replacement Theological approach. For a strict punitive Replacement Theological approach would not sit comfortably with Paul's very clear focus upon his fellow Jewish people and his passionate belief that despite Israel's stumbling (9:32) there remains a clear Jewish hope for salvation through the person and work of the Jewish Messiah. Also, within the proclaiming of this hope, there remains for Paul an eternal Jewish mission imperative, first declared in Romans 1:16.

Secondly, there is the conviction for some within contemporary Jewish encounters that verses such as vv2-3 with their apparent disingenuous undermining of the Torah, fuel an anti-Semitic agenda. The contention is that any commitment to living out Torah is seen through Christian eyes to be equated with ignorance, misplaced legalism and self-righteousness. I would argue that sadly such understanding does exist on the Christian side. In fact, such a view of the Torah is one consequence of a wider Replacement Theology shaping the life of the church. However, is this negative view of the Torah actually what Paul is presenting in these verses and elsewhere? I have argued in the comments on 10:4 and verses 5-8 that it is not.

Clearly Paul knows that some of his fellow Torah-observing Jews do have an attitude of misplaced legalism and a misplaced zeal. He himself knows of such things intimately from his own spiritual journey. Maybe even such legalism is the predominant position of the Rabbinic communities which Paul is interacting with at this time? However, Paul does not equate this legalism and self-righteousness uncritically to all Torah-observing Jews. If he did so, then a charge of possible anti-Semitic prejudice might have a hearing. What Paul is arguing for, and almost certainly pursuing himself,[46] is a right commitment to the Torah. This commitment implies that the Torah testifies to a righteousness rooted in a God-centered faith. Alongside this is the conviction that the Torah is a gift of the covenant between

God and Israel which will never be withdrawn or superseded.

Such faith/trust, argues Paul, must find its ultimate context in confessing and believing in the person and work of Jesus, namely that Jesus is Lord,[47] and directly linked to such a conviction is the reality of the resurrection of Jesus (10:9). It is important to state that one of the contours of Enlargement Theology (with its largely positive engagement with the contemporary Messianic Jewish movement) is a corresponding positive understanding of Torah. Enlargement Theology would see that any denigration of Torah or identification of Rabbinic Judaism as simply legalistic does not honour Paul's view of the Torah and ultimately undermines the presentation of the Gospel. Sadly there are presentations of the Gospel from a Replacement Theological perspective which, in order to celebrate the victory of the Gospel, falsely identify many aspects of Jewish spirituality with legalism and denigrate Torah.

Following on from this, the perception of the Torah and the living out of Torah from a Messianic Jewish position is of great interest. Within contemporary Messianic Jewish communities and individuals there is great diversity[48] found in how Torah is practised. However, there are, I would understand, two almost universally held points within contemporary Messianic Judaism: firstly, that Torah is a good gift of God which helps shape Jewish identity; and, secondly, that the Torah witnesses to faith in the Messiah. Apart from such personal faith in Messiah, no salvation can be found, and implicitly the Torah cannot be faithfully lived. It is of interest that for a number of Messianic Jewish believers, it is since coming to faith in Jesus that their commitment to Torah observance has been renewed. The point here that I suggest is at the heart of Messianic Judaism is not simply seeing faith in Jesus as an 'add on' to traditional Jewish practice or observing the Torah as adding Jewish flavour to belief in Jesus, but rather that faith in Jesus opens up a whole new and radical appreciation, restoration and reconstruction of Jewish identity and Torah practice rooted in Jesus.

This appreciation and reconstruction by Messianic Jewish

believers in regard to the Torah (and other related issues) must have wider implications for Rabbinic Jews and Christians. The quote by Harald Hegstad affirms this very point:

> The existence of Messianic Jews and a Messianic theology reminds us that the gospel is not originally Greek, German or Norwegian, but was originally expressed in a Jewish setting. To preach the gospel today in a Jewish setting is therefore something other than preaching the gospel in any other setting. Because the gospel is Jewish in its origin, it has to do not primarily with contextualisation, but with a restoration of the Jewishness of the gospel. As a restoration and not only as a new contextualisation, this process is of great interest for every other process of contextualisation. Perhaps we could propose as a criterion for any formulation of Christian doctrine in any context, that it might be communicated and understood in a Jewish-Messianic setting. If not, it is doubtful that this theological idea can be regarded as an expression of New Testament faith.[49]

Within contemporary encounters, it seems that the Messianic Jewish understandings and engagements with the Torah could well help open up fresh discussions and expose some false understandings about the purpose and place of the Torah between both Rabbinic Jews and Christians. This is an approach which supporters of an Enlargement Theological perspective would welcome.

Thirdly, Paul in this section strongly affirms the conviction that responding to what I have seen as the 'New Shema' (10:9) is open to all people and it is indeed necessary for all people in order to respond faithfully to God. This understanding connects to the third tenet of Enlargement Theology, namely that the 'New (enlarged) Covenant' needs to be entered into and embraced by all people, both Jews and Gentiles, through the outworking of faith/trust in the person and atoning work of the Messiah. This sense of 'open access' is affirmed by such inclusive words as 'anyone' (v 11) and 'everyone' (v 13).

Fourthly, connected with this 'open access' is the sense of

unity and equality expressed so clearly in verse 12. This sense of unity and equality directly engages with the fourth and fifth tenets of Enlargement Theology, which speak of God's purposes being worked out through mutually inter-related communities. This sense of unity and equality between Christians (both Jewish and Gentiles) is at the heart of much of Paul's teaching[50] about belonging to the one reconciled family of believers.

This unity is not just restricted to overcoming what is perhaps the core issue of potential division, namely that of the relationship between Jews and Gentiles, but such unity and equality impacts on all other divisions known to Paul, such as those between male and female and slave and free (Gal 3:28).

The essential conviction for Paul, I would argue, is that through the ministry of Jesus there is now open access for Gentiles to enter into 'full covenantal status' as 'God's people'. This is a fundamental issue at the core of Jewish-Christian relations, namely, from the Christian understanding, before the ministry of Jesus a Gentile was in some way 'removed from God's people'. Gentiles could begin to develop a relationship with God and with Israel by pursuing a path as a 'God fearing/righteous Gentile'. As such, the Gentile fostered this relationship with God through an appreciation of the life and witness of Israel as the Torah community.[51] Alongside this appreciation was also a consequential rejection of prevailing pagan practices. From this position as a God-fearing/righteous Gentile, a Gentile may take a significant further step and become a proselyte. In such a case, the Gentile comes to full covenantal status by firstly becoming part of Israel.

Paul argues now that, in the light of the ministry of Israel's Messiah and uniquely through the Messiah's death and resurrection, a Gentile who makes a faith/trust commitment to the Messiah (Israel's representative) has 'full covenantal status' not as previously through the path of becoming part of Israel (through becoming a proselyte) but directly through faith in the Messiah. Consequently, it is through the Messiah that the Gentiles discover their relationship with Israel and the

Torah, while previously it was probably understood that it was through some significant commitment to Israel and the Torah that a Gentile discovered their relationship with God.

This is at the heart of the 'new order' of relationships to be found within the New (enlarged) Covenant community. A Gentile enters into 'full covenantal status' through the Messiah and therefore the 'badges of belonging' to Israel such as circumcision, Sabbath and food law observances are no longer essential, because one enters the covenant through Messiah and not through firstly becoming part of Israel (which would have explicitly required the acquiring of such 'badges of belonging').

The 'badges of belonging' were the very things which defined the exclusive boundaries of the covenant with Moses. Now the boundaries have been redefined through the restoration and enlargement of Israel by the Messiah. Paul amongst many others who shared this 'Jewish hope', understood that this restoration of Israel had direct consequences relating to the inclusion of the Gentiles.

This new open access for Gentiles creates a new dynamic within the post-Messianic Jewish community/Christian church, namely both Jewish believers in Jesus and Gentile believers are 'one' and share equal status through the Messiah. In terms of this covenantal status of *being saved*, there is, in Paul's understanding 'no difference' between a Jew or a Gentile. There is a 'wonderful unity' in the Messiah based upon the total dependence expressed through faith/trust of each individual in the redeeming work of the Messiah. However, for Paul this 'oneness' in regard to covenantal status does not mean that there are not differences in terms of function and in certain aspects of identity within Christian communities.

A Jew who responds in faith/trust to the Messiah remains a Jew [52] in the same way that a Gentile remains a Gentile, or a man remains a man, a woman remains a woman, an English person remains English, etc. For the Messianic Jew, he or she has the privilege and responsibility of being fully a member of the Messianic community/church and fully part of the wider Jewish Community. Again this is a key point within the expression of mutually inter-connected communities from an Enlargement Theological perspective.

This conviction that the Messianic Jew is fully and appropriately part of two overlapping communities in which they stand at the intersection, is a core belief of Messianic Jewish theology and identity. The acceptance or rejection of such a belief is a major area of contention within the wider field of Jewish-Christian relations.

This oneness in terms of covenantal status does not, however, reduce the diversity within the Christian community. Within a Christian community, there must be a core unity in terms of 'salvation/covenantal status'. There can be no 'second class members'. However, in terms of function/identity there may well be many differences within some Church communities. For example, differences can be seen between 'ordained' and 'lay' members, between women and men, between young and old and between the 'strong' and the 'weak'. This difference may also include differences between some Jews and Gentiles, especially in terms of certain aspects of Torah observance. However, one must be very careful before taking sides and deciding which (if any) group from within any community which celebrates 'unity within diversity' of faith reflects 'strength' and which reflects 'weakness'. This is the very point Paul develops with immense pastoral care subsequently in Romans 14.[53]

Chapter Eight

Romans 10:14–21

Commentary on Romans 10:14–21

[14]How, then, can they call on the one they have not believed in? And how can they believe in the one of whom they have not heard? And how can they hear without someone preaching to them? [15]And how can they preach unless they are sent? As it is written, "How beautiful are the feet of those who bring good news!"

[16]But not all the Israelites accepted the good news. For Isaiah says, "Lord, who has believed our message?" [17]Consequently, faith comes from hearing the message, and the message is heard through the word of Christ. [18]But I ask: Did they not hear? Of course they did:

"Their voice has gone to the ends of the earth, their words to the end of the world."

[19]Again I ask: Did Israel not understand? First, Moses says,

"I will make you envious by those who are not a nation; I will make you angry by a nation that has no understanding."

[20]And Isaiah boldly says,

"I was found by those who did not seek me; I revealed myself to those who did not ask for me."

[21]But concerning Israel he says,

"All day long I have held out my hands to a disobedient and obstinate people."

Romans 10:14-21 (NIV)

8.1 General Comments

A number of commentators head this segment with the focus on Israel's unbelief and consequent lack of response. James Dunn for example uses the title "Israel's Failure to Respond to the Gospel" when introducing this text section in his commentary. While there is unquestionably an emphasis in the text on Israel's lack of response, I would understand that John Ziesler is probably correct when he argues that the main theme of the early section of verses 14–18 is dealing with the need for the Gospel to be heard in general terms. This is because the immediate preceding context is that of all people having the opportunity to hear and respond to the Gospel. In such a case, the context is probably the wider Gentile mission rather than, or as well as, the Jewish mission. The quote in verse 13 from Joel 2:32 gives a focus on the universal dimensions of God's redemptive purposes. Ziesler also makes the connection[1] that the use of the Joel quote is a good example of Paul's method of transferring the universality of God's purposes in the Old Testament to their specific fulfilment within the person and work of the Messiah.[2] Only later in this segment does the focus clearly turn from what is probably a universal setting to solely that of Israel (v16, v19 and v21) and Israel's largely but not exclusively negative response to the Gospel.

Once again Paul uses the method of a chain of questions and responses. David Stern outlines the view that the questions reflect the position of an imaginary Jewish opponent created by Paul:

> Sha'ul now utilizes a method he employed before (3:1; 6:1,15) one used by the Rabbis throughout the Talmud — he introduces an imaginary opponent to make objections and forwards his case

by answering them. This opponent is perhaps best thought of as a non-Messianic Jew defending Israel and looking for flaws in the argument of 9:30-10:13. He appears five times—by implication here (vv 14-15) and explicitly at v 18, v 19, 11:1-2 and 11:11.[3]

Within these perhaps imaginary questions, as Stern suggests, there is a progression of argument just as in verses 9-13, where Paul had mapped out the various steps that lead to 'being saved'. Here, through this rhetorical method, Paul sets out the steps which have occurred and are still occurring, which enables all people to respond to what is from Paul's conviction the universal principle, namely, that the gift of salvation is given to all who call upon Jesus as Lord. These steps are outlined in reverse order beginning with belief (v 14), which is dependent on hearing (v 14), which is preceded by preaching (v 14) which in itself is dependent upon the authority of the one preaching. Such authority for Paul implies being sent (v 15) which here implies probably Paul's own sense of his apostolic call and credentials. While Paul clearly affirms his calling and apostolic role, it is based on God's grace not upon his own merit.

This sense of Paul's dependency on God's grace flows from his own encounter with God's grace as part of what many commentators refer to as his 'conversion'. While I would question the appropriate use of the term 'conversion' in this context, nevertheless the emphasis on Paul's dependency on the grace of God is certainly central. This centrality is affirmed by Richard Bell:

Paul's conversion can be viewed as an act of the grace of God. Paul contributed absolutely nothing to his conversion — it shall therefore come as no surprise, that Paul was to stress the grace of God more than any other New Testament theologian. We shall also see that this experience was one of the clues for him in Romans as to how Israel will be finally saved.[4]

Through all of this outworking of God's grace the key point is that both Gentiles and Jews have 'open access' to the Gospel and both are now held accountable for their response, be it positive or negative. There is no excuse for rejecting the message, even though from Paul's teaching such (temporary) rejection and opposition from the majority of Israel is intriguingly within God's gracious sovereign purpose, as well as being simply Israel's own fault. Once again we see the complexity and 'multi-dimensional' aspects within Paul's teaching, which are especially apparent when relating to issues of Israel's identity, election and salvation.

The final general comment to make is to draw attention to the use of scripture in these verses. Paul quotes from Isaiah 52:7/Nahum 1:15 (v15), Isaiah 53:1(v16), Psalm 19:4 (v18), Deuteronomy 32:21 (v19), Isaiah 65:1 (v20) and finally Isaiah 65:2/Jeremiah 35:17 (v21). It is as if Paul is committed to showing, especially to his fellow Jews who have not accepted the Gospel message, that the authority which he claims is nothing less than the authority which flows from the Jewish scriptures. This focus on the authority of the scriptures is drawn out by Karl Barth:

> Thus the refusal to confess that Jesus is Lord—the demand which according to vv. 9-13 sums up all the demands of the Law, and in which its fulfillment as such is prescribed to a reader — can only be understood and characterised as disobedience. This refusal, unbelief, is not a misfortune. It is an action which is forbidden by the Law, and which for a reader of the Law is conceivable only as transgression.
>
> But Paul does not will that even this point should be established by his own authority. He wills, rather, that this point made in apostolic authority, should be established in such a way that the Synagogue Jew must recognise it as legitimate from the standpoint of his own presupposition, and therefore again from the standpoint of scripture.[5]

8.2 Specific Text Comments

Verses 14-15. The importance of calling linked to believing and hearing is stated here with the concluding focus on the role of the preacher. The role of the preacher and the link to hearing is a key component in the process which leads to faith and trust. This point is made powerfully by two key commentators, firstly Robert Jewett and then James Dunn. Jewett states:

> The expression "they might call upon him," that is, the Lord, as in 10:12-13, reflects the confessional response to missionary preaching as in Acts 22:16, "Rise up, be baptized, and wash away your sins, calling on his name." By selecting aorist subjunctive verbs, Paul draws attention to the events of missionary activity followed by conversions. The climax deals with this process in reverse order, beginning with the confession that marks the appropriate conclusion of the conversion process. The preceding pericope made it clear that such a "calling" involves confessing Jesus as Lord (10:9-10).[6]

Secondly, James Dunn states:

> The reference to hearing is not simply a logical link in the chain between believing and preaching; it also reflects Paul's self-consciousness as a preacher, as one who thought in terms of communication by the spoken word and whose success depended on winning the sort of attentive hearing which so often resulted in commitment among his hearers. Paul was well aware of how critical the transaction was between speaker and hearer—when mysteriously, not merely words are conveyed, but an understanding, a conviction, a life-changing commitment—and of how dependent as a preacher he was on the Spirit to make his word the word of God (1 Thess 2:13; 1 Cor 2:4).[7]

It is probable that at one level Paul is thinking of his own role as the preacher, as the previous quote from James Dunn suggests, yet the change to the plural in verse 15 (which is not in the Masoretic or LXX text), probably indicates that Paul is thinking either in terms of the large 'team of messengers'[8]

119

who have gone out faithfully preaching the news of Jesus, or the focus is on the role of Israel as the prime witness in the world to God's faithfulness. This second line of reasoning is promoted by Joseph Shulam:

> Paul's change to the plural therefore cannot be accidental. Neither can he refer to the "kerygma" or preaching of the church, however, since he is clearly giving a historical review. He thus seems to be referring to Israel's biblical task of being God's witnesses to the nations of the world.[9]

The other point to note in these verses is that the Isaiah quote is placed by Paul in the context of the proclaiming of the Gospel about Jesus rather than the immediate Isaiah setting of the restoration and renewal of Jews from captivity in Babylon. Such transferring is not out of step with some Rabbinic interpretations, as such texts were often seen by Rabbinic leaders as having a future 'Messianic age' context as well as an immediate 'historical' context and present application.

Verses 16-21. The witness of scripture confirms that which Paul has been wrestling with at such length and with such intensity, namely that of the mystery of Israel's unbelief. Yet such unbelief is always in the wider context of a faithful remnant. The faithful remnant has received the 'word of Christ'. Again there are a number of interpretations about the meaning of the 'word of Christ'. Is it the teaching/preaching of Jesus himself, or the word of the exalted Lord, or the preaching about Jesus Christ being carried out faithfully by the apostles and/or others? Whatever option or combination of options one selects, the key is that there have been, and continue to be, many opportunities for response.

Paul goes on to state, referencing Psalm 19:4, that the word has gone out into all the earth. Clearly Paul is not claiming here that every single person or group has heard the message, but probably Paul is making two rhetorical points. Firstly, that the Gospel of Christ and its proclamation is in its essence universal and secondly, that if the Gentiles have had meaningful opportunities to hear, how much more has Israel. Jewish excuses based on lack of opportunity (v 18) or lack of understanding (vv 19-20) will not be allowed to stand, especially in the light of so many Gentiles finding faith.

Paul's line of argument continues to develop, and certainly in the concluding verses of this section the scriptures themselves actually carry forward the main thrust of Paul's reasoning, rather than simply (as is normally the case in Paul's writings) providing a proof text or a wider context for his teaching. What is presented here then through Psalm 19:4, Deuteronomy 32:21 and the Isaiah texts is this multi-dimensional explanation of Israel's lack of faith, which leads to the conclusion that it is at one level simply Israel's fault. All the excuses fail. Yet within this 'failure' one can trace, at a deeper level, God's overall redemptive plan— a plan which for Paul is still being worked out and carried forward; a plan which leads not to an ultimate rejection or replacement of Israel, but a plan which continues to see the Lord 'holding out his hands' to his people. It is therefore from this conviction that Paul now concludes this section. Firstly, by reconnecting with the opening verses of this section, namely verse 20, with Isaiah 65:1 which links to 9:30 and then verse 21 with Isaiah 65:2 which has resonance with the concerns of 9:31. Then secondly, preparing the ground for the next key question, which is to be presented in 11:1.

8.3 Comments relating to the Development of Enlargement Theology

Again in this section Paul's teaching exposes inherent weaknesses within Replacement Theology and Two Covenant Theology. Firstly, in terms of Replacement Theology, which is based in part on the theological consequences of the understanding of Israel's terminal failure. With this in view, some Christians have taken verses in this section as an indicator of Israel's failure and have subsequently used such verses as the starting point for constructing a theology of replacement. Such a theological construct has huge implications for contemporary Jewish-Christian relations, especially in terms of creating, on the 'Christian side', a sense of triumphalism and arrogance towards anything Jewish. This reaction to anything Jewish would, by simple definition, also include the Messianic Jewish movement.

In regard to this first point of Israel's failure, I hope I have argued in the specific text comments that any sense of Israel's failure is only temporary and has within it the God-given purpose of in some way fostering Gentile acceptance. Therefore, any attempt to create a climate for an emerging Replacement Theology from these verses is largely flawed. As Joseph Shulam states:

> Paul understands Israel's "knowledge" in the light of what he says in 10:4, that God's righteousness is a gift in Yeshua to both Jews and Gentiles because it is based on faithfulness. God's purpose (τελος; telos) or goal, to which the Torah witnesses from the beginning (cf.3.21), is to make also the Gentiles righteous. On the other hand, however, part of this plan also includes the fact that the people of Israel have proved themselves disobedient to God. It is (partially) through this disobedience, which contains the element of not knowing or understanding the goal of the Torah, that opens the way for the Gentiles to be included in God's Kingdom. Finally, the Gentile believers will then "provoke Israel to jealousy" for their own God. God has revealed in Scripture through Moses and His prophets, that he would "call into being" a people who did not know Him, whom He had not chosen, nor with whom had He entered into a covenant relationship. His righteousness is not confined to Israel, His chosen people, nor to the revelation of His will in the Torah. Because it is also His will that the Gentiles receive His righteousness through faithfulness in Yeshua, He chose Israel to be His own people in order to include the Gentile nations as well, through Israel's temporary hardness of heart, and their (partial) rejection of God's Messiah (cf. Isaiah 65:1-2). This hardness, however, is proof of Israel's election, not proof of their rejection

by God. Israel will finally prove their election by being provoked to jealousy by those who formerly were not part of God's people but have now been "grafted in" to the commonwealth of Israel. This is the argument which Paul raises as the proper answer to the erroneous conclusion that God has in fact rejected Israel as His chosen people and replaced them with the Gentiles (or the "Church").[10]

This rejection of Replacement Theology clearly creates positive avenues for contemporary Jewish-Christian relations and prevents some of the worst forms of Christian arrogance, which may even today (as sadly in the past) lead to the justifying of anti-Semitic teachings and actions. However, if the line of argument to be followed which is explicit within Enlargement Theology, that Israel's ultimate purpose and destiny is only to be found by Israel's acceptance of Jesus as their Messiah and Saviour, then it may well be suggested that the 'Christian side' in any encounter will still have elements of triumphalism and arrogance at its heart. Such triumphalism and arrogance, it is argued, will be evident within the evangelistic ministry of Christians. If this is the case then in practice there will be no real practical differences in terms of Jewish-Christian encounters between those evangelical Christians who promote positions flowing from Replacement Theology and those adhering to an Enlargement Theology.

In the light of the above, it is therefore argued by many Jews and Christians who hold to a Two Covenant position that the only way to foster genuine Jewish-Christian encounters free from triumphalism and arrogance is to be free from both Replacement Theology and equally from the evangelistic ministry promoted by Enlargement Theology which also upholds the person and work of Jesus in exclusivist mission terms.

In response to such a line of reasoning, I think three points need to be offered at this stage. Firstly, an evangelistic Jewish ministry position which flows from the centrality and exclusivity of Jesus can be presented in a spirit of humility and gentleness. There can be, within such a position of conviction a genuine desire to listen and receive from the 'other side' and the willingness to refine and change one's own convictions. This issue of a readiness to refine and change by those who hold to an exclusivist position is made powerfully by Lesslie Newbigin. Newbigin, in holding to a personal exclusivist position, never sees this as a block to good relationships nor to genuine dialogue:

> The Christian partner must recognize that the result of the dialogue may be a profound change in himself . . . The Holy Spirit who convicts the world of sin, of righteousness and of judgment, may use the non-Christian partner in dialogue to convict the Church. Dialogue means the exposure to the shattering and up building power of God the Spirit. The Christian who enters into dialogue with people of other faiths and ideologies is accepting this risk. But to put my Christianity at risk is precisely the way by which I confess Jesus Christ as Lord-Lord over all worlds and Lord over my faith.[11]

It is of great importance that genuine dialogue and meaningful Jewish-Christian relations and ongoing encounters are not allowed to become the monopoly of those who hold to a Two Covenant position.

Secondly, I understand there is a fundamental difference between a Replacement Theology, which says God has finished with Israel and that the Jewish covenantal relationships are now null and void and the position of Enlargement Theology, which celebrates that God's gracious purpose is still being worked out within God's faithfulness to ethnic Israel and understands that Gentile believers in Jesus are being grafted into Israel's promises, even if one affirms that the final destiny of such a working out can not be removed from the person and work of Jesus.

Thirdly, I would argue that input from the Messianic Jewish movement is vital at this point. This is for two main connected reasons. It is again important here to state that Enlargement

Theology is shaped by a largely sympathetic engagement with the Messianic Jewish movement.

Firstly, input from the Messianic Jewish movement is not necessarily 'one-sided' within the wider field of Jewish-Christian relations. While it is broadly the case that the Messianic Jewish movement affirms the Christian position [12] in regard to the centrality and exclusivity of Jesus, however, there are often major challenges to some cherished 'Christian assumptions' which can come (only?) from engaging with the Messianic Jewish movement. Therefore, Messianic Jewish input in such Jewish-Christian mission encounters are never simply 'one-sided'. There is often, from the Messianic Jewish side, a robust criticism of Christian faith and practice as well as the wider faith and practice of Jewish communities. Such 'two-sided' informed and robust criticism is surely a key ingredient within any recipe for meaningful dialogue and mission encounter when core issues such as truth, destiny and identity are being openly explored.

Secondly, input from the Messianic Jewish movement changes the nature and tone of the evangelistic mission imperative of the church. [13] For many within the field of Jewish-Christian relations any form of evangelistic agenda is an anathema. This sense of the abhorrent nature of evangelism within such Jewish-Christian settings is presented powerfully by the following two Jewish theologians. Firstly Blu Greenberg:

> I know this general truth: whenever the Good News was combined with power, it became bad news for Jews. In every era in Christian Europe, the closer Christians got to their sacred texts, the more painful things became for the Jews. The more strongly Jesus was believed to have atoned for human sin, the more sins were committed against the Jews. [14]

Secondly, Susannah Heschel:

> There is no doubt within the Jewish community that Christian mission is abhorrent. It is especially disturbing after the Holocaust, because it represents its continuation, a spiritual genocide. Can

anyone really believe it is to the greater glory of God that there should be no more Jews left in the world? After the Holocaust, to pursue a Jew to convert to Christianity is to murder a soul.[15]

Such strong convictions as expressed above need to be taken seriously by Christians (and Messianic Jews) who are committed to sharing the 'word of Christ' within the Jewish community. Where such sharing has been insensitive, dishonest, abusive, manipulative or exploitative then the call to repent and to seek to make recompense must be heard and acted upon. However, it is my conviction that the correct antidote to the 'misuse' of mission is not 'non-use' as Blu Greenberg, Susannah Heschel and other proponents of a Two Covenant position would passionately advocate but 'right use'. Such 'right use' would see mission flowing from an Enlargement Theology which would see Christian mission to Jewish people not in terms of seeking to remove Jews from Jewish communities or to convert them out of Jewish identity, but rather to present Jesus as the fulfilment/renewal of Jewish hope. Such evangelistic mission is often done most sensitively, effectively and faithfully when there is a significant role for contemporary Messianic Jewish believers.

A useful model for this 'right use' of Christian mission is presented by Walter Riggans. Riggans argues that there should be a careful knitting together of dialogue and witness:

Our testimony to Jesus as Israel's Messiah has a rhythmic quality as it moves graciously and purposefully between the retrospective movement of learning and listening about God and our faith from Israel, and the prospective movement of witnessing to Israel about our God and our faith.[16]

Moving sensitively to such a rhythm and with the heartfelt passion shown by Paul himself, it is hoped that such a witness will challenge Rabbinic Jews and the wider Jewish community to (re)consider the person, work and claims of Jesus, without being distracted by the very real issue of Christian anti-Semitism, which is so often fuelled by a rigid Replacement

Theology. These are two separate issues and while for some within the Jewish community it is understandable that these two issues can not be set neatly apart, it seems that Christian witness must do all it can to make this separation a reality. If this separation cannot be adequately made and maintained then it is extremely unlikely that the truth claims of Jesus will be able to have a clear hearing within the various non-Messianic Jewish contexts.

On a final point, Christians who are committed to Jewish evangelistic mission believing it to be both a biblical priority (Romans1:16) and that the wider Gentile mission only has ultimate meaning within the wider context of God's redemptive purposes for Israel, are sometimes accused of being anti-Semitic as a consequence of such mission activity. To this charge the response by a Messianic Jewish believer [17] is extremely helpful. Stan Telchin states:

> I believe with all my heart that the most anti-Semitic thing a Bible believing Christian can do to the Jewish people is to deny them access to the good news of the Messiah Jesus . . . . Jesus himself embodied the perfect righteousness of God. And the Bible tells us that "without holiness no one will see the Lord" (Hebrews 12:14). Unless a man or woman can say that God, "has arrayed me in a robe of righteousness" (Isaiah 61:10), what hope does he or she have of standing in His presence? Which brings us to the matter of our guilt and shame for having disobeyed God in thought, word and deed. What solution has Messiah Jesus brought to this awful predicament? The solution is found in the cross. [18]

Chapter Nine

Romans 11:1–10

Commentary on Romans 11:1–10

¹I ask then: Did God reject his people? By no means! I am an Israelite myself, a descendant of Abraham, from the tribe of Benjamin. ²God did not reject his people, whom he foreknew. Don't you know what the Scripture says in the passage about Elijah— how he appealed to God against Israel: ³ "Lord, they have killed your prophets and torn down your altars; I am the only one left, and they are trying to kill me"? ⁴And what was God's answer to him? "I have reserved for myself seven thousand who have not bowed the knee to Baal." ⁵So too, at the present time there is a remnant chosen by grace. ⁶And if by grace, then it is no longer by works; if it were, grace would no longer be grace.

⁷What then? What Israel sought so earnestly it did not obtain, but the elect did. The others were hardened, ⁸as it is written:

"God gave them a spirit of stupor, eyes so they could not see and ears so they could not hear, to this very day."

⁹And David says:

"May their table become a snare and a trap, a stumbling block and a retribution for them.

¹⁰May their eyes be darkened so they cannot see and their backs be bent for ever."

Romans 11:1-10 (NIV)

9.1 General Comments

This section begins by presenting directly a core question which has been present[1] within the ongoing teaching and questioning from 9:1, namely, has God rejected Israel? This question for Paul is of the same nature as the question posed indirectly in 9:6 about the reliability of God's word and in 9:14 with the focus on God's justice. Paul will address this question by making reference once again to all three segments of scripture.[2]

This core question needs to be dealt with and Paul does this in a very overt way in the opening verse. This answer is translated as "By no means" (New International Version/Revised Standard Version/Good News Bible), "Heaven forbid" (Complete Jewish Bible), "God forbid" (Authorised.Version) and as "Of course not"(Revised English Bible). In this reply what we have from Paul is the conviction that any sense of rejection, replacement or repudiation must be seen as partial, (hence the theme of the faithful remnant) and also as temporary. That which is partial and temporary must also be seen, argues Paul, as part of God's overall redemptive purpose. Despite the pain and anguish of the substantial Jewish rejection and opposition (11:28) to the Gospel which Paul knows so deeply, Paul remains convinced that this partial and temporary rejection is a key ingredient to Gentile inclusion and subsequent restoration/salvation for 'all Israel.' This understanding will be spelt out fully in the next segments of Romans 11 (vv11-24 and vv24-36).

In dealing with this core question, Paul in this section is able to transition from focusing primarily on Israel in terms of past and present identity and election (9:6-10:21) to issues of future hope and destiny (11:11-36). In order to facilitate this transition Paul begins by proclaiming his own identity/testimony and then he re-introduces and focuses anew upon the theme of remnant first referenced in 9:27. This 'remnant theme', which is often spoken of as an 'Israel within Israel', clearly has a powerful resonance for Paul. John Ziesler, in commenting on this, states:

> It remains true that the majority have been 'hardened' (cf. 9 14-18), but a minority which includes Paul himself has not. The divine

purpose which always did work through an Israel within Israel, continues with that part of her, the remnant, which has responded in faith.[3]

This focus on the remnant is not simply a historical reminder as in this case with the focus on Elijah, but it also has for Paul contemporary relevance and acts as a catalyst for future hope. This point is developed by James Dunn:

> To substantiate his point Paul once again focuses on the theme of the remnant, not because that is the whole answer (as he will soon reveal) but because it is the first part of the whole.[4]

9.2 Specific Text Comments

Verse 1. This question of God's rejection of Israel reflects probably a growing conviction within some of the Christian communities within Rome, especially those with a growing Gentile leadership/membership, that in some way God had indeed rejected Israel and that the blessings and responsibilities of being Israel had now being given to the emerging mainly Gentile church communities.[5] This context would suggest that with this question Paul is addressing here mainly Gentile believers within the wider believing community in Rome. This is the view advanced by John Ziesler.[6] However, James Dunn[7] sees here Paul's first audience which he addresses as his fellow Jews. From my own reading of the text I would understand at this point in the development of the Christian communities in Rome the majority of such communities would be made up of an interwoven group of Jewish and Gentile believers. Yet it is worth noting that probably Gentiles in Rome who became active members within the 'Christian' communities were in most cases prior to their commitment to the Christian faith probably living as God fearers or proselytes. Therefore, in terms of 'ethnic allegiance' and 'religious expression' such believers were generally seen as belonging in a number of significant ways within the Jewish community. This understanding is developed further by Rudolf Brändle and Ekkehard Stegemann in their article on "The formation of the first 'Christian Congregations' in Rome in the Context of the Jewish Congregations." They state:

> It now seems little more than a truism that early Christianity was a product of this diffusion of Judaism into a society dominated by non-Jews. Its origins to be sure lie in an apocalyptic, esoteric movement within Palestinian Judaism. However, it gained its effective historical form, theologically and socially, in the tension filled encounter between Jews and non-Jews in the Mediterranean urban centers. Indeed it seems reasonable to say that the "Christian" movement, as it was named in the final quarter of the first century, at the latest to distinguish it from the Jews, was a new, self-supporting, although somewhat unstable form of reaction to the encounter between Jews and pagans. In substance it could perhaps best be characterized as a messianic-apocalyptic and charismatic movement in the grey areas between Jews, proselytes and God-fearers.[8]

Such 'replacement' convictions held by some Gentile believers may well have been fuelled by two main sources. Firstly, by the opposition to the message of Jesus Christ by many within the established Jewish community in Rome (and elsewhere). This opposition could lead to some Gentile believers deducing, that in the light of such opposition, Israel is now rejected. This line of argument is rejected by Paul powerfully in this section of Romans. Secondly, rejection of Israel seems to fit in with the reality of the earlier expulsion of the Jewish community (or some segments of the Jewish community?) under the edict of Emperor Claudius.[9]

Such convictions by some of the Christian community within Rome and the growing distance between some of the predominantly Gentile Christian 'house-churches' and the non-messianic Jewish synagogues clearly caused deep concern for Paul. Paul is determined to oppose in the strongest possible terms any notion of God's rejection of Israel, hence the powerful language of denial; 'By no means!' This sense of Paul's opposition to any sense of God's rejection of Israel is affirmed in the following comment by Richard Hays:

> Thus if in Romans 9 and 10, Paul deconstructs scripture's witness to Israel's favoured status, Romans 11, dialectically deconstructs the deconstructive reading, subverting any Gentile pretension to a position of hermeneutical privilege.[10]

To add weight to this denial, Paul once again (as in 9:3) affirms his own Jewish identity. Note here that Paul uses the term 'I am' not 'I was'. For Paul his Jewish identity is in no way diminished by his faith in Jesus Christ. In fact, for Paul such faith intensifies and refines his Jewish identity and reaffirms his hope for Israel and the world.[11]

The use by Paul of his own personal witness/Jewish identity is taken by David Stern[12] as a straightforward and important part of Paul's teaching tools. These claims of Jewish heritage, which Paul was making with special reference to his belonging to the tribe of Benjamin, could probably have been verified independently by the Jewish community argues Stern.[13] Robert Jewett makes a similar point and states:

> The oral tradition about this former zealot would surely have been as well known in Rome as in Galatia and Judea: "For you have heard of my former life in Judaism, how I persecuted the church of God violently and tried to destroy it" (Gal 1:13), while the churches in Judea "heard it said, 'He who once persecuted us is now preaching the faith he once tried to destroy'"(Gal 1:23). Although Paul had been a zealous opponent of the gospel, similar to current zealots who were seeking to "hinder us from speaking to the Gentiles" (1 Thess 2:16), he was not cast off by God. His conversion makes clear that the most fanatical opponents of the gospel can also be redeemed.[14]

The reference to belonging to the tribe of Benjamin may also have significance for, according to the teaching in the book of Judges (chapters 20-21), the tribe of Benjamin almost became extinct following 'civil war' yet was spared and later provided to the whole nation of Israel their first King.[15] This reference to the tribe of Benjamin and later to the prophet Elijah (vv2-4) may indicate Paul's own perception of his spiritual position of relative fragility and isolation in relation to the wider leadership within the Jewish community.[16] Yet I suggest that this also reflects his utter certainty in the promises of God and the irrevocable (v29) call of God being worked out through Abraham,[17] the tribe of Benjamin, the ministry of Elijah and Paul's own apostolic ministry within the church (including the faithful Jewish remnant) and his prophetic ministry to the wider Jewish community.

Stern also points out that Paul has used similar methods elsewhere[18] in his ministry. However, James Dunn helpfully develops this point in commenting on Paul's answer in 11:1,

> The answer at first seems rather ludicrous as though Paul was saying, "The fact that I have understood and believed the word of faith is sufficient proof that God has not rejected Israel," as though Paul was setting himself up as a representative of his whole people or even as a progenitor of a reconstructed people. But this is almost certainly not what Paul meant. The effect of such posturing, in studied disregard for all the other Jewish Christians, not an insignificant number, would be to trivialise the assertion. Certainly what comes to expression is Paul's consciousness of being one of the covenant people ("Israelite" 9:4), of being one of the seed of Abraham in whom God's promises and purposes are being fulfilled (4:13-18; 9:7-8), of his tribal identity (cf.Phil 3:5) But this is not an expression of egoistical aggrandizement, rather of indignation that a Jew could conceive of such a horrifying outcome. This is the utterance not of one self-confident in his own status over against his own people, but of one confident in God on behalf of his people.[19]

Verses 2-4. The issue of foreknowing points to the work of God's calling/election. Elijah is seen as a representative figure of this ongoing election but in a different way to the representatives of election in chapter 9. This point is made clearly by John Ziesler, in commenting on Elijah:

> He is used, however, differently from the figures of Isaac and Jacob in ch 9. There it was a matter of divine selection within historical Israel; here it is a matter of there having been apparently only one Israelite who remained faithful to God despite temptation to apostasy.[20]

Verse 4. The term 'χρηματισμος' translated God's answer (to him), is found only here within the New Testament. James Dunn comments helpfully on the possible significance of this striking 'divine response':

> It probably is not accidental that the two usages (2 Macc 2:4 and here) are both linked with visits to Mount Sinai (Jeremiah and Elijah): there may have been some tendency in Jewish circles to use this word in connection with the divine injunction which recalled Judaism to the revelation given at Sinai; moreover, it was at Sinai that Moses received the fundamental salvation-history revelation of God as "merciful".[21]

Also in verse 4 the remnant is numbered at seven thousand,[22] which has a sense of the completeness of Israel. However, it seems more fitting in view of Paul's understanding of God's saving purposes (based on God's grace)[23] to see the seven thousand in relation to the spiritual significance of the remnant of faithful Jewish believers in Paul's time and not as a strict and final total, but rather as a foundation for some larger future total. This line of argument and sense of future hope is affirmed by Richard Bell:

> Elijah was zealous for the Lord and despaired of the Israel he was facing. Paul was also zealous for God (his Christian zeal being quite different to his zeal as a Pharisee) and no doubt he also despaired of Israel (Rom 9.1-3).But here he introduces a note of hope. For just as in Elijah's day there were 7000 who had not bowed down to Baal, so in Paul's day there was a remnant chosen by grace. However this remnant anticipates a much greater salvation.[24]

In this outlining of the remnant of grace, Ben Witherington implies that there is a significant play on words by Paul:

> Verse 4 tells about those who God says are "left" (katelipon), so too now, says Paul, there is a leftover (leimna) that is a remnant. Paul uses the verb gegonen, which may be translated "has come into being" or "has happened". The point then is not that there are some Jews who never were outside God's elect people, but that God has by his free grace raised up (cf.11:6) a new righteous remnant from out of the midst of largely apostate Israel.[25]

Verse 7. The issue here identified by David Stern[26] is with the translation of 'ἐπιζητεῖ'as 'sought'[27](was striving) which implies that Israel is no longer striving for righteousness. Again the concern is that a theological worldview is dictating translation issues. The Complete Jewish Bible therefore replaces 'sought' with 'is striving'. Stern makes a similar point with the term 'forever' (11:10) preferring to use the term 'continually'. Stern states:

> "Continually" means "all the time, at present" while "forever" implies "always— now, in the future, and till the end of time." Here "forever" would be inconsistent with God's promises to Israel and also with what is said in vv.11-23 immediately following.[28]

Verses 7-10. Here is introduced the process of hardening. The verb 'πωρόω' points to a process of covering as in a callous covering skin.[29] Here Paul is again drawing out (as in 9:22-23 and :33) the judgment side of election. For Paul such hardening and Judgment is not just what is happening now with the opposition of many of his fellow Jews to the Gospel, but is what has happened throughout Jewish history. Such history is clearly witnessed to in the scriptures, hence the following quotations from Deuteronomy, Isaiah and Psalms.

In regard to these quotations, it is worth noting two points. Firstly, the reference to 'table' (v9) which has been taken as a possible criticism of kashrut.[30] While this is possible alongside possible references to cultic practices[31] it seems, I suggest, that if Paul was intending to apply the details in these quotations directly to his contemporary Jewish communities it would be more in keeping with the sense of general fellowship (or rather lack of it) associated with fellowship/festival meals within the Jewish community rather than a robust criticism of kashrut or cultic feasts. This view[32] is indeed advanced by David Stern:

> . . . If Jews who reject Yeshua have conversations purporting to be "words of Torah," then the dining table has indeed become for them a snare and a trap, a pitfall and a punishment — in the sense that when the worldview of non-Messianic Jewish life pervades the relaxed atmosphere of mealtimes, it becomes difficult for an individual Jew to recognise Yeshua and come to trust him.[33]

Secondly, the Deuteronomy text "eyes so they could not see" (v8) which is a description of Israel's lack of spiritual understanding and the Psalm text "may their eyes be darkened" (v9) which is the Psalmist's call for judgment upon his oppressors. Both of these texts may have been selected by Paul with emphasis on eyes and sight because Paul wanted to contrast the 'failing eyes' of non-belief in Jesus with the 'good eyes' of those who have faith/trust in Jesus. Paul probably knew that 'good eyes' were one of the three virtues within Rabbinic tradition of a true son of Abraham.[34] The true sons of Abraham for Paul would be clearly identified with both the historic and contemporary remnant of grace.

9.3 Comments relating to the Development of Enlargement Theology

In this section the theme of the remnant is a major focus. The remnant theme has a significant role within Enlargement Theology and contemporary Messianic Judaism.

Messianic Jews will draw from this remnant theme in identifying and defining their own identity. For Messianic Jews, they are part of the same faithful Jewish remnant as manifested in the time of Elijah, in the time of Paul and through the ongoing history of the church (where there has always been a Jewish believing element) up until the present. The key within this remnant for Messianic Jews is that this remnant should not (as in the case of Replacement Theology) be seen as a small anomaly which points to the excluding of the majority of the Jewish people as God's elect, but rather that the remnant is the 'first fruit' which witnesses to and in some way acts as a guarantee for the full harvest of Jewish fulfilment as outlined in Romans 11:26. This remnant understanding is therefore another weapon in presenting the 'no' to Replacement Theology. However, it is also a 'no' to some promotions of Two Covenant Theology by showing that the Jewish remnant (of which Paul is a part) has come into being because individual Jews have responded to the grace of Christ and are not part of the remnant as a result solely of their Jewish identity and calling, but this identity and calling must find its roots and fulfilment in a personal faith response to the person and work of Jesus the Messiah.

This identifying within contemporary Messianic Judaism which sees Messianic Jews within the role as the remnant clearly raises issues in contemporary Jewish-Christian relations. Firstly, some Christians especially one-covenant theologians would challenge the identifying of the remnant as solely a Jewish entity, but rather would see the remnant as referring to the elect which would consist of both Jewish believers in Jesus and Gentile believers. Secondly, by Messianic Jews claiming to be the remnant key issues are raised: how can such a remnant identify and interact with both the wider church community and the wider Rabbinic Jewish community, in what ways can it or should it seek to maintain a separate identity while wanting at the same time to be a helpful bridge between Jews and Christians?

In claiming to be the remnant, contemporary Messianic Jews are seeking to define themselves using a biblical concept in a contemporary setting. This is a momentous and far-reaching task. In some ways, this could be seen as a reactionary position.

This very point is taken up by the Messianic Jewish writer, Baruch Maoz:

> The modern Messianic Jewish movement among contemporary Jewish followers of Jesus is a reactionary position. It is a radical attempt to set the clock back and to make it as clear as possible that faith in Jesus does not involve a rejection of one's own Jewish identity but is an embrace thereof. [35]

Clearly issues around the defining of the remnant and resulting remnant theologies alongside Messianic Jewish self-definition will give rise to much material for Jewish-Christian dialogue. Such material will have significant ongoing impact in regard to the pursuit of Enlargement Theology which in its fourth tenet sees a key specific role for the remnant/Jewish believers in Jesus in relation to God's purposes being worked out through three different yet mutually inter-connected communities.

Chapter Ten

Romans 11:11–24

Commentary on Romans 11:11 – 24

[11] Again I ask: Did they stumble so as to fall beyond recovery? Not at all! Rather because of their transgression, salvation has come to the Gentiles to make Israel envious. [12] But if their transgression means riches to the world, and their loss means riches for the Gentiles, how much greater richness will their fullness bring!

[13] I am talking to you Gentiles. Inasmuch as I am the apostle to the Gentiles, I make much of my ministry [14] in the hope that I may somehow arouse my own people to envy and save some of them. [15] For if their rejection is the reconciliation of the world, what will their acceptance be but life from the dead? [16] If the part of the dough offered as firstfruits is holy, then the whole batch is holy; if the root is holy, so are the branches.

[17] If some of the branches have been broken off, and you, though a wild olive shoot, have been grafted in among the others and now share in the nourishing sap from the olive root, [18] do not boast over those branches. If you do, consider this: You do not support the root, but the root supports you. [19] You will then say, "Branches were broken off so that I could be grafted in." [20] Granted. But they were broken off because of unbelief, and you stand by faith. Do not be arrogant, but be afraid. [21] For if God did not spare the natural branches, he will not spare you either.

[22] Consider therefore the kindness and sternness of God: sternness to those who fell, but kindness to you, provided that you continue in his kindness. Otherwise, you also will be cut off. [23] And if they

*do not persist in unbelief, they will be grafted in, for God is able
to graft them in again. ²⁴After all, if you were cut out of an olive
tree that is wild by nature, and contrary to nature were grafted
into a cultivated olive tree, how much more readily will these, the
natural branches, be grafted into their own olive tree!*

Romans 11:11-24 (NIV)

10.1 General Comments

In this section Paul reaffirms that Israel's stumbling/failure is
not terminal but is part of the bigger concluding picture of God's
redemptive purposes which Paul will present in verses 25-36.
This picture of redemption will also be a picture of Israel's
restoration and fulfilment. However, before Paul can focus on
this concluding picture he needs to address specifically Gentile
'identity issues' within the Roman congregations. This (new)
primary focus upon a Gentile audience is seen by Paul Minear
as very significant:

This shift in address was very strategic; it continues, I believe
into ch 14. Paul's new target was to counter anti-Semitism among
members of Group Two in the Roman churches, those who
despised and ridiculed the weak in faith. Such anti-Semitism fed
anti-Gentilism.[1]

Minear then continues this line of reasoning:

If Gentiles accepted him, they must share his love for Israel, for he
took seriously 'the eternal triangle of forces' defining his vocation.
Gentile believers were obliged by their own faith, so strong in their
own eyes, to consider holy both the first fruits (Jewish believers)
and the whole lump as well (Israel as a whole, both believers
and unbelievers) The measure of a strong Gentile faith would be
whether the believer hoped for the salvation of all branches of this
tree whose root was holy (11:13-16).[2]

It seems probable that throughout Romans 9-11[3] Paul has in
mind specific questions and specific questioners. For example,
while the teaching from 10:14 will have significance for the

whole of the Roman congregation, clearly in the questions Paul presents (10:14, :18, :19, 11;1 and :11) he has a non-messianic Jew in mind. While in this section, from verses 13-24 certainly[4] and from verses 25-32 possibly, Paul has primarily Gentile believers in the forefront of his mind.

In addressing these Gentile believers, Paul is determined that faith in Christ, which has led Gentiles into the full covenant blessings of God, must not foster an arrogant or dismissive attitude to present unbelieving historical Israel and by implication make messianic Jews in some ways second class citizens. To address this pressing pastoral and theological issue, Paul introduces here the metaphor of the olive tree.

This olive tree metaphor enables Paul to explore, confront and heal tensions within the Roman congregation(s). As Robert Jewett states:

> . . . Paul was wise enough to know that one cannot deal with such prejudices by frontal assault. So he selects a natural allegory with persuasive power along with a "speech in-character" by a Gentile interlocutor whose prejudicial inclinations are exaggerated in a humorous manner. This enables the audience to gain perspective on itself by smiling at the foibles of the interlocutor. In the end, the audience is enabled to recognize that, despite its reluctance to support a mission that would augment the numbers of perceived competitors, there were nine very good reasons to reconsider the matter: "the salvation" (11:1), the "wealth" (11:12), the "reconciliation" (11:15), the "life from the dead" (11:15), the "welcome" (11:15), the "holy" (11:16), the "nourishing sap" (1:17), the "faith" (11:20), and finally, the "kindness and severity of GOD" (11:22). This passage which many interpreters have viewed as muddled, turns out to be a brilliant fusion of allegory and diatribe that would have functioned effectively with Paul's audience in Rome, drawing them in the direction of supporting his audacious mission to Spain that would provide a truly inclusive reconciliation of the world.[5]

The olive tree metaphor draws from 'Old Testament'

references such as Hosea 14:6 and Jeremiah 11:16. Also the olive tree metaphor allows for Paul to introduce and refine the concept of 'grafting in' and 'pruning out'. In addition to this, there was also a sense within Jewish understanding[6] that the olive tree always produced its very best crop at the final harvest. So it seems probable there is within this a sense of the 'eschatological fulfilment' that Israel will be fully restored and will fully prosper within God's purposes at the final hour. Here I suggest that we see for Paul that issues of evangelism and related soteriology must be understood within an eschatological framework. For Israel this means the consummation of the hopes of covenantal history and the created order. For Paul such consummation is to be found only through the ministry of the Messiah and the related outpouring of the Holy Spirit.

This metaphor of the olive tree shows both Gentile dependency within the covenant (v18) and the future hope of Jewish restoration and renewal (v15, v23 and v24). This shared hope is a core component of Paul's apostolic ministry to the Gentiles. This shared hope is also in part to be fulfilled through Paul's jealousy motif (v14). Paul does not explain how this jealousy motif will be fully realised. In fact it appears to be a very strange 'mission strategy'. This very point is picked up by Ernst Käsemann:

> Paul seriously counts on it that the Gentile mission will make Israel jealous and lead to its conversion. This hope can be imagined only if the conversion itself stands beyond any doubt and only the way to it is obscure. The theology and practice of the apostle cannot be adequately understood unless attention is played to this conviction. The fact that it seems absurd to us should underscore rather than reduce its importance for Paul and his interpretation.[7]

In whatever way one sees this potential outworking of the jealousy motif, it seems to be dependent upon the grace of God enabling the full functioning of the new 'olive tree' community — a community which displays not its own strength and credentials, but is fully reliant upon the awesome redemptive power of God. As John Lodge states:

> The present state of 'unbelief' is part of God's doing. God has broken off the branches for the sake of the Gentiles. Their suffering in the light of the future glory, however is not a punishment but a fulfillment of the psalmist's words: "For thy sake we are being killed all day long" (Ps 44:22 [44:23 LXX] Rom 8:36) They cannot be separated from the love of God. The new olive tree—made fantastically from wild, natural and broken-off branches—includes both Jews and Gentiles, not as one or the other (pro-Israel or anti-Israel), but as a people called into being by the power of God (Dunn).[8]

10.2 Specific Text Comments

Verses 11-12. At first reading verse 11 appears to be simply a repetition of the earlier question in 11:1. However, I think Stern is helpful here in drawing out the following distinction between 11:1 and v11:

> This is not, as some commentators think, a repetition of the question in v.1. There it was whether God has acted to abandon Israel; here it is whether Israel's rejection of Yeshua has as its necessary consequences the permanent self-exclusion of the Jewish people from the purview of God's promises, without any positive action on God's part. If Sha'ul answers "Yes," his whole Gospel will be unacceptable to Jews, again not because it offends them, but because it contradicts the Tanakh, which presents God's promises to Israel as unconditional (vv.28-29).[9]

Paul in these verses seems to be gathering together the remaining few strands of his teaching focusing on the questions and concerns of non-messianic Jews prior to the shift in focus to the Gentiles. In this final gathering together Paul has this growing sense of expectation as he glimpses at the outworking of God's purposes. The whole thrust of Paul's argument here is focused on the apocalyptic. Terms such as 'how much more'[10] (v12 and v24) and 'life from the dead' indicate this expectation. Paul does not spell out how this fullness will come[11] or exactly how this fullness will be measured,[12] but for Paul there is without doubt the hope that the faithful remnant and the whole of Israel may be inseparable at the concluding of God's redemptive purposes. As John Lodge states:

> In the light of the eschatological scenario there must be an incredible bond between Israel and believers in the gospel, the Jew first and also the Gentile.[13]

Verses 13-15. Paul here is aware of the importance of his ministry as the apostle to the Gentiles, yet this critical ministry is seen by Paul within the bigger purposes of God, namely, that this Gentile ministry has at its heart the desire and purpose to save Jewish people. This affirms the place of the Gentile mission within the redemptive purposes of God. Equally, the accomplishment of the largely Gentile mission is reliant in part on Jewish acceptance (v15) of the gospel message which Paul is committed to proclaiming to both Jew and Gentile. In this section of teaching we have this interdependency of Gentile and Jewish mission. This interdependency is helpfully expressed by Timothy Butlin:

> Paul is not only concerned for the salvation of Israel but the process by which this will take place. Paul perceives God as having a cycle of grace at work in which Israel and the Gentiles both have opportunities for receiving mercy. Furthermore it is God's purpose that each is to be the means by which the other receives mercy. In historical times Paul not only reflected that the hardening of Israel was the moment of opportunity for Gentile salvation but also that as a result of that salvation the flow of blessing would return to Israel.[14]

While at times, for geographical or sociological/theological reasons, Paul may distinguish between specific mission to Jews and Gentiles[15] in the bigger picture of God's overall gospel (Rom 1:1) the mission to Jews and Gentiles has an inherent unity. James Dunn comments on this inherent unity:

> Both partners in this eschatological minuet must learn to acknowledge the role of the other.[16]

This essential unity connects with Paul's understanding of the unity of God in terms of being the God of all, not just of the Jews but also of the Gentiles (Rom 10:12). For Paul the wider link here to the doctrine of God is of great importance.

The term 'life from the dead' (v15) in line with many other key phrases in Romans 9-11 has been the subject of much debate. The main thrust of the arguments[17] seems to present three main lines of interpretation. Firstly there is a vague interpretation which in David Stern's words would mean:

> . . . something even more wonderful, in what we will have when the Messianic Age has fully come.[18]

The second line would follow a more metaphorical interpretation. Moo outlines such an interpretation with an interesting footnote to Luke 15:24 as meaning:

> . . . a way of referring to a great and unprecedented blessing, whether this be a spiritual quickening of the whole world or the "spiritual coming back to life" of Israel.[19]

While the third literal interpretation preferred[20] on balance by Moo and Dunn would suggest that the term means as Stern states:

> . . . nothing less than the consummation of salvation in bodily resurrection (as in 8:11-24), a hope Pharisees held then, as Orthodox Jews do now. The resurrection will be delayed until the Jewish people, as a nation, come to faith in Yeshua; therefore Sha'ul feels duty bound to follow the Jewish pattern of hasting the Messiah's (second!) coming (see 2 Ke 3:12 & N) by evangelizing the Jewish people indirectly (vv.13-14) as well as directly (Acts 9-28, 1 C 9:19-23).[21]

Verse16. As with the debate about the precise interpretation of 'life from the dead'(v15), here there is a similar debate about the identification of the firstfruits and the 'root'. Verse 16 marks the introduction of the olive tree metaphor which shapes Paul's teaching through to verse 24. However, initially the olive tree metaphor begins with the picture of supplementary offerings drawn from Numbers 15:20-21 and Leviticus 6. In commenting on this Joseph Shulam sees that Paul is creating a midrash on the theme of the 'holy stump' which runs through the following verses and he creates a verbal analogy between Israel as the tree (olive) and the giving of the tithe portion. Joseph Shulam states:

> In Isaiah 6v13, the stump of the terebinth or oak is associated with the olive tree. Paul connects the stump of the tree with the "tenth of the . . . . seed of the land or the fruit of the tree" which is "holy to the Lord" (Num 27:30) He thus describes Israel as a "holy seed" Although the root is indeed holy the tree may be felled (cf. "fallen" in 11.11) if its members (branches) do not obey the commandment to be holy as the Lord is holy (cf. Lev 19.2).[22]

In relation to the identification of the earlier metaphor[23] of firstfruits or the following metaphor of the root, three main views are promoted, yet they all stand on the common perception that the outworking of God's redemptive purposes grow out of the history of Israel. Firstly, the identification is made with the faithful believing Jewish remnant of Paul's time (messianic Jews). Secondly the identification is made with the patriarchs (11:28) with special reference to Abraham (4:12-17). This is the view favoured by David Stern[24] in view of the chronological progression of Paul's teaching in this section. However, John Ziesler is probably helpful here when on balance he states:

> . . . perhaps we should take it that Paul is not here making a sharp distinction between the true Israel of old and the true Israel now . . . .[25]

Thirdly, and probably the least favourable, is to identify the firstfruits/root with the person and work of Jesus Christ. This would draw from 1 Corinthians 15:23 which proclaims Jesus

Christ as the first fruits of the resurrection. While in this segment of Romans the theme of resurrection is addressed (v15), the context is very different and such an identification of first fruits/ root with Jesus is difficult to fit, although it is favoured by many of the early church Fathers[26] and by Karl Barth:

The church was of course convinced from the very outset of the special dignity of the patriarchs and the seven thousand. But it could hardly be a matter of course — for its non-Jewish members at any rate — to hear the latter summarily described as the holy root by which all branches are sanctified and they themselves are sustained. This kind of statement was possible for the church of Jews and Gentiles only if Jesus Christ was meant by the root.[27]

The next key area for interpretation is the issue of identifying the (natural) branches (v16, v17, v18, v19, v21 and v24) of the olive tree to which the Gentile believers have been grafted in. Four main lines of interpretation have been promoted, namely: every true Jewish believer (the faithful remnant of the past and the present future/ Messianic Jewish believers); secondly, simply every Jew; thirdly, all believers in Jesus (Jews and Gentiles); fourthly, the Jewish people as a whole nation, though not specifically every single Jewish person.

On balance, the case for the third option seems weak, for while Gentiles are grafted in and are part of the branch structure of the tree (the wild olive shoot of verse 17) they are clearly not the natural branches as identified in verse 21. Yet any full understanding of the olive tree structure must honour the place of Gentiles as part of the 'people of God',[28] but the picture here of natural branches simply does not fit. Equally, the first two options do not fit easily either because the branches are not all being seen in the same way, hence the term 'some' (v17). Some of the natural branches have been cut off (yet with the hope of future regrafting back in vv23-24) while clearly some of the natural branches have remained fruitful and have provided a 'grafting in' point for Gentile believers (the wild olive shoot of v17). Therefore, to see that the natural branches refer to all

Jews or all Messianic Jews disconnects with the overall flow of Paul's carefully chosen natural metaphor.

How one identifies the branches has direct correlation to the identification of 'all Israel' in verse 26.[29] It seems to be vital that in any unwrapping of the olive tree metaphor/theology, one must hold in tension the conviction that God's electing purposes have an essential unity, yet these purposes are being worked out at times within three distinct expressions/groups, namely messianic Jewish believers, Gentile believers (who are grafted into the cultivated olive tree) and the Jewish people as a corporate ethnic identity. This understanding is at the very heart of contemporary Messianic Jewish Theology and of what I have been presenting and developing in part under the heading of Enlargement Theology.

Verse 18. In this teaching one of the main thrusts of Paul's argument is designed to prevent Gentile boasting, hence the call in this verse, 'do not boast' and the similar call of verse 20, 'do not be arrogant'. Maybe such tendency to boast has been stimulated by the particular context of the situation within the Roman congregations. One possibility would be the return of some of the Jewish believers to Rome (this is probably indicated by the greetings in Romans 16 which lists a mixture of Jewish and Gentile believers present within the congregations) following the edict of the former Emperor Claudius. Such a return may have led to tensions and possible conflicts over leadership roles within the emerging congregations. The second main possibility would be that some of the synagogue communities may have initially welcomed and responded positively to the gospel, but later became hardened to the outworking of the gospel; this point is developed by William S Campbell:

> Some such sentiments seem to surround the scornful words of Rom. 11.13-24, 'Branches were broken off so that I might be grafted in', which are perhaps an indication of self-definition in the face of the 'other'.

Such a statement implies a very specific context because it presupposes both a connection to, or a relationship with, the Jewish community and simultaneously a distancing from it.[30]

The significant point is that, whatever the particular cause or causes for boasting, such attitudes are completely inappropriate for anyone who stands by faith.[31] Standing by faith is rooted in God's action, namely his kindness[32] (v22) and gives no room for pride or arrogant boasting. This particular point is made powerfully by James Dunn:

Consequently the appropriate response for the gentile believer to the present stage of salvation-history is not pride or status, but fear— fear not of the potter (the inscrutable ways of divine providence or whatever) but fear of the creator who is also the judge, and whose response to the pride and presumption of the creature will always be one of wrath and condemnation (chaps1-2).[33]

Dunn continues:

... the history of Israel shows how quickly faith can be corrupted into unfaith, how easily grace can be perverted into human presumption. Individual gentile Christians should not assume that what has happened to them is something final and irreversible; the only security derives from a sustained and unreserved reliance on God's grace alone. [34]

Verse 21. John Lodge raises the issue here as to the precise intent of the term 'did not spare', asking in what sense is this a direct Christological reference? In what sense if any does Paul interpret the present fate and future destiny of Israel Christologically? Lodge states:

The genuine implied reader will recall that Paul said God did not spare (ουκ εφεισατο) his own Son (Rom 8:32) Paul uses the same language to describe Israel's destiny as he did to talk of Jesus' death. The implied reader may even recall Abraham who did not spare Isaac on account of the Lord (ουκ εφεισω, Gen 22:12 LXX). The *apistia* of some in Israel is not so much a reference to their actions as to a state in which they find themselves. The broken branches find themselves in a state of 'faithlessness' as their role in salvation. "Israel's present unbelief is ordained by God; Israel cannot and may not yet come to a full understanding of Christ" (Stuhlmacher). Israel undergoes '*apistia*' for the sake of the world, bearing suffering vicariously. We might even paraphrase Rom 11:21 "For if God did not spare his own Son, neither will he spare Israel." And the outcome for both is the same: "life from the dead" (11:15).[35]

10.3 Comments relating to the Development of Enlargement Theology

I will focus here on one main issue. The issue which is raised here (and throughout Romans 9-11, elsewhere in Paul's writings[36] and in the wider New Testament context)[37] relates to the understanding of who constitutes 'God's people' and what is/are the relationship(s) between the various potential constituents. This is clearly a key issue in the development of Enlargement Theology and within any theological system which attempts to identify and define relationships between groupings such as 'church', 'Israel', 'Jewish people', 'the remnant' and 'the elect'.

In terms of the understanding of the term 'God's people', I understand that Paul sees 'God's people' in terms of three united yet distinct entities, namely: unbelieving Israel, believing Israel and believing Gentiles. I see that this understanding of 'God's people' is a true reflection of Paul's teaching especially in relation to the olive tree analogy outlined in Romans 11:16-24. Equally, I believe that such an understanding does not make Paul's teaching in any way supportive of Replacement Theology or any supersessionist position. This is because Paul's understanding clearly affirms a significant and ongoing role within 'God's people' and purposes for ethnic Israel. However, my view in seeing Paul's position as not being supersessionist is a view which is robustly challenged by many within contemporary Rabbinic Judaism and within the wider field of contemporary Jewish-Christian relations.

One such robust challenge comes from Daniel Boyarin.[38] Boyarin argues that Paul's understanding of the nature of 'God's people' is full of ambiguity as Paul wrestles with the relationships between ethnic Israel and the new reality of Gentile believers in Christ.[39] Yet within this ambiguity, argues Boyarin, there is unquestionably an inherent form of supersessionism. This conviction is based on the view that while as Boyarin states the signifier Israel remains central in Paul's theology, it has evolved in Paul's thinking to take on a new allegorical meaning.[40] This new meaning links Israel to the new community of Jews and Gentiles who believe in Jesus and consequently excludes those Jews who do not. This is not classical Replacement Theology/Supersessionism as appears later in the theological writings of Justin Martyr because Paul is not saying that God has totally rejected Israel or that Israel now refers only to Gentile Christians, but rather that supersessionism can be seen on different levels. Boyarin argues that Paul is seeking to persuade Gentile Christians away from one form of supersessionism.[41] Yet what Paul actually states is from a contemporary Jewish perspective still another, if a somewhat modified form of supersessionism. Boyarin states:

> Now the crux of Paul's argument is for the continuing significance of the Jewish People. If the Christian part of the People is holy, so is the rest. Paul, however, subtly shifts the ground on which he is standing. On the one hand, he argues that the Christian Jews are merely a saving remnant, such as the one that the same prophetic texts would speak of from Elijah to Jeremiah. Here, however, is where the shift comes in, for the saving remnant is no longer, as it was in the prophets, those Jews who are faithful to the commandments, the works of the Torah, but is now defined by grace alone . . . . A new, if temporary, election has been added to the original one. Although ultimately God has not abandoned the original election by grace of Israel, a new act of grace has taken place which replaces those who are faithful to the original covenant with those who have faith in Christ as the remnant of Israel. Surely, those left behind will in the end be gathered into the community

of faith, so God's honesty has not been impugned, but for the moment at least, Jews who have not accepted Christ are simply left by the wayside. Precisely, however, as that moment stretched into millennia, this doctrine became inevitably one of supersession even without—indeed, as it may have stood against—the sectarian formulation and violence of a community such as the one that later would produce John's gospel.[42]

Boyarin in continuing this line of argument is at pains to stress that Paul's doctrine as it stands is not anti-Judaic[43] and that the emerging doctrine of supersessionism found here in Romans 11 is vastly different to those later fully developed Christian doctrines of supersessionism. Boyarin draws his argument to a conclusion:

> Precisely because we understand "grace" and "works" as sociological markers, then we must understand Romans 11:5-6 as reflecting a replacement of the historical, physical Jewish tribe, with its cultural practices, by another kind of community, defined by grace. Indeed it has always been the case that only part of Israel are the elect, but election until now has been defined through commitment to Israel's historical practice and memory. The remnant is now defined through the grateful acceptance of Christ. No longer Israel according to the flesh, but Israel according to the Spirit—that Israel signified by the physical and historical one.[44]

In terms of contemporary Jewish-Christian encounters, Boyarin's contribution is helpful inasmuch as his arguments show the various nuances within Replacement Theology and supersessionist thinking. Yet I do not share his conclusion that Paul's position in Romans 11 is supersessionist. Paul is not arguing that Israel has been replaced or superseded in any sense, but Paul, as a prophet to Israel, is saying that a process of transformation has taken and is taking place because of the person and work of Jesus Christ. This transformation, which enlarges the 'people of God' and redefines the boundary markers through the recognition of Gentile believers, is fully in keeping with the faithful outworking and fulfilment (not as Boyarin describes the replacement) of the prophets, the commandments and the works of Torah. This emphasis on grace/faith in the person and work of Jesus Christ is not, as Boyarin argues, a 'new arbitrary election'[45] but it is the explicit consummation of that which was implicit within (to use Boyarin's phrase) 'the original covenant'.[46]

In addition to this fundamental difference between how one defines such a transformation, either as a 'fulfilment' which is in continuity with the promises and purposes of God or as a 'replacement' which brings about a discontinuity within the purposes and promises of God, or to some extent a mixture of both, I see three other weaknesses in Boyarin's position which, in relation both to the development of Enlargement Theology and to contemporary Jewish-Christian encounters need to be addressed.

Firstly, Boyarin makes no reference to the role of Messianic Jewish believers; in fact he appears to see that as a Jew belief in Jesus would mean the abandonment of his Jewish practices and commitments.[47] This is the very point which both Enlargement Theology and Messianic Jewish Theology and practice would fervently confront.

Secondly, he sees that, through Paul's teaching, unbelieving Israel has no present role and is "simply left by the wayside".[48] This is not the understanding which flows from Paul's teaching. Paul, while seeing that 'unbelieving Israel' is currently outside the present full purposes of God (because of such unbelief, in terms of receiving the fullness of grace through faith in Jesus Christ), nevertheless sees this Israel as part of the wider Israel which still has a significant role for the gifts and call of God are irrevocable. Such a role would suggest that within elements of religious practice,[49] national and community life, the promises of the land, etc, God's riches, blessings, grace and truth can be seen within all 'Israel', both believing and (at present) unbelieving Israel.

Thirdly, Boyarin sees that within John's Gospel there is an explicit sectarian and violent form of supersessionist theology, the early seeds of which he sees Paul is rightly opposing in Romans 9-11. However, I think Boyarin overplays the supersessionist/anti-Judaic interpretation of John's Gospel. This is in part to help contrast what Boyarin sees as Paul's nascent doctrine of supersessionism with the more fully developed and hardening doctrines of supersessionism which clearly developed subsequently into full blown Replacement Theology within the predominant Gentile church. I think it is however possible to see the 'anti-Judaic' material within John's Gospel just as Boyarin sees similar material within Romans 9-11, namely as 'an inner-Jewish discourse and an inner Jewish controversy'.[50] Clearly later some of the material within John's Gospel was used in an anti-Judaic way by many promoters of Replacement Theology and by those with anti-Judaic agendas, but it is I believe highly questionable to state that this was the original intent of the author or of that original faith community.

Chapter Eleven

Romans 11:25–36

Commentary on Romans 11:25–36

[25]I do not want you to be ignorant of this mystery, brothers, so that you may not be conceited: Israel has experienced a hardening in part until the full number of the Gentiles has come in. [26]And so all Israel will be saved, as it is written:

> *"The deliverer will come from Zion;*
> *he will turn godlessness away from Jacob.*
> *[27]And this is my covenant with them*
> *when I take away their sins."*

[28]As far as the gospel is concerned, they are enemies on your account: but as far as election is concerned, they are loved on account of the patriarchs, [29]for God's gifts and his call are irrevocable. [30]Just as you who were at one time disobedient to God have now received mercy as a result of their disobedience, [31]so they too have now become disobedient in order that they too may now receive mercy as a result of God's mercy to you. [32]For God has bound all men over to disobedience so that he may have mercy on them all.

> *[33]Oh, the depth of the riches of the wisdom*
> *and knowledge of God!*
> *How unsearchable his judgments,*
> *and his paths beyond tracing out!*
> *[34]"Who has known the mind of the Lord?*
> *Or who has been his counsellor?"*

^{35}*"Who has ever given to God,*
that God should repay him?"
^{36}*For from him and through him and to him*
are all things.
To him be the glory for ever! Amen.

Romans 11:25-36 (NIV)

11.1 General Comments

This final part of the reading of Romans 9-11 shows the unfolding of the merciful redemptive plan of God. This redemptive plan has the entire world in view.[1] Within this unfolding, there is a strong sense of the revealing of God's ultimate purposes. The final mystery is being revealed. For Paul, at the heart of these purposes is the utter faithfulness of God to his people. To understand the outworking of this faithfulness, Paul knows that a full understanding of who 'God's people' are and how they will receive his mercy must be explored. Paul is determined that his brothers (v25) (here in this context probably mainly Gentile believers) should not be ignorant of, or misunderstand the fullness of God's faithfulness to his people, both Jew and Gentile. Such ignorance could easily lead to an arrogant and conceited attitude which was reflected in part in the earlier statement of verse 19. Paul clearly states (v26) that the covenantal call to Israel is not transferable; for Paul, despite the serious nature of Israel's sin, Israel's election remains.

The first stage of this exploration of who 'God's people' are took the form of the olive tree analogy which immediately preceded this section. Now this exploration includes understanding of future key terms and events such as "the full number of Gentiles" (v25), "all Israel" (v26) and "all men" (v32). Such affirmation of God's faithful purposes are, for Paul, in keeping with the clear witness of scripture (hence the quote in verses 26-27 from Isaiah 59:20-21 and 27:9) and the eschatological hope that has shaped and driven his own ministry both as an apostle of the church and as a prophet to Israel.

In the light of this outworking of God's merciful promises

which will vindicate Paul's 'gospel of God' (1:1), Paul breaks into a rich declaration of praise, verses 33-36. It is fitting that Paul concludes this major section of teaching with such praise, for praise and worship must be the ultimate concluding point for any true engagement with the purposes of God. Also this engaging with the purposes of God traced throughout Romans 9-11 began with such a declaration of praise (9:5) and so fittingly also concludes with praise. Within this praise, there is also a deep sense of trust. Paul does not explain how this wonderful working of God's purposes will take place but as John Ziesler states:

> He (Paul) therefore simply asserts that all things are in God's hands, and may safely be left there.[2]

This placing all into 'God's hands' and Paul's use of mystery is also helpfully commented upon by Rowan Williams:

> Frequently as I read Paul's epistles I read the impatient inarticulacy of someone whose vision is bigger than his language and that is what makes Paul so intensely worth reading . . . . There is an extraordinary moment when Paul realizes that he has dug himself in far more deeply than he originally intended to in an argument and suddenly breaks away saying "I don't know where this is going but . . ." as he does, of course so memorably at the end of his most agonized excursions— Romans 9-11. How am I going to bring all these ideas together, Paul asks at the end of 11 when he has been wrestling with the fate of Israel and he can say only, "O the depth and mystery of God." And this is not a short cut because you have watched him getting there.[3]

11.2 Specific Text Comments

Verse 25. Paul here introduces the final outworking of God's merciful purposes with the term 'mystery'. This term is one which is frequently used in the Pauline corpus.[4] In each case, the term refers not to something which is beyond comprehension or something which is shown only to a select inner group as in the case of Greek mystery cults, but, as Romans 16:25-26 makes clear, mystery refers to a truth which can only be known by God's revelation and this revelation has been and is taking place through the person and work of Christ, the outpouring of the Holy Spirit and the preaching of the Gospel. This preaching of the 'mystery' is of crucial importance. As Karl Barth eloquently states:

> Revelation and election pass bluntly by the Church, by every Church. This whole situation constitutes a mystery from which there is no escape. It is of paramount importance that we should not be ignorant of this mystery, for it is the God given riddle, in which we verily encounter God.[5]

The term 'mystery', as C E B Cranfield also points out,[6] has strong eschatological connotations. Paul here sees what is happening namely with the large positive response of Gentiles, the Jewish remnant and the hardening of the majority of Israel as part of God's overall redemptive plan. As John Ziesler states:

> The salvation of all Israel depends on the ingathering of the Gentiles, which in turn depends on the recalcitrance of the majority of the Jews. The argument is thus partly historical, partly theological, and as the use of the term 'mystery' hints, partly intuitive. Rightly interpreted, the contemporary situation shows the divine strategy effectively at work.[7]

A similar point to that made by Ziesler is made by James Dunn:

> He (Paul) had not solved the puzzle of Israel's lapse by his own intellectual ability or by his skills as an exegete. God had revealed the solution to him, perhaps through the scripture he is about to cite though it is equally possible that the verses were seen to have such a full eschatological significance only in the light of this revelation received independently of them. Either way, Paul's claim is that God had resolved the puzzle of Israel's failure by revealing to him that Israel's fall always had been part of God's purpose for the climax of history.

The mystery he now invites them to share is precisely the confirmation of the possibility already envisaged. "A hardening has come in part on Israel . . . ." Paul does not attribute the hardening here to God, but in the light of what he has already said (9:18; 11:7) he does not need to. In this summary fashion the mystery of the dark side of election is again affirmed, and again with reference to Israel itself. The blindness is partial as both temporary and as afflicting what Paul hopes will in the end be a relatively small proportion of his people.[8]

The partial hardening of Israel is only for a time and for a purpose, namely that Gentiles may become full covenantal members of 'God's people'. The term 'full number' of Gentiles has been understood in three main ways. Firstly, following from a universalistic agenda as 'every single non-Jew'. Secondly, as the full number of the elect amongst the Gentiles, throughout history. Thirdly, as the completion of the missionary task amongst the Gentiles. The issue here is not precise numbers, one can only speculate if the fullness means all, most or many individuals but the term refers to the full and inclusive representation of Gentile identity, namely all who God calls and all who will respond to this call, by calling upon God.[9] As David Stern states:

> Sha'ul wrote when the Gospel mission to the Gentiles was just beginning; but already he foresaw what Yeshua had prophesied, that "this Good News about the Kingdom will be announced throughout the whole world as a witness to all nations (or "to all Gentiles"). It is then that the end will come" (Mt 24:14). Later Yochanan would see in his vision countless multitudes "from every nation and tribe and people and language" (Rv 7:9). The fullness of the Gentile world comes in when all components and subgroups of humanity are contributing people to the Kingdom. [10]

The term 'the full number of Gentiles' may also have some echoes with Luke 21:24, where Jesus refers to "the times of the Gentiles". Luke 21:24 could also connect with Genesis 15:16. The Messianic Jewish theologian Dan Juster, in commenting on the meaning of the fullness of the Gentiles, does indeed make reference back to Genesis 15:16:

> This (Genesis 15:16) implied the fullness of the stored up iniquity of the Amorites, whereby it would be the right time for Israel to be used as God's instrument of judgment in history.

Dan Juster then continues with a helpful contemporary reflection:

> Surely, the period of Auschwitz, when 6,000,000 of our people were slaughtered while nations watched in apathy has brought God's judgment. Israel's history in the Diaspora, although a severe discipline, has also been a test for the nations; and we can discern in the historical maltreatment of Israel a corresponding correlation in the decline of the people who acted unjustly. Israel's prophetic purpose thus continues even in the age of Diaspora; but now that Israel is in her own land, as predicted in Scripture, one can even now hear the steps of Messiah approaching.[11]

In Luke 21:24, the hope is that the Gentile oppressive yoke on Israel will be removed. This removal is part of the process for Israel's redemption,[12] yet Paul also sees Israel's redemption not just through the removal of the Gentile yoke, but also through the faithfulness of the Gentiles to the Gospel message. Here we have the linking of the destiny of Israel with the destiny of the Gentiles.

Verse 26a Within the term "and so", it is better to understand the 'so' as referring to the way in which all "Israel will be saved" rather than the issue of timing. For Paul wants to declare that clearly the timing of Israel's salvation is different to the majority of the Gentiles who have already in Paul's immediate context come to faith in Jesus. It seems to Paul that all Israel being saved is to be an event linked primarily to the Parousia. However, while the general timing is different, the method of this salvation will be no different to that of the Gentiles for the source, content and gift of salvation is the same, namely the person and work of Jesus. The focus, therefore, is on the process of how all Israel will be saved. Paul sees in these verses that in some way[13] the Jewish rejection of Jesus opens up the way for significant Gentile acceptance of Jesus.

This reality is at the heart of Paul's eschatology that even Israel's predominant rejection of the person and work of Jesus has major significance in terms of completing God's redemptive purposes. This significance is partly shown in that Israel's rejection of Jesus opens up a way as already stated for a significant Gentile acceptance of Jesus, which in turn will help to create a new openness in Jewish people leading to the promise that "all Israel will be saved". However, Pieter W Van der Horst[14] argues against James Dunn[15] and David Stern[16] by presenting the more unusual temporal sense, which could render the phrase as 'then all Israel' or 'thereafter all Israel'. Van der Horst argues that this temporal sense, with an emphasis on the issue of the timing of Israel's salvation rather than the method of such salvation, is in keeping with other possible New Testament usage such as Acts 7:8, 22:17 and 1 Thessalonians 4:16-17. It is, however, worth noting that the model sense and the temporal sense are not necessarily mutually exclusive.

Verse 26b "All Israel will be saved". This key statement can be understood in four ways. David Stern notes[17] that these four ways echo the four possible meanings of 'loaf' and 'branches' in 11:16.

The first line of meaning draws in part from Galatians 6:16, namely that all Israel means all the elect, both Jew and Gentile. However, this surely makes no sense of the way Israel is used in verse 25 and does no justice to the clear contrast between Gentiles and Israel which has been a main theme of Paul's argument outlined in verses 11-32.

The second line of meaning is that all Israel means the elect within Israel, namely, the faithful Jewish remnant of Paul's time alongside Jewish people of future generations who will respond to the Gospel. However, this, as in the first line of meaning, would be stating the obvious and would fail to make any sense of the mysterious hope of some great act of wider redemption anticipated by the promise of how much greater riches will their fullness bring (v 12), of their acceptance (v 15), of the promised grafting in of what had previously been broken off (vv 23-24) and of the irrevocable nature of God's call (v 29). This line of argument also fails to take into account Paul's 'inclusive' use of Israel. This point is made by William S Campbell:

> What is most significant from our analysis of Paul's use of Israel terminology is that having made a distinction within 'Israel' between the 'remnant' and the 'rest' (11.7), he does not disinherit either group by employing the term to refer exclusively to one party or the other.[18]

The third understanding is to see 'all Israel' as the whole nation of Israel which includes every individual.[19] The fourth view simply nuances the third to emphasis that the whole nation of Israel does not automatically or necessarily mean every single individual. Clearly this fourth position is in keeping with the way the term is used in 1 Samuel 7:5, 1 Kings 12:1, 2 Chronicles 12:1 and Daniel 9:11. Also in support of this fourth position the Mishnah[20] speaks of "All Israel" having a share in the world to come, while this is then followed by a list of those to be excluded. This fourth position is the one favoured strongly by a large consensus of commentators, for example David Stern,[21] C E B Cranfield,[22] James Dunn,[23] Douglas Moo,[24] John Ziesler[25] and James Boice.[26]

Following on from the defining of the term "All Israel", two further questions relating to the saving of all Israel from the text must be addressed. Firstly, the issue of 'how' this salvation will take place and secondly, 'when' this salvation of all Israel will take place.

In regard to these connected questions, Paul has already presented the view that the saving of all Israel is part of the larger process of God's redemptive purposes which has included Israel's hardening (9:30, 10:21, 11:26), the establishing and maintaining of a faithful remnant (11:1-6), his own prayer ministry (10:1) and the completion of Gentile inclusion (11:25). Now this process will be completed by the deliverer who will come from Zion and will renew the covenant and remove godlessness and sin. This deliverer, in keeping with Isaiah 59:20, could refer to Yahweh, but in keeping with Paul's teaching in 7:24-25 and 1 Thessalonians 1:10 it seems here that Paul's prime intention is to show that the deliverer is Jesus Christ. While, as stated earlier, the timing is different, the 'process of salvation' for 'all Israel' is not. For such salvation will follow a turning away from unbelief (v23) and a calling upon and trusting in Jesus. This understanding is affirmed by all the commentators listed in the footnotes 20 to 25 and by Robert Jewett.[27]

On balance, all the listed commentators except for David Stern[28] would place this event within the setting of Jesus Christ's second coming/Parousia. I will outline the following four quotes to give a flavour of this teaching and to introduce some of the nuances within the teaching.

Firstly, from C E B Cranfield who helpfully makes reference to Mt 10:23 when commenting on 11:26 (a):

> . . . it seems more probable that Paul was thinking of a restoration of the nation of Israel as a whole to God at the end, an eschatological event in the strict sense. We cannot help wondering whether this half-verse and Mt 10:23b may not perhaps have some light to throw upon each other. Could it be that the meaning of Mt 10:23b (whether its authenticity as a saying of Jesus is accepted or rejected) is that the conversion of 'all Israel' will not be accomplished until the Parousia? [29]

Secondly from John Ziesler, who explores around the Two Covenant approach (and in so doing references the work of K Stendahl),[30] he states:

> How will they be saved: by finding faith in Jesus Christ or without doing so? It has been suggested that, as Paul never states that they will become Christians, he allows for the possibility that somehow

at the end God will bring together those who have followed two different tracks to being his people; the track taken by the remnant and by believing Gentiles, the Christian track; and the track of historical Israel, relying on God's grace in his ancient covenant with them. This suggestion avoids any theological anti-Semitism, but it is scarcely congruous with Paul's argument and in particular with his argument towards the end of the olive tree passage. [31]

Thirdly, from James Dunn, who introduces the theme of the content of early Christian teaching about the second coming of Jesus Christ. Dunn concludes that in dealing with the second coming Paul here certainly does not give precise details. However, this has not stopped much speculation around the eschatological framework of Romans 11:26-27. In terms of Messianic Jewish Theology, the framework is often pre-millennial with a subsequent emphasis on the millennial reign of Jesus Christ. It is through the presence of Jesus Christ and the ongoing preaching of the Gospel that all Israel will be saved. The emphasis on the continuing millennial preaching is in part to refute any notion of Two Covenant Theology, by showing there is, always has been and always will be only one way of salvation, namely by grace through faith in Jesus Christ.[32] James Dunn goes on:

Paul would also certainly identify the redeemer as Christ (cf 1 Thess 1:10), and since he refers the scripture to the eschatological climax he would not be thinking of Jesus' previous historical association with Jerusalem, rather of his Parousia from heaven to Jerusalem or from heavenly Jerusalem (cf. again 1 Thess 1:10; also Gal 4:26). This is the first and only time Paul speaks of Christ's second coming in this letter. He could no doubt assume that this was a well known element in the new movement's teaching (cf. 13:11-14) which needed no fuller exposition in this final summary dealing with a different issue. What role Christ's return would actually play in the end events is by no means clear, not least how it would "turn away ungodliness from Jacob" and how this fitted in with Israel's being provoked to jealousy by the gentile influx. But a lack of clarity and precision on the interrelation of the end events is a feature of the early Christian eschatology and Paul presumably was no wiser on these matters. His contribution to the early Christian eschatological thought at this point is simply in the revelation given to him that Israel's salvation is to the climax of salvation-history, not a precise schedule or agenda of coming events.[33]

Fourthly Karl Barth states:

We have spoken to unredeemed humanity of the Last Things, of the miracle of the divine 'Yes', of the Parousia of Jesus Christ who is the fullness of the Gentiles. Jesus Christ is the redeemer, the individual standing existentially before God. In Him duality has become unity, for in Him rejection has been overcome and swallowed up in election. He comes out of Zion that is from above, from the unobservable Origin of the Church. He comes from the glory of the throne of God, whence came the rejection of the Church; and with Him come regal dignity and regal power. His appearing is the creation which takes place at no time, for it is the mystery in which all time is dissolved and established. His coming is eternity, and His work is ineffable — He shall turn away ungodliness from Jacob. He tears away the veil which now hides the unobservable Church of Jacob. What is this veil but the inevitable contingency and perversion of the Church of Esau? He inaugurates the new covenant of God Himself, of God alone. He turns away, clears out, quenches, demolishes, annihilates, both sins and Sin. He restores to men the union with God which they have now lost. Once again we have to break off; for we stand once more at the point where what we have to say is unutterable. Yet this boundary is the end of hardening, the incomprehensible goal of the road to God.[34]

Within all of the above quotes the emphasis I would suggest is that for Paul both judgment and salvation are still not yet fully realized. Paul's eschatology is best not seen as a 'closed book'.[35] Paul's eschatology is not an 'over-realized' eschatology, and means that Paul and his readers will need to engage with aspects of temporary uncertainty and present imperfection.[36]

Verses 28-32. Following on from the great climax of verses 26-27, Paul then moves on to sum up the current position and future hope with emphasis on the faithfulness of God (expressed in part by his gifts and call to Israel which remain valid despite the majority of Israel being in positions of unbelief/disobedience) and his merciful intentions to all (v32). The term 'irrevocable' or 'without repentance' (King James Version) is placed at the beginning of the sentence with significant emphasis. Here Paul may well be making a connection back to 9:6 with his emphasis that God's word which reflects God's faithfulness has neither failed nor become invalid.

The reference to 'you' (v30) again within the flow of this segment is a reference probably to Gentile believers, while the 'all' (v32) refers to and in some ways unites both groups. For some in hearing of God's universal desire for mercy, the question is posed about universalism. John Ziesler helpfully states:

> It is important to note that here obedience and disobedience are not matters of ethics, but concern about being or not being God's people. Least of all is Paul talking about individual morality. This is one reason why it is inappropriate to ask if Paul is putting forward the theory that in the end all men and women, all individuals will be saved. He is neither affirming that nor denying it. He is talking about the responses of peoples, Jews and Gentiles respectively. Nevertheless it is important to reiterate that at the end of this long discussion from 9:1, Paul sees the divine purpose as embracing not just a few Jews here and there, but the people of historical Israel as a whole. [37]

Verses 33-36. The concluding doxology celebrates the greatness, glory and goodness of God. Ernst Käsemann in commenting on these verses and their relationship to the rest of Romans 9-11 and Paul's wider writings, states:

> The doxology has the same sense as 1 Cor 2:16c and later Eph 3:5ff. Pneumatics know about what is hidden from the world because God has revealed his will and way to them. They know about that

which according to 1 Cor 2:9ff no eye has seen or no ear heard nor has it entered any human heart, for they know what God has prepared for those who love him and what his grace has given us. As the apostle sees it, there has been this kind of disclosure in chs. 9-11 and especially the conclusion.. The mystery of Israel is not concealed from him. He responds to that with astonished praise.[38]

In these verses there is a striking threefold arrangement[39] which alludes to the three key areas of God's power (v36), namely creation (from him), revelation (through him) and redemption (to him). Also in this "Pauline hymn" with its nine ascending lines Paul[40] once again draws from scripture. Appropriately the first source is Isaiah (40:13) which has been the major scriptural source for Paul in this letter. The second source is from Job (41:11). Steve Motyer, in referring to these two scriptural sources also helpfully draws parallels between Paul's situation and those of Isaiah and Job:[41]

Isaiah sought to understand the providence of a God who promised an everlasting commitment to Israel while sending her into exile and apparently abandoning her. Job wrestled likewise with an inscrutable wisdom which decreed suffering, deprivation and death as part of a perfect ordering of his servants' circumstances. Paul knows that he has been facing precisely the same problem, and that the answer is the same too. He reaches with Job the point at which he confesses wonderment for what he can understand, and adoration for what he cannot.[42]

11.3 Comments relating to the Development of Enlargement Theology

In drawing from the conclusions within the specific comments outlined above, the first key point in the development of Enlargement Theology is to see that God's eternal purposes are being worked out not just through the church, as would be a self evident truth of Replacement Theology, but also through the faithful Jewish remnant and Israel as a whole. This realization of the multi-faceted and diverse identity of God's people and purposes must give vibrancy and a depth of appreciation within contemporary Jewish-Christian relations. At the very least, from a Christian perspective, there must be a commitment to pray for God's blessing upon Israel and to hope that, through such prayer, dialogue and expressions of love, Jewish people can come to see that the gospel message presents the fulfilment of the awesome hope for the Jewish people, such hope which flows from the Torah, patriarchs and the prophets.

From a Messianic Jewish perspective there is also a sense of the responsibility and privilege of their identity. An identity in terms of their calling as Jewish people and their salvation through faith in the person and work of Jesus Christ. In commenting on "All Israel will be saved," David Stern makes this helpful point about how such a statement impacts contemporary Messianic Jews:

> A Messianic Jew experiencing the poignancy of rejection by his own people, perhaps even by his own family, makes these glorious words his expectation and refuge and prayer. For him it is a joy to contemplate God's answer to the plea of the Kaddish, "May he (God) establish his Kingdom during your life and during your days and during the life of all the house of Israel, speedily and at a near time; and say ye, Amen. [43]

As an addition to the above quote from Stern, in which he speaks of the rejection Messianic Jews feel from many of their Jewish contemporaries, there is also at times a separate sense of rejection and misunderstanding from the wider Christian church. Again if the wider Christian community takes seriously the role of Jewish believers in Jesus there must be a real level of appreciation and support for such believers.

The engagement with the multi-faceted and diverse identity of 'God's people' must however be balanced by the understanding (assuming the line taken in the reading/ application of the Romans 9-11 text) that this diversity also coalesces in and finds fulfilment only through the person and atoning work of Jesus Christ. Such an understanding would rule out a Two Covenant approach with its explicit 'no' to Jewish evangelism. This no to Jewish evangelism, however, is not just the result of the outworking of a Two Covenant position, but can also have some currency in certain aspects of dispensational theology which maintains a strong delineation between the church and Israel. This point is explored by Stephen Sizer:

The return of Christ is seen by all millennial traditions as the consummation of God's purposes on earth and synonymous with the Day of Judgment. Dispensationalism, with its rigid distinction between Israel and the Church and its doctrine of a secret rapture and tribulation, is based on a rather more complex eschatological chronology. There is a diversity of opinion as to the purpose of Christ's return as well as the basis of his judgment. Scofield, for example, having divided the world into three classes of people, sees the return of Jesus Christ as having a 'threefold relation: to the church, to Israel, to the nations. He claims that after the Day of Judgment and the removal of the church there would still be 'a world wide Gentile conversion and participation in the blessings of the kingdom', at least for those who survive Armageddon and are left on earth during the millennium. This is one reason why some dispensational organizations such as the ICEJ regard evangelism among Jewish people as inappropriate or unnecessary with the present dispensation.[44]

In conclusion, from my reading/application of the Romans 9-11 text, the position of Christians and Messianic Jewish believers participating in the wider field of Jewish-Christian relations must be that of celebrating and engaging with the multi-faceted identity of 'God's people', while at the same time proclaiming the central and unique salvation role belonging to the person and work of Jesus Christ. This understanding is at the heart of Enlargement Theology, which I will focus upon in the final two chapters. This is clearly a demanding and testing position which will be robustly challenged by various sides, especially by holders of Replacement Theology and by holders of Two Covenant Theology. At times, there will be conflict and misunderstanding. Successful and faithful engagement will call for humility and openness (especially in the maze of eschatological teaching), love and wisdom encircled by a deep trust in God. These are the very qualities displayed by Paul as he proclaims the beauty, power and the mystery of the gospel of God in Romans 9-11.

11.4 Concluding Key Understandings from Romans 9-11

The exploration of Romans 9-11 within this book has resulted in the presentation of a number of key understandings about Paul's teaching in Romans 9-11. While there is unquestionably much within Romans 9-11 which remains open to a number of legitimate lines of interpretation and application, this book nevertheless presents strongly the following five key understandings. It is also the conviction underlying this thesis that these understandings have significant relevance in the light of the development of Enlargement Theology alongside the emerging contemporary Messianic Jewish Movement and in regard to engagement within the wider field of Jewish-Christian relations.

The five key understandings are outlined in the following five headings:

(i) Romans 9-11 is an integral part of the 'Gospel of God' outlined in Paul's letter to the Romans.

Romans 9-11 is not in any way an excursus or an appendix.[45] The theme of Romans is Paul's teaching of 'the Gospel of God' (1:1, 15:16). This teaching is addressed originally to the mixed (Jewish/Gentile) congregation(s) in Rome, with the initial intention of helping to prepare for his visit to Rome; and then with the subsequent hope that Rome, in turn, would become the starting point and the vital resource base for Paul's new apostolic endeavours focusing westwards towards Spain (15:24). Within the outlining of the gospel of God in Romans, there are many important components which give a structure to this epistle. It would be misleading to claim that any one component was the dominant one, or to state that any one component was an unnecessary excursus or an appendix. Each component has a role in presenting the full picture of the gospel of God (1:1). For example, one can see the focus of God's righteousness (1:17) and faithfulness (3:3). The focus on human sinfulness (3:12). The focus on justification through faith in Christ (3:21-5:21). The focus on sanctification/ life in and through the Holy Spirit (6:1- 8:27). The focus on Israel's election, partial hardening, faithful remnant and future vindication within the purposes of God (9.1-11:36). The focus on living out the implications of this gospel (12:1-15:13) with its emphasis on love, fellowship, submission, acceptance and unity. All of these are part of a full gospel presentation. If any one focus was missing the overall picture would be diminished or distorted in some way.

(ii) Paul shows an unswerving passion for and commitment to Israel.

This passion for Israel shows that, for Paul, Israel is not a side issue within the proclamation of the Gospel of God (1:1), but that Israel is central to God's purposes.

On balance, my reading of Romans 9-11 understands, that for Paul, in his eleven uses of the term Israel (Ἰσραηλ) in Romans 9-11, Israel primarily refers to all (or the vast majority)[46] of the Jewish people.[47] Yet, at times, a case can be made for recognition that Paul uses the term 'Israel' when he is in fact referring to a subset within Israel. For example, to those Jews who have not (yet) come to faith in Jesus[48] (unbelieving Israel), or the opposite, namely that Israel is used in referring to the faithful (Jewish believers in Jesus) remnant of Israel.[49] My reading of Romans 9-11 does not support the understanding that the term 'Israel' in Romans 9-11 can be taken to refer to all the 'elect' in Christ. In fact, Israel is contrasted to the elect (11:7). The only place within Paul's writings where such an identification of Israel with the elect is permissible is in Galatians 6:16. Although this is dependent upon how one interprets the general context of this verse and more specifically how the conjunction (και) is used.[50]

While at times the term Israel in Paul's usage may have within it, dependent on particular contexts, a focus on a particular subset (unbelieving or believing in Jesus) within Israel, the prime meaning which remains for Paul is that 'Israel' is an inclusive term for all (or the vast majority of) Jewish people. In this, the term 'Israel' has as its prime mark of identity a physical belonging to the Abrahamic covenant people rather than any specific individual religious affiliation/commitment or lack of any such religious affiliation/commitment. Such a passion for Israel is shown clearly in texts such as Romans 9:1-5 and 10:1. This passion is not reduced by Paul's faith in Jesus or his Gentile mission, but on the contrary Paul's passion for Israel and his own identity as an Israelite (11:1) is enhanced by his faith in Jesus and by his ongoing apostolic ministry primarily, but never exclusively, to the Gentiles (11:13). This passion is also from Paul's understanding a reflection in part of God's ongoing faithfulness towards Israel (9:21), a faithfulness which is not undermined by Israel's unbelief or Israel's failure to attain righteousness (9:31). For Paul, this passion for Israel is ultimately to find its fulfilment in all Israel being saved (11:26). Within this ultimate salvation, Paul sees that the previous unbelief, disobedience and hardness of Israel are part of the wider process of God's mysterious plan of salvation— a plan which includes a special role for the faithful remnant of Israel, of which Paul and his fellow Jewish believers in Jesus are a valued part. Also there must be space made within this 'salvation plan' for the full inclusion (11:25) and contributions of Gentile believers in Jesus.

(iii) Paul shows a clear rejection of Two Covenant Theology. While Paul is obviously not addressing contemporary Two Covenant Theology, what he does state about the plan and purposes of God can be applied subsequently to make the case for a clear rejection of Two Covenant Theology. As stated above, if one is to be an advocate for a Two Covenant approach one must look elsewhere for support for such a position.

This looking elsewhere would result in a by-passing of Paul's passionate concern for the salvation of Israel and of Paul's clear line of teaching about Jesus as the only Lord of all, both Jew and Gentile, which Paul presents in Romans and throughout his other epistles.[51]

Thus far, in exploring the text and in the earlier discussion 'Comments relating to the Development of Enlargement Theology' (starting at 11.3) we have embarked upon five[52] clear assertions that impinge on Two Covenant Theology. In each case, as we are (hopefully) discovering, no support is found for the position of Two Covenant Theology.

While Two Covenant Theology may have a helpful emotional resonance for Jews and Christians engaged in dialogue and deepening relations especially in the light of the horrors of the Holocaust (*Shoah*), it has no support from a plain reading of Romans 9-11. It is clearly possible to argue that, in the light of the Holocaust, a new revelatory event has taken place. Such revelation may lead to the promotion of Two Covenant Theology. Such Two Covenant Theology may also be enhanced by a growing pluralist worldview, which participants in Jewish-Christian relations may or may not adhere to, but in terms of clarity and transparency it is important to state that Two Covenant Theology does not fit into the plain meaning of Romans 9-11 and of the wider context of the teaching and missionary practice of Paul or that of the early church.[53]

For Christian participants within Jewish-Christian relations who hold to a high view of the authority of scripture, a dialogue paradigm which is not based upon the plain meaning of scripture (as is the case I would argue in Two Covenant Theology) must be revoked. It is then of paramount importance that a new paradigm should be sought which reflects the clear thrust of scripture.

(iv) Paul shows a clear rejection of Replacement Theology.
In the exploration of the text and the subsequent discussion
under the heading 'Comments relating to the development of
Enlargement Theology' there are seventeen[54] direct discussion
references to Replacement Theology. It is our conviction
(despite the space given to the argument presented by Daniel
Boyarin[55] which centers on the conviction that, from a Jewish
perspective, Paul's theology remains supersessionist, even
if originally Paul's teaching stood against certain aspects of
Gentile supremacy) that Paul argues consistently against any
sense of God rejecting Israel, or that the promises to Israel are
simply transferred to the 'church'. Clearly for Paul there is
a redefining of Israel taking place. Yet this redefining is part
of the ongoing story of Israel as God's people (9:6-29). Such
redefining is not for Paul the same as the transferring of God's
purposes and the removal of the blessings which is explicit
within Replacement Theology. This redefining may be seen
as an enlarging of God's promises and his people, but not as a
replacing of his promises or people.

For Paul, God remains faithful to Israel. God's word to Israel
has not failed (Rom 9:6). Yet Paul is not hesitant in proclaiming
Israel's disobedience. Paul acts as a prophet to Israel, as well
as an apostle of the church. Paul as part of the great Jewish
prophetic tradition does not seek to hide in any way the fact
that Israel has stumbled. Indeed, the majority of Israel missed
the mark. In terms of the advancement of the Gospel many
are for now enemies (11:28) of his work and his apostolic
ministry. There has been a severe hardening of Israel (11:25).
This hardening consistently moves Paul to prayer (10:1) and
to experiencing a deep anguish (9:2).

Paul also argues passionately against a false view of Torah or
Jewish heritage which removes or bypasses the need for faith
in Jesus. Elements of this teaching by Paul have been taken
by some (especially when the context of such teaching is to
do with opposing 'Judaizing legalism' and upholding Gentile
inclusion through faith in Jesus)[56] as a source for promoting

forms of Replacement Theology. Yet Paul's intention was never to deny God's faithfulness to Israel in the past, present, or future. Paul as a prophet to Israel is calling for Israel to recognise this faithfulness so wonderfully worked out through God's process of election and the person and work of Jesus Christ. Paul is determined both to show the Gentile believers in Jesus their debt to Israel for their present position (11:18) and to encourage them to look to Israel for the outworking of future hope (11:12 and :15). There is also in Paul's teaching no justification given for the emergence of Gentile arrogance (11:25), which often is associated with Replacement Theology. Equally, there is no justification either for any sense of Jewish supremacy (3:12, 10:13 and 15:7) which, like Gentile arrogance, undermines unity within the church.

For Paul Israel has stumbled, yet, in this stumbling, Israel has not fallen beyond recovery (11:11). Unbelieving Israel has been cut off, yet they will be grafted in (11:23). God did not reject his people (11:1), for God's gift and his call are irrevocable (11:29). Ultimately this gift and call will result in all Israel being saved (11:26). For all of this faithful outworking of God's promises to Israel Paul concludes his theological arguments with an in-depth outpouring of praise to God— 'To him be the glory for ever! Amen' (11:36).

(v) God's purposes are being worked out through a threefold understanding of God's people.

Within the term, 'God's people' there is unity and diversity. There is a unity in God (11:36), yet diversity within God's election and call. Within God's calling, Paul sees three distinct yet connected groups. For Paul, there is firstly unbelieving Israel. This is the Israel which has not yet accepted the good news (10:16). This reality breaks Paul's heart (9:2) and leads Paul to address fundamental questions about God's trustworthiness (9:6), justice (9:14) and human accountability (9:19). This Israel has been broken off from the olive tree (11:17). Yet this Israel remains within the purposes of God, for

God's gifts and call are irrevocable (11:29). This Israel will, in the fullness of God's purposes, be saved and grafted back into the olive tree as all Israel receives her deliverer (11:26).

Paul also sees that there is, in addition to unbelieving Israel, a believing Israel — the faithful remnant, those Jews who like himself have fully embraced Jesus as Messiah and Lord. These Jewish believers in Jesus have the unique privilege and responsibility of being both fully part of Israel and fully part of the church. Within the church such Jewish believers in Jesus are fully united with Gentile believers in Jesus. They together (believing Israel with believing [called in] Gentiles) form a new community[57] which Paul serves as an apostle. This community is called to witness to the unity of Jew and Gentile (10:12) yet this unity does not result in uniformity but allows for specific identities and callings to flourish under the Lordship of Jesus. This community is called to witness in word and action, to witness both to God's judgment on Israel, yet also to God's faithfulness and future restoration/deliverance of (all) Israel. This community is also equally called to witness to the Gospel of God (1:1) in the wider Gentile world, a world where many know little or nothing of the 'Gospel of God' or the outworking of God's faithfulness to Israel shown through the promises and history of Israel's covenantal faith. These groups of Jewish believers are the natural branches of the olive tree which have not been broken off. They have remained faithful and have entered the ongoing promises of God. It is into these branches that the Gentile believers (wild olive shoot) are now being grafted, and by which they are to be supported.

The Gentile believers in Jesus, which constitute the third group within the 'people of God', are called to witness alongside Israel to the kindness and mercy of God. This kindness and mercy of God has brought them into the very heart of 'God's people' and purposes. This was not done by their becoming Jews and taking upon themselves the badges of Jewish identity, but rather through faith in the Jewish Messiah who is Lord of all. They who were once not 'God's people' are now 'God's people' (9:25). For Paul the boundaries of the 'people of God' have now been enlarged beyond the ethnicity of Israel in order to embrace fully Gentile believers in Jesus. This (new) faith of the Gentiles and their faithfulness to God and their partnership with their Jewish believers in Jesus in a new community (10:12) is the very thing which Paul sees that God will use to bring unbelieving Israel into the fullness of God (10:19 and 11:13-14). Exactly how and when this will happen, Paul does not teach. Yet Paul is content to know of the faithfulness of God to His threefold people: unbelieving Israel, believing Israel and believing (grafted in) Gentiles.

In conclusion, Romans 9-11 is a closely argued part of Paul's teaching. Paul raises and seeks to deal with many questions,[58] as he leads through the deep issues of God's election, sovereignty and saving purposes. Paul also deals with the past, present and future for the people of God. Paul sees that the present unity within the church between Jew and Gentile must be worked out in real practical community. Hence the teaching about the weak and the strong[59] which follows in chapters 14-15 with the emphasis on bearing with, caring for and accepting one another.

We conclude in regard to Paul's teaching in Romans 9-11 that these five key understandings stand in the face of robust challenges — moreover these understandings have significance not just in terms of the interpretation and application of the text, but also within the wider development of Enlargement Theology which is a key resource in helping move beyond the impasse within contemporary Jewish-Christian relations. This impasse is caused in part by the promotion of Replacement Theology (with its numerous supersessionist mindsets), Two Covenant Theology and a failure to engage with the emerging Messianic Jewish movement.

Chapter Twelve

Enlargement Theology

12.1 A Model for Encounter and Engagement

The contours of this thesis so far have been an exploration of the key impasse within Jewish-Christian relations. This impasse has taken shape as a consequence of far reaching historical, sociological and theological reasons. The key reasons for the development of this impasse have been presented in the opening three chapters of this thesis. Following on from this presentation I then focused in chapters 4 to 11 on the key biblical text (Romans 9-11) and have argued from this text that there exist inherent weaknesses in both Replacement Theology and Two Covenant Theology.[1]

It is my argument that there are five key understandings resulting from a robust engagement and a specific reading of the Romans 9-11 text, namely that:

- Romans 9-11 is an integral part of the proclamation of the 'Gospel of God' outlined in Romans.
- Paul shows an unswerving passion for and commitment to Israel.
- Paul shows a clear rejection of Two Covenant Theology.
- Paul shows a clear rejection of Replacement Theology.
- God's purposes are being worked out through a threefold understanding of 'God's people'.

In the light of these five understandings, the initial building blocks are in place for a new theological method to develop. This new method is what I am presenting under my heading of Enlargement Theology.

As stated, I present my arguments for Enlargement Theology, believing these to be a faithful and coherent response to the key text, but also believing that Enlargement Theology draws from, enhances and complements insights from certain aspects of Jewish Christian relations, specifically the emerging contemporary Messianic Jewish movement.

Enlargement Theology engages sympathetically with the contemporary Messianic Jewish movement in relation to finding 'common ground' with what I understand as the four core epistemic convictions of the emerging Messianic Jewish movement.[2] These four core epistemic convictions are as follows:

- The validity of and the conviction to build and sustain vibrant Messianic Jewish communities.
- The universal evangelistic proclamation of Jesus (Yeshua) as the crucified and risen Messiah of Israel and the Son of God.
- The continuing election of the Jewish people.
- 'Messianic Jewish Theology' must be faithful to the Bible.[3]

In the light of the above, Enlargement Theology is to be presented as a faithful response to the key biblical text and core convictions of the emerging contemporary Messianic Jewish movement. Enlargement Theology is not to be viewed as a complete theological system, but is a way of focusing on the Church's relationship with Israel, Jewish people and the emerging Messianic Jewish movement. The manner of this focusing is intended to stimulate responses free from the current theological impasse within Jewish-Christian relations.

12.2 The Tenets and Development of Enlargement Theology

This presentation of Enlargement Theology upholds and is built upon five connected key tenets listed below:

- God's covenantal relationship with the Jewish people is eternal yet this relationship is not static.
- Gentiles are brought fully into this covenantal relationship through the covenant being reshaped/enlarged (and not replaced) through the person and work of Jesus.
- This enlarged covenant needs to be entered into and embraced by all people, both Jews and Gentiles through the outworking of faith/trust in the person and atoning work of Jesus.
- The ongoing purposes of God are being worked out through three different yet mutually inter-connected communities.
- The understanding of God is faithfully expressed within Trinitarian models and this has a creative link to the 'people of God' as three different yet mutually inter-connected communities.

12.2.1 The First Tenet of Enlargement Theology

In terms of the first tenet of Enlargement Theology: this covenantal relationship grows, deepens and is renewed again and again through God's gracious dealings with his people. Such gracious dealings can be traced through God's call to key biblical covenantal characters such as Abraham, Moses and David. God continually shapes and reshapes Israel by his call to his covenantal people.[4] For Enlargement Theology, the meta-narrative of the Bible is the God of the covenant who creates in order to bless. This ongoing covenantal history ascribes to God an identity which is rooted in particularity. God deals with and is revealed primarily as the God of Abraham, Isaac and Jacob.

Ultimately, Enlargement Theology teaches that such reshaping and renewal is working towards completion in the person and work of Jesus. This completion in and by Jesus is understood as a fulfilling of the covenant promises spoken by the prophets.[5] Yet this completion in Jesus is still awaiting full consummation. This full consummation is linked in Christian teaching to the second coming of Jesus.[6] This sense of future hope being revealed alongside the 'now but not yet' of God's kingdom is a key eschatological tension which needs to be addressed in any Christian theological model. This eschatological tension is exactly what Paul is addressing in Romans 8:18-21 and 11:25-27.

Enlargement Theology is not drawn into promoting any particular eschatological timetable.[7] However, Enlargement Theology does work within the general Christian eschatological framework which recognizes the 'now but not yet' nature of the kingdom established by the person and work of Jesus.

Enlargement Theology, from its explicit understanding of the eternal faithfulness[8] of God's covenant to Israel, stands against any concept which seeks to undermine or replace God's covenantal relationship with Israel. Enlargement Theology states that any concept which seeks to undermine or replace God's covenant with Israel tears at the very heart of God's redeeming purposes. A good illustration of this would be that the promise of Romans 11:26 of the saving of all Israel is understood as a promise to the physical descendants of Israel. It is therefore understood as primarily an 'ethnic/physical' designation, rather than as a 'spiritual' reinterpretation. Such a 'spiritual' reinterpretation should be resisted when referring to the term 'Israel'. In this sense Enlargement Theology stands against interpretations of Israel as a 'type' of the church.[9] In this sense, Enlargement Theology is critical of a form of linear logic which is implicit within Replacement Theology which is firmly rooted in a promise-fulfilment hermeneutic. Clearly there is some validity in a promise-fulfilment hermeneutic, but the danger which Enlargement Theology attempts to resist is simply seeing all the covenantal promises to Israel as only 'types' and 'shadows' which have little or no reality within God's purposes today.

This focus on the promise to ethnic/physical Israel within

Enlargement Theology is based upon the understanding that the covenant is made with all Israel. Israel can not be used to refer solely to the church community, or to just a present Jewish spiritual remnant. Therefore, as stated earlier, Enlargement Theology stands against interpretations which replace physical Israel with the church, or variations within such replacement schemes. One such variation would be that of N T Wright,[10] who appears to read Romans through a framework that presents Jesus as the new Israel replacing Israel. For Wright, this replacing occurs through the restoring of Israel which has already taken place[11] at the point of Jesus' resurrection. Yet within Enlargement Theology, 'all Israel' will only be fully restored/saved through a future event. This event is the welcoming of the deliverer from Zion. This future hope however, does not invalidate, for those holding to Enlargement Theology, the current need for ongoing culturally sensitive evangelism to Jewish people.[12]

Enlargement Theology, in upholding the view of the eternal nature of God's covenant with all Israel, nevertheless equally states that God's covenantal relationship with Israel is not static and there must be space for renewal and enlargement. Any theology which fails to give space to this renewal and enlargement fails in the view of Enlargement Theology to honour the covenant, in ways which are equally damaging as those ways which seek to replace Israel with the church or other variations flowing from a replacement perspective.

This process of renewal and enlargement is expressed in many ways throughout Israel's story. One of the most significant ways in which this is seen is in terms of the inclusion of the Gentiles into the fullness of the covenant. This is the second key tenet of Enlargement Theology to which we now turn.

12.2.2 The Second Tenet of Enlargement Theology
Enlargement Theology affirms that Gentiles are brought fully into this covenantal relationship through the covenant being reshaped/enlarged and not replaced. This enlargement is made

possible only through the person and work of Jesus, the Jewish Messiah. This enlargement is understood as being in keeping with and a fulfilment of the promises of God (Romans 1:2). In the light of this sense of fulfilment there tends to be a general emphasis in Enlargement Theology on the continuity of the ministry of Jesus with the purposes of Israel and the 'Old Testament' rather than an emphasis on certain elements of discontinuity. It is also affirmed that Gentiles, in becoming fully part of the covenant, do not become Jews, but they are grafted into the true life of Israel (Romans 11:17). By so doing, they come to share fully and equally within the ongoing purposes of God.

12.2.3 The Third Tenet of Enlargement Theology

Enlargement Theology affirms that this enlarged covenant needs to be embraced by both Jews and Gentiles, for both stand in equal need and both enter on the same basis, namely by grace though faith/trust in the person and atoning work of Jesus. Yet this entering can be seen to take place in differing contexts.[13] For a Gentile enters from the outside of the ongoing benefits of a covenantal relationship. For the Gentile there is a grafting into the true life of Israel from a non-covenantal past.[14] Such a grafting in could well be appropriately described as a religious conversion. Yet, for an observant Jew who comes to faith/trust in Jesus, he or she is not embracing the covenant relationship for the first time, but is finding true faithful expression of the growing and deepening covenantal identity to which Abraham, Moses, David and the prophets gave and still give eloquent witness. The term 'conversion' in this context is deemed to be largely inappropriate. Enlargement Theology would tend to speak in terms of such Jewish People as finding 'completion' or 'fulfilment' in Jesus. This sense of fulfilment/completion points to the wider truth which Enlargement Theology upholds, namely that the person and work of Jesus must and can only be fully seen in the wider context of the fulfilling of the Jewish covenantal hope.

12.2.4 The Fourth Tenet of Enlargement Theology

Enlargement Theology affirms that God is working his purposes out through three different yet mutually connected communities. This is based upon Paul's metaphor[15] of the olive tree. The *first community* is Israel (the historic and ethnic community[16] of the Jewish people) and despite, or perhaps because of the present 'no' of the majority of this Israel to the call of Jesus Christ, God has not finished with Israel but remains faithful to her. The *second community* is the community of Messianic Jews (the faithful remnant within Israel) who have said 'yes' to the call of Jesus Christ and are partnering with Gentile believers in this 'new' community of Jewish and Gentile believers in Jesus.[17] This saying 'yes' to the call of Jesus Christ does not, in the view of Enlargement Theology, in any way imply a leaving of Israel. The *third community* is made up of Gentile believers in Jesus, who are those Gentiles who have said 'yes' to the call of Jesus Christ, the Messiah of Israel and the Lord of all, and have been grafted into faithful Israel and share in this 'new' community of Jewish and Gentile believers in Jesus. For Enlargement Theology, this understanding of God's one ultimate purpose being worked out within three contradictory communities (yet communities which share significant mutual and reciprocal identities) raises some real and present creative tensions. Enlargement Theology affirms that these present tensions point to a future hope (which will be and indeed is being realized), where resolution and true unity between these communities of contradiction will be found.[18] This true unity is rooted in Paul's understanding that division between Jew and Gentile is conquered through the person and work of Jesus. Yet the distinction between Jew and Gentile remains today and will persist into the era of the future consummation[19] of all things. This understanding rests on seeing the essential difference between uniformity (which is often based on a reductionist hermeneutic implicit in Replacement Theology) and true unity which is based on multi-dimensional richness, which is often displayed in Hebraic thought and through covenantal relationships. This line of understanding is powerfully summed up by William S Campbell:

> In real history Jews remain Jews. One cannot simply take over the good name and identity of another without fraudulent activity taking place . . . . To claim therefore that Christians, especially gentile Christians, are the real Jews is to seek to attain a laudable goal by the wrong means. In making this claim Christians are acknowledging gentile indebtedness to Israel. They are acknowledging their dependence on Jewish roots, their need for a proper identity. But the way to achieve this identity is to allow Paul's paradigm of the relation of Jew and gentile in the light of the Christ-event to guide our reflection. In this pattern or blueprint of identity, gentiles do have status as gentiles by virtue of their relationship to Christ as Messiah and of his and their relation to the historic people of God.[20]

12.2.5 The Fifth Tenet of Enlargement Theology

Enlargement Theology, in wrestling with the 'unity within diversity' of contemporary Messianic Jews and Gentile believers while also holding together the three-fold constituency elements which make up the 'people of God', proclaims that it is through the upholding of Trinitarian concepts of God that insight and creative models of community can be explored. For example, God is one, Father, Son and Holy Spirit, perfect in unity yet with distinct diversity. The three persons of the godhead are not to be confused. It is only by holding together the unity of relationships within the Trinity of God that one is given a glimpse of the model for developing a similar 'unity with diversity' in relation to the threefold 'people of God'. This point is helpfully developed by John Kelly, who in commenting on elements of weakness within Barth's doctrine of God, states:

> His Trinitarianism collapses into an undifferentiated monotheism which cannot ultimately find 'room' for Israel beside the Church.[21]

In upholding the distinctive relationships within the Trinity, one is able to see the church, Israel and Messianic Jews as distinctive entities within the one 'people of God'. Yet, this also raises many questions. For example, Messianic Jews are within the contours of Enlargement Theology both fully part of the church and Israel. What is of interest here is that the current emergence of Messianic Jews recreates something of the creative historical fluidity of Jewish-Christian relationships which existed before the formal separation of church and Israel into two divergent entities. Clearly this time of historic fluidity is the very time in which Paul was writing his letter to the Romans and presenting the olive tree metaphor.

For upholders of Enlargement Theology the current emergence of a Messianic Jewish reality creates at the very least an opportunity for a robust re-appraisal of Jewish-Christian relationships. This very point is made powerfully by John Kelly:

> Messianic Jews could therefore find room to be the living embodiment of an open, mutual and reciprocal relationship between Church and Israel, so taking matters beyond mere 'fellowship in contradiction' towards a fuller maturity. [22]

In presenting the above five tenets of Enlargement Theology there is much which warrants further exploration, especially in relation to engagement within the wider field of Jewish-Christian relations. I will turn now to the following three. Firstly, to exploring issues of diversity and unity within a faith community. I will use the heading; 'Exploring community within communities'. This has direct connections with the second, fourth and fifth tenets of Enlargement Theology. Then I will turn to the issue of the legitimacy of the church's evangelistic mission to Jewish people which has direct connections with the third tenet of Enlargement Theology. Thirdly, I briefly explore the issue of how Enlargement Theology engages with Israel and the promises of the land.

12.3 Exploring community within communities

Enlargement Theology also engages with what I have listed as the first core epistemic conviction of the contemporary Messianic Jewish movement,[23] namely, the desire to build and sustain Messianic Jewish communities. Such communities can, at times, be in conflict with and in contradiction to the wider church communities and other established Jewish communities. Yet equally, at other times, such Messianic communities can be in real partnership and mutual belonging to both church[24] and other Jewish communities. It is in reflecting upon this 'community within communities' that one comes to the very heart of issues within contemporary Jewish -Christian relations. Therefore, an Enlargement Theology which upholds the understanding that God is working his purposes out through three different yet mutually connected communities gives a vital framework/theological model for exploring such issues in contemporary Jewish-Christian relations. Such a framework for encounter and exploration does not (and, I would argue, cannot) in fact exist to the same extent in theological models which flow out of Replacement Theology or Two Covenant Theology.

Enlargement Theology teaches that there are a number of boundary markers within the communities of 'God's people'. The prime boundary marker which divides the current majority Israel from Messianic Jews and the church community is faith/ trust in the person and work of Jesus. Yet other markers exist and are of importance. For example, the marker of Jewish ethnic identity, namely Jewish people are physical descendants of Abraham, through Isaac, and are inheritors of the gift of the Torah which defines Jews as distinct from Gentiles.

The following three metaphors, 'the juggler', 'the bow' and 'the river' all draw inspiration from the prime biblical metaphor of the olive tree and they seek to explore issues around community within communities. In the olive tree metaphor, the apostle Paul presents 'God's people' as one community represented by the one olive tree. The natural branches of the olive tree are those Jewish people, like Paul himself, who have put their faith/trust in Jesus. Yet unfaithful natural braches (unbelieving Israel) have been broken off while wild shoots (Gentile believers) have been grafted into the growing olive tree and are supported by the faithful natural branches. This picture of branches having been broken off in judgment and the grafting in of wild shoots through faith/trust in Jesus is then followed by the promise of a future restoration for the broken branches which means their re-grafting back into the one olive tree.

In exploring the three metaphors we turn firstly to the Messianic Jewish theologian David Stern who in upholding what he describes as Olive Tree Theology[25] teaches through the metaphor of the juggler:

> Traditional Jewish theology sees God as throwing one ball into the air, the Jews. Christian Replacement theology sees him as having thrown the Jewish ball into the air in the past, but now he has let it fall and is juggling the Christian ball. Two Covenant theology and Dispensationalism sees God somewhat more coordinated — he can juggle two balls at a time, both Jews and Christians. But only "olive tree theology" credits God with being able to juggle all three balls at once. Gentile Christians, Messianic Jews and non-Messianic Jews, without letting any of them drop to the ground.[26]

The metaphor of the juggler is helpful in seeing the existence of three communities. Yet in this metaphor the balls all appear to remain separate and distinct from each other. This makes Stern's metaphor weak and oversimplified for, from the perspective of Enlargement Theology, there is the conviction that in the case of the Messianic Jewish 'ball', this ball must not be seen as always remaining separate and distinct, but must somehow be seen to merge with and become one with both of the other balls. For Messianic Jews are fully part of Israel and fully part of the church. This conviction breaks the usefulness of the juggler metaphor.

Secondly, we turn to Karl Barth who presents the metaphor of the bow.[27] The difficulty I perceive with the bow metaphor is simply that the complexity of the relationship between Israel and the church cannot be held within such a simple singular image, namely a bow. The bow of the one covenant of God. Barth's understanding, unlike the threefold understanding of God's elect community as presented by Enlargement Theology, focuses in on two forms of God's elect community, namely Israel and the church. This two form emphasis is similar to the understanding of Two Covenant Theology and certain aspects of Christian dispensationalist thinking in the sense that God's purposes are being worked out within two separate communities. However, there is no way in which Barth can be seen as a Two Covenant theologian. This is because for Barth there are not two separate communities relating to two separate covenants and ways of salvation, but one covenant of grace stretching over both communities, Israel and the church. However, Barth understood that for the Christian this grace is shown both in terms of promise and fulfilment, while the Jew simply inherits the promise. This Barthian understanding was challenged by the Orthodox Jewish Rabbi, Michael Wyschogrod who in conversation[28] with Barth reasoned that if God makes a promise then the fulfilment is assured. Barth pictured this fulfilling and stretching of grace in terms of a bow which arches over both Israel and the church. If Barth, in regard to grace finding fulfilment uniquely through the person and work of Jesus, is not therefore a Two Covenant Theologian, he is equally not a promoter of Replacement Theology, as Barth affirms the present reality of grace/election for Israel. This point is made clearly by George Hunsinger, who states:

His repudiation of the belief that Israel has forfeited its election could not be stronger. Nor does he subscribe to the belief, still more virulent, that God has disavowed Israel in order to punish it for (supposedly) crucifying Christ. Barth is as responsible as anyone in recent theology for recovering the normative apostolic teaching that God has not rejected his people, that God's gifts and promises are irrevocable, and that all Israel will be saved (Rom 11:1-2, 26, 29).[29]

Barth's position is based on three key principles. The first principle is that of the authority of God's word within the Bible. It is the engagement with scripture which is the source for his theology. Secondly, the link between Israel and the church must be grounded upon belief that Jesus is the Christ and that his death, resurrection, ascension, and the gift of his Spirit is the only place of transition and definition within and between the two communities. Thirdly, Barth understands that the community of God exists in two dispensations which co-exist together[30] and are linked by the one covenant of grace:

There are two forms of the elected community. The two poles between which its history moves (in a unilateral direction from here to there) but in such a way that the bow of the one covenant arches over the whole. For all the necessary sharpness, therefore restraint is also needed. The antithesis between the two cannot be formulated in exclusive terms. Behind and above the human obduracy characteristic of the Israelite form of the community stands indeed the divine rejection, but there stands also God's election in which He has determined Himself to take upon Himself the rejection. And behind and above the divine calling characteristic of the Church form of the community there stands also the rejection that God Himself has taken upon. The ineffaceable differentiation of the two forms of the community has certainly to be noted. But it has also to be noted that thereby its indissoluble unity is also brought to light.[31]

For Barth, unlike Stern's metaphor and the Enlargement Theology model, there is no separate role or identity for Messianic Jews although Barth affirms the role of the faithful Jewish remnant, for example he states:

The elect in Israel witness to the election of Israel itself.[32]

Barth, also drawing from the olive tree metaphor in Romans, affirms the permanency of Israel's election:

Without any doubt the Jews are to this day the chosen people of God in the same sense that they have been so from the beginning, according to the Old and New Testaments. They have the promise of God, and if we as Christians from among the Gentiles have it too, then it is only as those chosen with them as guests in their house, as new wood grafted onto the old tree.[33]

In terms of the role of Messianic Jews, it would be of great interest in relation to exploring Barth's metaphor of the bow to consider how the two-fold nature of God's community (promise and fulfilment) would be modified if Barth had been able to engage with the contemporary Messianic Jewish movement. For many within the Messianic Jewish community would suggest that the reality of Messianic Jewish life would be the very place where the 'ineffaceable differentiation' and the 'indissoluble unity' within and between Israel and the church of which Barth spoke is most clearly and significantly manifested.

Thirdly, we turn to my own Enlargement Theology metaphor of the river. The river represents the community of 'God's people'. The river flows through time beginning to mark a definite course from the initial spring, namely the covenant call to Abraham. The river continues to widen and deepen as it is fed by the gifts of the covenant (Rom 9:3-5) yet at times the course of the river shrinks and appears dry as a result of God's judgment and times of exile for Israel. However, in the fullness of God's covenantal purposes the river is wonderfully refreshed and enlarged by flowing through a new spring, namely the person and work of Jesus. Here the river draws in a new tributary, the in-gathering of the Gentiles. Yet at this very point of enlargement the river is divided, part of the river appears blocked, a hardening takes place. From this point the river begins to form a delta with three distinct yet connected streams. As the streams flow into the one delta, it is difficult at times to trace out the future courses of the streams as at times the streams flow in isolation, while at times within shared boundaries. However, the promise remains that the three distinct yet connected streams within the one delta will become one, when the river reaches its final goal of the sea. Here the sea represents the full consummation of God's covenantal purposes.

As with any metaphor there are always limitations and lack of precision.[34] However, the metaphor of the river is, I hope, useful in attempting to show the continuity and discontinuity, the connectedness and disconnectedness, the unity without uniformity of the threefold 'people of God' within the constraints and insights of Enlargement Theology.

In terms of this 'river metaphor', I also want to show that in Enlargement Theology the one covenant of God to Israel is renewed and enlarged through the person and work of Jesus, the Jewish Messiah. This enlargement gives the context for non-Jews to enter fully into the covenant, not by becoming Jews, but by their grafting into faithful Israel through trust/ faith in the Jewish Messiah. Such an enlargement also gives the context for and acts as the catalyst for the formation of what I am defining as the church (the universal community of Jews and Gentiles who have put their faith/trust in Jesus).

Enlargement Theology teaches that the community known as the church is the prime witness to and the prime channel of God's kingdom purposes[35] in this present age. Yet God continues to work out his purposes through historic/ethnic Israel as well. For as Paul states, the gifts and call of God to Israel are irrevocable (Rom 11:29). Clearly, the content of these gifts and call have changed due to the coming of Jesus and the subsequent life of the church community. This change for Enlargement Theology would be seen as stated that the church is the prime channel of God's purposes. However, Enlargement Theology would uphold that within the faithful community life of Judaism, which draws from the promises of scripture and biblical Torah, the outworking of these gifts and call can be partially seen, proclaimed and experienced yet can only find full consummation through the person and work of Jesus.

It is at this point in upholding the role of Israel, yet also in speaking of the prime missionary role of the church that one comes face to face with the issue of the legitimacy of the church's evangelistic mission to the Jewish people. In this, there is a significant point of decision for Enlargement Theology. The point has already been decided for advocates of Two Covenant Theology with a resounding 'no' to evangelistic mission. In fact the convictions and contours within Two Covenant Theology make the question of Christian evangelistic mission to Jewish people seem simply irrelevant. Equally, there is, for advocates of Replacement Theology, a simple 'yes' to evangelistic mission. For there is within Replacement Theology, no question of the ongoing validity of Israel within God's saving purposes. Yet for Enlargement theologians, Messianic Jews and for others who are seeking to find a path free of the theological constraints of Two Covenant Theology and Replacement Theology, the question is not so easily or overtly settled. It is to this question we now turn.

12.4 The Legitimacy of the Church's Evangelistic Mission to Jewish People

A good example of one of those seeking an answer to this question of legitimacy (and appropriateness) is Peter von der Osten-Sacken. His seminal work, *Christian-Jewish Dialogue*[36] is unusual in this field of contemporary Jewish-Christian relations in giving a very positive role to Messianic Jewish believers and their ongoing search for identity:

> They are the ecclesiological bridge joining Israel and the Gentiles, the lack of which is unimaginable. And they have the task of witnessing to and emphasizing, in the light of the gospel especially, the indissoluble bond between the two.[37]

However, for Osten-Sacken, this honouring of the position of Messianic Jews (alongside his exegesis of Romans 9-11) does not lead as one may expect[38] to a positive affirmation of a relationship between the church and Israel based on a evangelistic mission paradigm to the Jewish people. In fact, he argues against such a mission paradigm. This is based in part on his understanding of the delay of the Parousia[39] which raises for Osten-Sacken significant questions about the ministry of Jesus and of the church. Also, Osten-Sacken sees that the promise of

Romans 11:26 is not conditional upon Israel having faith/trust in Jesus (the deliverer from Zion). The "and so" of Romans 11:26 does not he argues point to Israel coming to have faith/trust in Jesus, but rather to the full ingathering of the Gentiles. In concluding this point, Osten-Sacken states:

> This means that, in the light of Paul's gospel, where theology and the church (as institutions of gentile origin) have a bearing on Israel, they are called simply and solely to recognize God's enduring relationship of love for his people. It is this they have to affirm, and it is from this that they have to draw conclusions for themselves in their theological and practical relationships to the Jewish people. Here, if anywhere, the Pauline gospel must prove itself.[40]

From the perspective of Enlargement Theology, Osten-Sacken is right in regard to the point that it is at the place of God's enduring love for Israel that Pauline teaching must prove itself. However, Enlargement Theology would say that Osten-Sacken's 'no' to Jewish evangelistic mission is misplaced.

The reason for this is that while Osten-Sacken is right in suggesting Romans 11:26 is not explicit in saying that the saving of Israel is linked to the acknowledgement of Jesus as Lord and Saviour by Israel, nevertheless, the whole tone of Paul's argument in Romans and his apostolic work (with its emphasis on the proclaiming of the gospel) points to the explicit understanding that for Paul the process of 'being saved' is based upon confessing and believing in Jesus as Lord (Romans 10:9). There is no difference between Jew and Gentile in this way of and need for salvation (Romans 10:12-13). To say that Paul is silent on the 'how' of salvation for Israel as Osten-Sacken does clearly state,[41] is simply not true. Paul is clear on the 'how' of salvation. The gospel Paul proclaims contains the how, and this same gospel states explicitly, within this how, that there is an absolute priority of Jewish mission (Romans 1:16). Also, there is no indication given that this methodology or priority will change with the passing of time or the coming of the Parousia/second advent of Christ.

It is true to state, however, that Paul is silent on the when of the saving of all Israel and that Paul concludes Romans 9-11 with a doxology of praise rather than with a detailed evangelistic mission strategy or salvation timetable. It is also true that, following the opposition from part of the Jewish community in Corinth, Paul turns his missionary focus on the Gentiles (Acts 18:6). However, this turning to the Gentiles is not defining a new Gentile strategy at the expense of Jewish mission, for soon Paul is shown once again sharing the gospel with Jewish people largely within the context of a synagogue community (Acts 19:8). For Paul, his apostolic focus to the Gentiles and his desire to "preach the gospel where Christ was not known" (Romans 15:20), in no way undermines his conviction of the vital importance and the complete appropriateness of an ongoing mission led by Jewish and Gentile believers in Jesus towards Israel.[42] Also for Paul, the promise of a future saving of all Israel does not invalidate the ongoing mission of the church to Israel. In fact, the opposite could well be argued, in regard to seeing that a strengthening of the Jewish remnant (messianic Jewish believers in Jesus) alongside and in partnership with vibrant and faithful Gentile believers could be part of the 'jealousy motif' (Romans 10:19) and hasten in some way the full restoration of Israel and the consummation of God's kingdom purposes.

It is also the case that for Paul, the significance of Israel's 'no' (Romans 11:15 and :25) does not remove the mission imperative from the church towards Israel. For Paul, God's righteousness demands an ongoing mission to Jews and Gentiles. Without such a dual focused mission, the essential purpose and unity of the church would be in danger of being lost. At the heart of this mission to Israel for Paul is the conviction that if Jewish people (individually in the present age or as part of 'all Israel' corporately in the future) come to faith/trust in Jesus, this coming to faith/trust in Jesus in no way will result in the undermining of Jewish identity or the standing of Israel within God's purposes. Paul, even when his main focus is predominantly on Gentile mission, continues to strive and hope for the salvation of some of his own Jewish people through his present and future ministry (Romans 11:14). For Paul, his own largely Gentile focused ministry is part of God's wider mission agenda to the whole world. This point is well made by Anthony Guerra:

> Paul maintains that the successful completion of his mission to the Gentiles, which he seeks to realize by his proposed efforts in the west, is the necessary precondition for the salvation of πα Ιοραηλ. Further, Paul has expressed throughout Romans 9-11 considerable appreciation for Jewish traditions, the patriarchs and scripture. Indeed, the abundant use of biblical quotations is outstanding, exceeding that in all other genuine Pauline texts. He has attempted to demonstrate that the course of Christian missionary expansion is repeating a pattern of rejection and salvation discernible in the biblical record. Furthermore, he has argued that the stages of the history of the Christian mission—beginning with a small number of Jewish Christians, then a greater number of Gentiles following the rejection by the majority of Jews, and finally the inclusion of "all Israel" after the completion of his mission to the Gentiles—are all "events" testified/predicted by the scriptures.[43]

Enlargement Theology would uphold that the church's mission to Jewish people when carried out with gentleness and care has an honourable place within each subsequent generation of church life as part of a wider mission of the church to all people. Evidence from the book of Acts suggests that this dual mission approach became the established method of the church in the first generation[44] in which Paul, as both an apostle of the Gentiles and prophet to Israel, was arguably the key theological advocate and active participant. This position is powerfully affirmed by Richard Bell:

> Paul's theology demands a mission to the Jewish People. I believe therefore there are no theological or ethical objections to a mission sensitively directed towards Jewish People, even a mission carried out by Gentiles.[45]

In view of this understanding of the validity of the church's mission paradigm to Jewish people, the metaphor of the river must contain an expression of both the ongoing importance of God's purpose within Israel and with Israel's 'no', yet at the same time show the importance of the church's ongoing mission to Israel, in terms of seeking Israel's present and future 'yes'. This may be hard to illustrate, but Enlargement Theology would affirm that this dual desire and ambition is theologically and pastorally essential.

12.5 Israel and the Land

Enlargement Theology would present the understanding that the promise of the land is implicit with the outworking of the covenant promises. These covenants remain as God's everlasting gift to Israel.[46] Paul states that the covenants remain as an ongoing part of the inheritance of the people of Israel (Rom 9:4) and Paul also affirms that God's gift and call are irrevocable (Rom 11:29). The gift of the land promised within the Abrahamic covenant and Israel's subsequent entering, possessing, being exiled from and promised restoration to the land is also rooted in the rich prophetic history of Israel. In the 'Old Testament' there are 109 occasions[47] in which the land is described as a promise or gift to the people of Israel. On 35 of these occasions the context is a solemn oath made by God.

Enlargement Theology recognises that certain aspects of God's covenantal promises to Israel are fulfilled in the coming of Jesus. Some aspects of a promise-fulfilment hermeneutic, as already stated, have validity. For example, aspects of the Mosaic covenant are conditional and temporary (Hebrews 10:1). The outworking of the New Covenantal promises brings into place a new intimacy and a new community of 'unity within diversity' of Jews and Gentiles brought into being through God's enlargement of his gifts and call. This results in some aspects of the covenant with Moses becoming obsolete (Hebrews 8:13), especially as the Jerusalem Temple and the nature of Priesthood become redefined and find fulfilment in the light of the person and work of Jesus within New Covenant teaching.[48] However, Enlargement Theology does not uphold the view that the promises of restoring Israel to the land can be dismissed using a promise-fulfilment hermeneutic. This is primarily because of the nature of the Abrahamic covenant (as an eternal and non-conditional covenant) and the promises of God contained within. In the light of this, Enlargement Theology would present the case relating to the restoring of Israel to the land as follows:

- God's character is verifiable in and through history.
- The modern day ingathering of the Jewish people and the related restoration of the Jewish people to the land is a fulfilment of key biblical promises.
- The land of Israel and the Jewish people clearly have a distinctive role within the ongoing purposes and promises of God. This must have implications for the just treatment of Palestinians[49] and the ongoing commitment to seek justice, reconciliation and peace for all people.

In concluding this segment on Enlargement Theology as a model for encounter and engagement, we now turn to the concluding chapter of this book. In doing this I will explore if the five tenets of Enlargement Theology (worked out alongside the threefold understanding of exploring communities within community, the legitimacy of the church's evangelistic mission to Jewish people and the understanding of Israel and the land[50]) will have an opportunity to make a significant contribution to the contemporary state of Jewish-Christians relations. The question which will be posed is this: "Is there any space at the table?"

Chapter Thirteen

Enlargement Theology and Contemporary Jewish-Christian Relations

'Any space at the table?'

13.1 The Current Context

The main focus of contemporary Jewish-Christian relations appears to be largely devoid of any meaningful engagement with Enlargement Theology and/or the wider contemporary Messianic Jewish movement. It is not, in most cases, that the question of Enlargement Theology and/or Messianic Jewish input has been addressed, explored and rejected, but rather that the question has simply not been considered. For example, many of the key contemporary books[1] in the area of Jewish-Christian relations give no consideration, or at best only fragmentary consideration, to Messianic Jewish Theology, the wider Messianic Jewish movement and of related groups such as Jews for Jesus and the Church's Ministry among Jewish People (CMJ). However, there has been some limited significant input from the perspective of Messianic Judaism. For example, the contribution by Arthur Glasser, in the book *Christians and Jews Together*,[2] the contribution by Wolfhart Pannenberg in *Jews and Christians: People of God*,[3] the book *Your People shall be my People*,[4] by Don Finto and the book, *Christian-Jewish Dialogue* by Peter von der Osten-Sacken.[5] In addition to these books there have also been some key articles in a number of Journals, for example, both the Princeton Theological Review[6] and the Journal of Ecumenical Studies[7] alongside a number of ongoing articles within the Mishkan Journal.[8]

The writers who present the case for Messianic Jewish involvement argue that, as the contemporary Messianic Jewish movement strengthens its influence and refines its theological convictions, the movement will gain credence and achieve a status which demands that it should be worthy of serious consideration by all participants within the wider field of Jewish-Christian relations. This view is presented clearly by Wolfhart Pannenberg:

> One of the new developments made possible by the reestablishment of a Jewish state in Palestine has been the emergence of groups of "messianic Jews" within Israel, Jews who confess their faith in Jesus the Messiah without leaving the Jewish community and a Jewish way of life. Since the end of the Jewish congregation of Jerusalem in the first century, this is the first time that a Jewish-Christian church reemerges so that a Jew need not turn to a gentile church when he or she comes to believe in Jesus the Christ. The "messianic Jews" intend to remain Jews while professing Jesus to be the Messiah. Sooner or later Christian-Jewish dialogue will have to take notice of this fact.[9]

A similar plea is made as the concluding statement in his Ph.D thesis by Walter Riggans:

> It is without doubt hopelessly naive for Messianic Jews to even imagine that they could act as a bridge community between the church and synagogue, but on the other hand it is surely tragically immature and self-serving of both the church and synagogue to refuse Messianic Jews any participation at all in the modern movement to build bridges among religious communities. If it is decided that Messianic Jews can not be considered to be authentic members of the body of the Messiah, or that they do not qualify as authentically Jewish, then let that decision emerge from a genuine meeting of minds and spirits.[10]

The various teaching resources outlined above, which seek to make the case for a greater appreciation of and openness towards the Messianic Jewish movement have, as stated earlier, had little influence within the wider field of Jewish-Christian relations. The prevailing general line within this wider field is that such input from Messianic Jewish circles is at best an unhelpful side issue and at worst a major distorting factor which could well destroy the whole process of dialogue and genuine encounter. There appears, therefore, to be a general mindset of rejecting the legitimacy of the Messianic Jewish movement and therefore its place at the table of authentic dialogue for three connected main reasons.

Firstly, there appears to be for many from the Rabbinic Jewish side an 'innate inner conviction' that any credence given to the Messianic Jewish movement is simply unacceptable. This has led to the insistence that one of the key ground rules for dialogue and encounter meetings is that Messianic Jews are excluded.[11] Such a ground rule clearly limits, in advance of any dialogue encounter, both the breadth of issues to be explored and by implication the possible acceptable conclusions of any such encounters. Such a pre-judging of issues prior to dialogue and opportunities for encounters seems somewhat inappropriate. This point is well documented by Mitch Glaser,[12] who outlines this insistent position from the Rabbinic Jewish community by quoting from a public letter addressed to Dr Paige Patterson (Former President of the Southern Baptist Convention – USA) from Gedale B Horowitz (President of the Jewish Community Relations Council, USA). Horowitz writes:

> All the movements within Judaism have jointly averred that conversion to Christianity removes one from participating in Jewish communal life and that Christian belief in, and worship of, Jesus is incompatible with any authentic Jewish practice.[13]

This view expressed by Horowitz is at the very heart of the Rabbinic Jewish reluctance to engage with the Messianic Jewish movement. Yet it does not necessarily reflect the overall position of the various Rabbinic Jewish communities. For example, Glaser in his article draws attention to the potential acceptance of Messianic Jewish input into wider dialogue resulting from new works flowing from a general pluralist position outlined by the Reconstuctionist Rabbi Carol Harris-Shapiro[14] and the Reformed Rabbi Daniel Cohn-Sherbok.[15] It may be somewhat of an irony that it is arguments from a Jewish pluralist position which open up opportunities for Jewish-Christian dialogue and further encounters for Messianic Jews and Christians who generally hold to exclusivist positions and who have associated evangelistic agendas. Daniel Cohn-Sherbok concludes his book by drawing out the logical necessity of his pluralist convictions:

> On the principle that it is always better to listen to people than to spit on them, the pluralists argue for an open model. In accordance with this, the seven-branched menorah in which all denominations, including Messianic Judaism, are represented, is the only reasonable starting point for inter-community relations in the twenty-first century.[16]

Secondly, there is a fear that Messianic Jewish involvement will inevitably confuse and restrict the dialogue process. As David Novak states:

> (Hebrew Christians) pose a special problem for both the Jewish and Christian communities, that problem is neither an antecedent nor a consequence of the dialogue. When this happens the relationship is no longer the relationship of Jews and Christians in which each faces the other from a distinctive origin. One that always transcends the meeting between them—rather the dialogue becomes an encompassing reality in which Judaism and the Christianity of the participants become moments that are then overcome in a reality whose dynamic is its own momentum.[17]

Thirdly, alongside this fear of confusing and distracting the genuine dialogue process is the commitment to the vision of inter-faith dialogue, which affirms that such dialogue must not merge into some form of syncretism. The involvement of Messianic Jewish believers will, it is argued, undermine the 'purity' of the dialogue by inevitably blurring and complicating the demarcation lines between Judaism and Christianity.[18] Such blurring could, it is argued, give rise to a syncretistic model. Hans Ucko explores this very argument:

> In inter-religious dialogue the partners try to be inclusive and such inclusiveness is sometimes misunderstood as syncretism, sometimes described as the "illegitimate mingling of different religious elements." But inter-religious dialogue actually affirms the very opposite of syncretism. It affirms diversity and recognizes plurality, without seeking to blend or mix the different religious traditions.[19]

13.2 Towards a New Paradigm/Moving Beyond the Impasse

This issue of blurring or as Hans Ucko stated, 'illegitimate mingling' is the core issue of contention. For those opposed to 'space being made at the table' for Messianic Jewish input the conviction is that such involvement (perhaps not necessarily intentionally) inevitably leads to an unhelpful blurring of the issues. Yet for those who argue for making significant room at the table of Jewish-Christian relations for the Messianic Jewish movement and Messianic Jewish Theology/Enlargement Theology (be it from a general pluralist position, a Messianic Jewish position or an evangelical Christian position) do not deny that such involvement may well at times, blur and disturb the normative demarcation lines between Judaism and Christianity and Jew and Gentile. However, such blurring and disturbing of the demarcation lines should not, it is argued, be viewed as a negative thing to be avoided, but rather should be viewed as a potentially positive development. Such a 'disturbing' is needed for it will contribute towards the 'breaking open' of the prevailing limited mindsets and bring forth new and creative avenues for dialogue and genuine encounters.

A willingness by participants within Jewish–Christian dialogue towards such a 'breaking open' is surely a key part of any process of dialogue and genuine relationship-building as one must be free to move beyond pre-existing constructed categories of identity and faith in order to respond to new insights and fresh understandings. In addition to this breaking open of the demarcation lines between Judaism and Christianity and Jew and Gentile, the Messianic Jewish movement in partnership with an Enlargement Theology, both in terms of practice and wider theological reflection, robustly contributes to a number of important areas within the wider framework of Jewish-Christian relations. In terms of these contributions, this thesis would affirm the significance of the following six:

- Exposing the flaws within and the subsequent opposing of Two Covenant Theology.
- Exposing the flaws within and the subsequent opposing of Christian Replacement Theology.
- Helping to give a new perspective on the teaching of Paul in Romans 9-11.[20]
- Helping to question and then in reformulating some core issues of Jewish identity. For example, the conviction that Jewish identity is not forfeited or undermined but renewed by faith in Jesus as Messiah and Lord.
- Helping contribute towards new avenues[21] for engagement, exploration and reflection in the wider field of Jewish-Christian relations.
- Presenting as the meta-narrative of scripture, God's covenantal faithfulness to Israel. This includes God's particularity as the God of Abraham, Isaac and Jacob alongside God's universal desire to bless all peoples through the outworking of the covenant promises.

As a result of these six insightful contributions by the Messianic Jewish movement alongside Enlargement Theology it is the conclusion of this thesis that when 'space at the table' is made for contributions from the emerging Messianic Jewish movement alongside Enlargement Theology, in a spirit of openness, honesty and respect, a new paradigm within Jewish-Christian relations will be in the process of being established.

In seeking to establish a new paradigm, the Messianic Jewish movement working in partnership with a developing Enlargement Theological model is not seeking to dispossess or to disenfranchise other participants within the process of Jewish-Christian relations. Sadly, Messianic Jews have often been dispossessed or disenfranchised by elements within both the Rabbinic Jewish community and the church. Rather, the Messianic Jewish movement in partnership with a developing Enlargement theology is seeking to find ways in which the Messianic movement can contribute fully within the field of Jewish-Christian relations and have its own present identity and future hope appropriately tested, recognized and perhaps even celebrated.

13.3 Concluding Plea

Such a new paradigm will, in the view of this thesis, not result in an unhelpful blurring of religious identity, but rather the opposite, namely, moving beyond the current impasse in Jewish-Christian relations to a new position. This impasse has been maintained as a result of the promotion of Replacement Theology or Two Covenant Theology, which have both drawn from and been built up from the classic paradigm rooted in historical and theological assumptions which resulted from the so called 'parting of the ways'[22] of Judaism and Christianity. This paradigm contributes to a view that Messianic Jews simply have little if any value, as they do not fit into the prevailing structures of Jewish or Christian life. A classic Christian historical expression of this way of understanding is that of Jerome who, in commenting on the Ebionites, stated:

> Since they want to be both Jews and Christians, they are neither Jews nor Christians.[23]

This thesis argues that Messianic Jews when understood within the wider framework of Enlargement Theology should not be regarded as ill-fitting pieces to be discarded neither as 'proper' Jews or Christians, but rather, when understood within this wider theological framework, Jewish believers in Jesus should be seen as key pieces. Such key pieces are vital in establishing the bigger picture, a bigger picture which presents the call and gifts of God to Israel and now enlarged to all people. Such call and gifts are shown in God's faithfulness to his people Israel, both in the past and here in the present age and, as Paul so faithfully perceives in Romans 9-11, on to the future final fulfilment:

For the deliverer will come from Zion; he will turn godlessness away from Jacob.[24]

For God has bound all men over to disobedience so that he may have mercy on them all. Oh, the depths of the wisdom and knowledge of God! How unsearchable his judgments, and his paths beyond tracing out! "Who has known the mind of the Lord? Or who has been his counsellor?" "Who has ever given to God, that God should repay him?" For from him and through him and to him are all things. To him be the glory for ever! Amen.[25]

Notes

Chapter 1

[1] Within this area of Jewish-Christian relations terminology is extremely important. This is because sensitive issues of identity are being explored and defined. I use the term 'Jew' here and the term 'Jewish' in the title believing it to be the most appropriate descriptive term. Later I consistently use the term Rabbinic Judaism to refer to the Jewish religious community which began to develop or to reconstruct itself initially in the period alongside the emergence of Christianity. The exact timing of this process of developing or reconstructing is a major debating point, with views ranging from as early as the early apostolic period of church life to as late as the fourth or fifth centuries. Other terms such as Post Biblical Judaism or Normative Judaism have been used for this descriptive task. For a fuller discussion on the use of the term 'Jewish' see article by Menachem Benhayim, 'Jewish survival and its significance for the Church', *Mishkan*, 4, (1986), pp43-48.

[2] As with note 1 above, I use the term 'Christian' here believing it to be the most appropriate and straightforward descriptive term. I am aware that some would prefer the term 'Christian' was not used for the early period of the church community which consisted of mainly Jewish believers in Jesus/Yeshua. This is because the term Christian is heard by many, especially Rabbinic Jews, in terms of someone opposed to or separate from the Jews. Terms such as Messianic Jews or Jewish believers in Jesus are therefore sometimes promoted. See article by Michael L Brown, 'Messianic Judaism and Jesus Jewish Research', in which he argues; "Because 'Christianity' quickly developed into a predominantly Gentile religion, at times quite hostile to Jewish roots, I believe scholarly references to 'Jewish Christianity' may present an unnecessary oxymoronic problem. Terms such as Messianic Jewish and Messianic Judaism may be a more appropriate descriptive and in fact, accurate when applied to the first followers of Jesus", *Mishkan*, 33, (2000), p 44. Against the use of the term 'Messianic Jew' promoted by Brown, Oskar Skarsaune also writing in the Mishkan Journal states; "I have spoken consistently about Jewish believers (in Jesus) . . . . The most popular modern self-designation is "Messianic Jew". Applying this latter term to Jewish believers in any century before the 20th is, however, anachronistic", *Mishkan*, 35, (2001), p71. In terms of writing protocol in regard to Messianic Judaism I will follow the path of using the capital to describe messianic in relation to Judaism in the modern era but not in the early Christian period.

[3] Michael Hilton, *The Christian Effect on Jewish life* (London: SCM Press, 1994), p4.

[4] This understanding of polarised positions flows largely from the prevailing understanding that Christianity and Rabbinic Judaism were shaped by a definitive parting of the ways which was almost entirely completed by the second century; however this view has been challenged. See A Becker and A Read (eds), *'The Ways that Never Parted: Jews and Christians in Late Antiquity and the early Middle Ages'* (Tubingen: Mohr Siebeck, 2003). See also footnote 11.

[5] Marcel Simon, *Verus Israel* (London: Littman Library, 1996).

[6] Hans Schoeps, *The Jewish Christian Argument* (London: Faber, 1963).

[7] N T Wright, *The New Testament and the People of God*, 4th edn (London: SPCK, 1992), p161.

[8] G Reith, *Justin Martyr—Dialogue with Trypho* (Edinburgh: Ante-Nicene Christian Library, 1867). It is worth noting here that there is some dispute about the genuine nature of this dialogue and the identity of Trypho. Within this, there is some dispute regarding how fairly Trypho represents 'Rabbinic Judaism/Pharisaic opinions'. While this account gives us somewhat of a slanted Christian version, it is generally seen as being much more of a genuine encounter than much of the later (medieval) period of 'forced dialogue' or polemic promoted by the powerful Church.

[9] F C Conybeare (ed), *Dialogue of Athanasius and Zacchaeus and Timothy and Aquila*. (London/Oxford: Society of Biblical Literature, 1898). This encounter took place in approx 200 CE.

[10] F C Conybeare (ed), *Dialogue of Athanasius and Zacchaeus and Timothy and Aquila*. (London/Oxford: Society of Biblical Literature, 1898). This encounter took place in approx 325 CE.

[11] This line of thought regarding a clear common history, shared beginnings and therefore a subsequent parting of the ways has been challenged in the writings of Jacob Neusner. See, *Jews and Christians: The Myth of a Common Tradition* (Binghamton: Global Academic publishing, 2001).

[12] Marcel Simon, *Verus Israel* (London: Littman Library, 1996), p384.

[13] A Roy Eckardt, *Elder and Younger Brothers* (New York: Charles Scribner's and Sons, 1967), p51.

[14] See E P Sanders, *Paul and Palestinian Judaism* (London: SCM Press, 1977), pp550-552.

[15] James Dunn, *Word Biblical Commentary—Romans 9-16* (Dallas: Word Books, 1988), p546.

[16] Acts 1:15 states this group numbered about 120. Later in Acts we see the rapid growth of the group. See Acts 2:41, 4:4, 6:7 and 21:20.

[17] N T Wright, *The New Testament and the People of God*, 4th edn (London: SPCK, 1992), p359.

[18] This 'normative' process is sometimes presented as four stages while others would argue that repentance and faith belong together as one stage. Clearly throughout the book of Acts the process does not always

follow the same order. In Acts 10 for example baptism in the Holy Spirit precedes water baptism. Also in Acts 8 what occurs is seem by most commentators as exceptional rather than normative. For a fuller discussion see commentaries on Acts. I have found the commentaries by John Stott and H A Guy to be helpful on this point, see the bibliography for details. Therefore, this normative process can be best seen not as a rigid formula but rather as a single cluster containing the necessary three or four key elements which make up the reality of Christian initiation.

[19] See Romans 9-11, Galatians 3, Ephesians 2:11-22, Ephesians 3, Philippians 3:1-9 and Hebrews 8.

[20] David Stern, *Jewish New Testament Commentary*, 6th edn (Clarksville: Jewish New Testament Publications, 1999), p261.

[21] There is a significant point of debate as to the question if the term Minim refers to Jewish believers in Jesus or to other unspecified 'heretical' groups. For a fuller discussion of this question, see James Dunn, *The Parting of the Ways* (London: SCM Press, 1991).

[22] Ebionites rejected core 'Orthodox Christian' views, such as the virgin birth, and moved away from seeing the 'full divinity' of Jesus as they promoted the understanding of a deified man. They practiced a strict yet reformed view of Torah observance and also rejected the authority of Pauline writings. It may be that the Ebionites had strong resemblances (condemnation of the sacrifice system of the Jerusalem Temple, elements of dualism and the practice of ritual washing) with elements of the Essene communities. For fuller discussion, see Kenneth Latourette, *A History of Christianity* (London: Eyre and Spottiswoode, 1964), pp121-123.

[23] Similar to Ebionites and founded by Elkesai who claimed to have received special revelations by an angel identified as the Son of God. This movement gained support in the early 2nd century but shortly disappeared.

[24] Arnold Fruchtenbaum, 'The Quest for a Messianic Theology', *Mishkan*, 2, (1985), p9.

[25] The term Replacement Theology is a known theological term which refers to a broad theological approach with special reference to how the church relates to Israel and the covenantal promises of God. See ch.2 of this thesis for a fuller exploration of Replacement Theology.

[26] See Franz Rosenzweig, *The Star of Redemption* (London: Routledge and Kegan Paul, 1971). Also see his discussions with Rosenstock and Ehrenberg. These took place in 1913-1916 but were only published in 1969. Also see ch. 3 of this thesis for fuller outline of Franz Rosenzweig.

[27] See his dialogue with K L Schmidt outlined in *Two Types of Faith* (London: Macmillan, 1951).

[28] As in footnote 1and 2, I use the term here not to divide Christianity along Jewish or Gentiles lines but rather to refer to the reality of many Jewish believers in Jesus who, in various ways, have sought to express

their faith in ways which honour their Jewish identity.

[29] Oskar Skarsaune, 'The Jewish-Christian Dialogue in Ancient and Modern Times', *Mishkan*, 3, (1985), 21.

[30] For a helpful introduction on the 'New Perspective of Paul' see Douglas Moo, 'Paul and the Law' *Scottish Journal of Theology*, 40, (1987).

[31] Such as the meetings of Christians and Jews in Seelisgburg (1947), Frankfurt (1962) and Cambridge (1966).

[32] See Helga Croner, *Stepping Stones to Further Jewish-Christian Relations* (London/New York: Stimulus books, 1977).

[33] Torleif Elgvin, 'The Church and Israel-Dialogue and Witness' *Mishkan*, 36, (2002), 1-2.

[34] The term Two Covenant Theology is a known theological term which refers to a broad theological approach with special reference to how the church relates to Israel and the covenantal promises of God. See ch.3 in this thesis for a fuller exploration of Two Covenant Theology.

[35] It is however important to note that while the Two Covenant model and the approach of Replacement theology are hugely significant in terms of the establishing and outworking of Jewish-Christian relations there are many church groups and individual Christians who do not perceive themselves as falling into either of these camps. In this regard it is probably fair to say that Replacement theology and Two Covenant theology are not as influential in certain Christian circles as they once were. Yet there is no question that the field of Jewish-Christian relations is still as problematic as ever, especially as one engages with the many nuanced positions within the theology of contemporary Jewish-Christian relations. These positions relate to a vast range of theological subjects especially in the areas of eschatology, evangelism, ecclesiology and religious identity.

[36] David Ford, 'A Messiah for the Third Millennium', *Modern Theology*, 16, (2000), p78.

[37] Torleif Elgvin, 'The Church and Israel-Dialogue and Witness', *Mishkan*, 36 (2002), p3.

[38] David Stern, *Jewish New Testament Commentary*, 6th edn (Clarksville: Jewish New Testament Publications, 1999), p416.

[39] Walter Kaiser, *Towards an Old Testament Theology* (Grand Rapids: Baker Books, 1978), p264

[40] The exact relationship between the teaching of the church in the context of Replacement Theology and numerous anti-Semitic activities throughout church history is impossible to fully gauge. In terms of the link with the Holocaust the following quote from Hans Küng gives a useful perspective, "The mass murder of Jews by the Nazis was the work of Godless criminals but without the almost 2000 year history of Christian anti-Semitism it would have been impossible. The killing of the Jews in the Twentieth century was the final result of a tradition of denigration

and rejection of Jews and Judaism dating from early in Christian history, which also tried to strip Jesus of his Jewishness to produce a homemade God and saviour, a Gentile hero". (Quote taken from Holocaust article in the London Times Newspaper, (April 1985). Also cited by Derek White in his book *Replacement Theology* (London: CFI communications, 1997).
[41] See A Roy Eckardt, *Elder and Younger Brothers* (New York: Charles Scribner's and Sons, 1967), p49.

Chapter 2

[1] Marc Saperstein, *Moments of Crisis in Jewish-Christian Relations* (London: SCM Press, 1989), p2.

[2] Jonathan Sacks, *Faith in the Future* (London: Darton, Longman and Todd, 1995), p103.

[3] Replacement Theology is my preferred term believing that the term gives a clear description of the theological process. However, supersessionism is the term used by many theologians such as R Kendall Soulen (see footnote 6) and David Ford. See David Ford's article, 'A Messiah for the Third Millennium', *Modern Theology*, 16, (2000). On p78, Ford states: "Supersessionism is intrinsic to the Christian pathology in relating to Jews".

[4] Often in terms of Replacement Theology the focus is on the New Covenant replacing the Old Covenant. The Old Covenant is spoken of in the singular. Therefore the emphasis tends in terms of the number of Covenants to be that of Two (Old replaced by New). In contrast to this in terms of the number of covenants some Christians would emphasize that there is only One covenant of God which embraces both the Old and New dispensations, while other Christians would emphasize the different nature of the Old Covenants and speak of at least four major Old Testament Covenants.

[5] The first author to claim direct identification of the term Israel with the church was Justin Martyr in his dialogue with Trypho. The main New Testament text used in this argument is Galatians 6:16.

[6] R Kendall Soulen, *The God of Israel and Christian Theology* (Minneapolis: Fortress Press, 1996), p 181.

[7] For a contemporary reflection on the use of such terms see James Moore's article; 'The Passion of the Christ-A Protestant Perspective', *Shofar*, 23, (2005).

[8] When the Jews are described in negative terms such as; "You belong to your father, the devil, and you want to carry out your father's desire." (John 8:44), the issue is that the context is one of internal Jewish debate, namely one Jewish person rebuking another Jewish person. When later such texts are used to justify anti-Jewish convictions or actions the point which needs to be put forward is that such a text has been wrenched out

from the original authorial intent, namely that of recording an internal dispute. The issue of authorial intent is critical in claiming if the text itself is anti-Jewish rather that the later interpretation and application of the text. For further study see Stephen Moyter, *Your Father the Devil?* (Exeter: Paternoster Press, 1997) and Glenn Balfour, 'Is John's Gospel Anti-Semitic?' *Tyndale Bulletin*, 48, (1997), pp369-72.

[9] Jules Isaac, *Jesus and Israel* (New York: Holt, Rinehart and Winston, 1971).

[10] The view I hold is that Paul is the author of 13 New Testament letters. However, this point is probably a minority view in terms of modern scholarship and is strongly challenged by those who would argue against Paul's authorship of many of these 13 'Pauline' New Testaments letters. This challenge often begins with the pastoral letters but also includes other parts of the traditional Pauline corpus such as Ephesians and Colossians. A good example of this approach is that advanced by J C Beker, *Heirs of Paul* (Minneapolis: Fortress, 1991) A useful balanced discussion of the issues is given by David Horrell, *An Introduction to the Study of Paul* (London/New York: Continuum, 2000) pp116-122. For a defence of my view see Donald Guthrie, *The Pauline Epistles—New Testament Introduction* (London: Tyndale Press, 1961), p11-12.

[11] I understand here that the writer to the Hebrews is speaking of aspects of the covenant with Moses and not the irrevocable core promises made to Israel in the Abrahamic covenant. This issue will be explored further in sections dealing with the Romans 9-11 text and especially in exploring Romans 10:4 from a mainly teleological perspective.

[12] Origen (185-245) cited in *Ante-Nicene Christian literature* (Edinburgh: 1867).

[13] Hilary of Poitiers (315-367) cited in *Ante-Nicene Christian literature* (Edinburgh: 1867).

[14] John Chrysostem (347-407) cited by E Flannery in, *The Anguish of the Jews* (New York: Paulist Press, 1985), p43.

[15] See R Kendall Soulen, *The God of Israel and Christian Theology* (Minneapolis: Fortress Press, 1996), pp17-18.

[16] Ecumenical Council of Antioch (341).

[17] Ecumenical Council of Antioch (341).

[18] Ecumenical Council of Orleans (538).

[19] Ecumenical Council of Chalcedon (451).

[20] From the Church of Constantinople—The Assemani code cited by H.Schonfield, *The History of Jewish Christianity* (London: Duckworth Press, 1936).

[21] Calvin does not argue along classic Replacement Theology lines in regard to identifying the elect as the Church which replaces Israel, but rather sees that the church is grafted into the elect. He states, "We must be

numbered in his (Abraham's) family in order to be the children of God. Now what would be more absurd than that Abraham should be the father of all the faithful and not have even the lowest place among them? But he cannot be excluded from that number, not even from the most honourable station, without the destruction of the whole church." (Calvin, Institutes, Book 2, 10, p474 translated by John Allen, 7th American Edition 1936). Calvin develops this line of argument by stating that those who hold to the view that no spiritual blessing was ever promised to the carnal seed of Abraham, or that such promises were confined only to present and corporeal enjoyments as being "greatly deceived." Calvin continues by affirming that for the sake of the promise, the blessing of God still remains among the Jewish People, and; "It will never entirely depart from them; for the gifts and calling of God are without repentance" (Calvin Institutes, Book 4, 16, p617) He concludes this argument with reference to Exodus 20:6 in which he states: "Shall we say this promise in cancelled? That would be subversive to the Law, which on the contrary Christ came to establish as a rule for holy life. It ought to be admitted therefore beyond all controversy, that God is so kind and liberal to all his servants as for their sakes, to appoint even the children who shall descend from them to be enrolled among his people". (Calvin, Institutes, Book 4, 16, p618).

[22] Many of the Reformers spoke in regard to the Jewish people in tones very much in keeping with the polemic of the early church fathers and the prevailing mindset of Replacement Theology. See for example Martin Luther's work; *On the Jews and their lies*, published in 1543. However, it should be noted that this particular work belongs to the period near the end of Luther's life and reflects a growing anti-Jewish tone. In early periods of Luther's teaching , he had a much more 'positive' attitude towards the Jewish people as he hoped that the Jewish people would embrace the Christian faith when it was presented to them with the clarity of the newly Reformed Church. For many, this reformation within the Church was seen to mark the beginnings of the 'end times'. When no significant turning of Jewish people to the Christian Gospel took place then a more negative tone, like that expressed in the work "On the Jews and their lies" developed.

[23] An Anabaptist Minister from London. He published in 1792 the book, *The Signs of the Times*.

[24] The term Israel for example occurs 11 times in the key teaching passage of Romans 9-11. Romans 9:4, :6 (x2), :27, :31, 10:19, :21, 11:1, :2, :7 and :25.

[25] Pre-Millennialism is one theological reading of eschatological events outlined in the Book of Revelation. The other two broad theological approaches are A-Millennialism and Post-Millennialism.

[26] Kelvin Crombie, 'Early Christian Zionists', *Mishkan*, 26, (1997), p49.

[27] Groups such as the London Society for Promoting Christianity amongst the Jews (Established 1809) the Hebrew Christian Testimony to Israel, the American Board of Missions to Jews, and the Hebrew-Christian Alliance (Established 1866). See also key work undertaken by individuals such as Charles Simeon, Joseph Frey and Lewis Way.

[28] See for example the ministry of Michael Solomon Alexander the first Anglican Bishop of Jerusalem following an act of the British Parliament in 1841.

[29] From the Roman Catholic side leaders such as Cardinal Bea with a post- second Vatican council outlook were able to usher in a new era of Catholic-Jewish dialogue with a new emphasis based on a clear repudiation of anti-Semitism and a desire to find mutual understanding through friendship, dialogue and joint Biblical studies. On the Protestant side valuable contributions were made by A Roy Eckardt, James Parkes and Richard Niebuhr amongst many others.

Chapter 3

[1] The term "Two Ways" or "Dual Covenant" are sometimes used when referring to this theological position.

[2] Jonathan Sacks, *Faith in the Future* (London: Darton, Longman and Todd, 1995), p120.

[3] For a full exploration of the Marranos Jews and their theological developments see Peter Hocken, *The Marranos – A History in Need of Healing, Towards Jerusalem Council 2*, booklet Series, No. 3, (2006).

[4] There has been and still is within Rabbinic Judaism different strands (Hasidism, Orthodox, Conservative, Reform, Reconstructionist etc) of religious thought. Such differences can be seen in many areas including issues around the validity of seeking to make converts from the Gentile community. In the New Testament period the text Matthew 23:15 suggests that some Jews were active in seeking proselytes. However, when the Church, under the rule of Constantine, came to a position of official ascendancy, further Jewish attempts to proselytise became illegal. Today some Reform movement Jews actively reach out to Gentiles with a 'converting' agenda. However, this is not the position of the majority of 'religious Jews', and even when Gentiles seek to enter the Jewish faith, this is sometimes resisted. Some would argue that this is because the tendency born out of a diaspora 'survival instinct' is to exclude rather than include. Others would see the motivation as one of compassion in terms of not wanting to place the full demands of the Torah upon God-fearing Gentiles.

[5] These laws are reflected in part in the rule given to Gentile Christians in Acts 15. These laws prohibit idolatry, blasphemy, incest, murder, castration, robbery, and occult practices. The Jewish philosopher Maimonides argued that a Gentile who keeps the Noachide laws is more

honoured than a Jew who neglects the Torah (See *Encyclopedia Judaica*, vol 7, p1387).

[6] Micah 4:4-5.

[7] This teaching sought to show that Christians were not idolaters by their affirming the divinity of Jesus and the Holy Spirit. This was done by defining idolatry in different ways for Jews and Gentiles. See for example Berger and Wyschogrod, *Jews and Jewish Christianity* (New York: Seabury Press, 1978), pp32-33 and pp61-63.

[8] In the majority of cases the culture would be Christian yet also the same principle applies to interaction with Islamic culture.

[9] Rosenzweig studied jurisprudence, philosophy and theology at the Universities of Leipzig, Freiburg and Berlin.

[10] Maurice Bowler, 'Rosenzweig on Judaism and Christianity', *Mishkan*, 11, (1989), 2.

[11] Franz Rosenzweig, *The Star of Redemption* (London: Routledge and Kegan Paul, 1971). This work was first published in Frankfurt in 1921. Franz Rosenzweig died in 1929.

[12] Franz Rosenzweig, *The Star of Redemption* (London: Routledge and Kegan Paul, 1971), p12.

[13] Quoted by N.Glatzer in *Franz Rosenzweig, His Life and Thought* (New York: Schocken Press, 1985), p163.

[14] Franz Rosenzweig, *The Star of Redemption* (London: Routledge and Kegan Paul, 1971), p416.

[15] See article, 'Judaism and Christianity', published in the *Journal of Bible and Religion*, (1953).

[16] See article, 'Rosenzweig on Judaism and Christianity', published in the *Journal of Conservative Judaism*, (1956).

[17] See article, 'The Covenant', published in the *Anglican Theological Review*, 64, (1982).

[18] Cohen argues that the separate existence of the Jewish people is necessary until the Messianic age is established. Israel is seen as a symbolic vision of the Messianic age to come. Cohen also argues that authentic Jewish monotheism is the only sufficient ontological ground for universal morality. See *The Natural and Supernatural Jew* (New York: Pantheon books, 1962) and *Tremendum* (New York: Crossroad publishing, 1988) Cohen is cited by Novak in *The Election of Israel* (Cambridge: Cambridge University Press, 1995), p65.

[19] See *Two Types of Faith* (London: Macmillan Press, 1951). Also, *Israel and the World* (New York: Schocken Press, 1963).

[20] See article, 'Jewish-Christian Relations: a Jewish perspective', *The Journal of Ecumenical Studies*, 21, (1983).

[21] See Kenneth Cracknell, *Towards a New Relationship* (London: Epworth, 1986).

[22] See James Parkes, *A History of the Jewish People* (London: Pelican, 1964).

[23] See P Van Buren, *A Christian Theology of the People of Israel* (New York: Seabury, 1983). Also, A Theology of the Jewish Christian Reality (San Francisco: Harper and Row, 1988).

[24] See M. Brearley, *Jerusalem Past and Present in the Purposes of God*, P W L Walker (ed), (Carlisle: Paternoster Press, 1994), pp99-124.

[25] See Matthew Fox, 'Creation Spirituality in the Aquarian Age', *Anvil* 9.2 (1992) cited by M. Brearley, Christian Jewish research paper, 22.2, (1989).

[26] P W L Walker (ed), *Jerusalem Past and Present in the Purposes of God* (Carlisle: Paternoster Press, 1994), p121.

[27] Arnulf Baumann, 'The Two Ways/Two Covenants Theory', *Mishkan*, 11, (1989), pp37-38.

[28] Quoted in Marc Saperstein, *Moments of Crisis in Jewish Christian Relations* (London: SCM Press 1989), p16.

[29] Quoted in the Sigtuam conference papers of the consultation of the Church and the Jewish People World Council of Churches, (1988).

[30] Jacob Taubes, 'Argument and Doctrine', *Jewish Publication Society Journal* (1970), p441.

[31] Richard Robinson, 'My Yiddishe Paul', *Mishkan*, 20, (1994), p20.

[32] Alan Segal, *Paul the Convert: the Apostolate and Apostasy of Saul the Pharisee* (Yale University Press, 1990), p281.

[33] Richard Robinson,'My Yiddishe Paul', *Mishkan*, 20, (1994), p21.

[34] David Torrance, 'Two Covenant Theology', *Mishkan*, 11, (1989), p34.

[35] Mitch Glaser, 'Critique of the Two Covenant Theory', *Mishkan*, 11, (1989), p64.

[36] Arnulf Baumann, 'The Two Ways/Two Covenants Theory', *Mishkan*, 11, (1989), p42.

Chapter 4

[1] Thomas Merton, *A vow of conversation* (New York: Farrar, Straus and Giroux, 1988), p7.

[2] This work contains a wide range of Roman Catholic and Protestant documents from differing geographical and ecclesiological settings. The work was published by Stimulus books in 1977.

[3] Other texts which are referenced within the documents include, Matthew 5:17, 16:16, :23, :26,:27, Luke 13:35, 23:34, John 1:17, 20:21, Acts 1:7, 2:23, :10, :15, :23, Romans 3, 1 Corinthians 10:15, Galatians 3, 4:5, Ephesians 1:10, 2:11-22, Colossians 1:16-18, 2 Timothy 3:16, Hebrews 7, 8, James 2 and 1 Peter 2:9.

[4] Helga Croner, *Stepping stones to Further Jewish-Christian Relations* (London/New York: Stimulus, 1977), p32.

[5] Ibid., p33.

[6] Ibid., p47.

[7] See bibliography for full publication details.

[8] David Stern, *Jewish New Testament Commentary*, 6th edn (Clarksville: Jewish New Testament Publications, 1999), p385.

[9] John Lodge, *Romans 9-11: A readers-Response Analysis* (University of South Florida: Scholars Press, 1996).

[10] See especially *Paul, the Law and Jewish People* (Philadelphia: Fortress, 1983) and *Paul and Palestinian Judaism* (London: SCM Press, 1977). Also, see for current reflections on the New Perspective *Justification and Variegated Nomism*, vol 2, D Carson, Peter T O'Brien and Mark A Seifrid (eds), (Tubingen: Mohr Siebeck, 2004).

[11] The statement from the Basis of Faith submitted by the Evangelical Alliance is a helpful summary of my position. In terms of scripture the basis of faith states: "We affirm the divine inspiration and supreme authority of the Old and New Testament scriptures, which are the written Word of God—fully trustworthy for faith and conduct."

[12] Cornelius Van Til in his introduction to B B Warfield, *The Inspiration and Authority of the Bible* (Philadelphia: Presbyterian and Reformed Publishing Co, 1964), p3.

[13] See Romans 1:19-20.

[14] See the four steps within my exegetical method outlined on pp46-48 of this thesis.

[15] B B Warfield, *The Inspiration and Authority of the Bible* (Philadelphia: Presbyterian and Reformed Publishing Co, 1964).

[16] *Explaining Hermeneutics: A Commentary on the Chicago Statement on Biblical Hermeneutics* (Oakland, California: International Council on Biblical Inerrancy, 1983).

[17] W Randolph Tate, *Biblical Interpretation*, 3rd edition (Peabody, Massachusetts: Hendrickson, 2008), p223.

[18] Grant R Osborne, *The Hermeneutical Spiral* (Downers Grove: IVP Academic, 2006) p411.

[19] The view expressed by B B Warfield was often referred to as 'the classical high Protestant doctrine of the Bible'.

[20] See comments by Sussanah Heschel on p116

[21] At a recent Tyndale Fellowship lecture (June 2009) Professor Wayne Grudem spoke on the perspicuity of scripture. He stated that scripture affirms that it is able to be clearly understood and applied but with six qualifications, namely – not all at once, not without effort, not without ordinary means, not without the help of the Holy Spirit, not without human misunderstandings and never completely.

[22] This approach is sometimes referred to as the harmony of scripture principle. In this approach no part of scripture may be interpreted in a way which contradicts another part of scripture. Proper application of

hermeneutical principles will resolve apparent discrepancies. The key here is the word "proper" for exegetical mistakes can sometimes result from an ill-informed approach which attempts to over-harmonize scripture. I think it is helpful to carefully apply the harmony of scripture principle alongside the progressive revelatory principle of scripture.

[23] For example, there can be an arrangement of material based on the principle of association of ideas.

[24] I realize that for some commentators who in attempting to 'reconcile' John's account with the Synoptic accounts suggest that there were in fact two cleansings of the Jerusalem Temple (John reports the first occasion). While this may be possible, it is not necessary from my hermeneutical perspective to insist on this solution in order to confront alleged 'discrepancies' within the inspired text. Different groupings of material does not necessarily bring one author into conflict with another.

[25] Richard Bell, *Israel and the Irrevocable Call of God* (Tubingen: Mohr Siebeck, 2005) See especially Chapters 4 and 8.

[26] I think Bell would see the 'change of mind' reflected within Paul as a positive process of mature reflection rather than inconsistency.

[27] This approach is part of the outworking of the Grammatico-Historical method which is embraced virtually by all evangelical exegetes. The historical background principle affirms that each part of scripture was composed in a specific culture at a particular point in time.

[28] Grant R Osborne, *The Hermeneutical Spiral* (Downers Grove: IVP Academic, 2006) p32.

[29] Ibid, p33.

[30] Context can be explored in a number of ways, for example, there is the context of the word itself (semantics) or the context of sentences and phrases (grammar) as well as the wider context of the historical background of the text.

[31] Manfred Oeming, *Contemporary Biblical Hermeneutics*. Trans by Joachim Vette (Aldershot: Ashgate Publishing, 2006) p16.

[32] When this is the case the focus of interest becomes either the text itself in isolation (as far as this is ever possible?) from external/historical factors, or the understanding given to the text by the reader. In as much as the reader with his or her presuppositions and cultural nuances is understood as being the only arbiter of meaning. For it is argued, the text only ever has the 'meaning' given to it by the reader.

[33] In a way this is similar to a medieval nuanced allegorical approach see Manfred Oeming, *Contemporary Biblical Hermeneutics*. Trans by Joachim Vette (Aldershot: Ashgate Publishing, 2006) , p12.

[34] I use the term inductive to mean that a particular argument or theological understanding must be built upon what the text clearly states rather than from a more 'deductive' model which allows for the use of logical/

philosophical reasoning to deduce an understanding.

[35] See pp47ff.

[36] I think here especially in terms of Jewish believers in Jesus trying to maintain significant relationships both within the church and within wider Jewish communities.

[37] The writer expressed such a meaning as a result of the inspiration of the Holy Spirit. I understand that this inspiration is best described in terms of God's guidance not dictation. God inspires through the writer's personal and community experiences, personality, vocabulary etc.

[38] Grant R Osborne identifies seven types of literature—narrative, poetry, wisdom, prophecy, apocalyptic, parable and epistle. See *The Hermeneutical Spiral* (Downers Grove: IVP Academic, 2006) p149.

[39] See for example, Philippians 3:2

[40] I would suggest that Paul's use of scripture in Romans 9-11 is shaped by his Jewish middot.

[41] A good example of this method is in the discussion around Romans 11:26 on pp160ff. Here I take the line (in the light of Paul's previous teaching, especially in Romans 10) in affirming that the way in which Israel will be saved cannot bypass the person and work of Jesus.

[42] This four-way discourse may become a somewhat 'closed circle' of conversation in which one's own personal predilections and theological insights are not challenged by other insights or by even the text itself. This danger needs to be acknowledged for any hermeneutical approach probably has aspects of closed circular language, however it is vital in attempting to address this concern to robustly pursue the process outlined in step 4 of my method, in order to keep the so-called circle open as far as is possible.

[43] Paul also used a scribe identified as Tertius (Romans 16:22) to help him. The issue of Pauline authorship of Romans has no serious challenge unlike some other 'Pauline works' such as the Pastoral Epistles. The issue around authorship which is however debated is dealing with the integrity of the text especially the place of Ch 15/16 (See John Ziesler, *Paul's letter to Rome*, London: SCM Press, 1989), pp19-31 for an outline of this debate.

[44] The term 'Christian community' is one filled with difficulties (see footnote 1 on page 1 of this thesis). In one sense using this terminology could well be seen as an anachronism as believers in Jesus were probably seen by the vast majority of the population as religiously and ethnically inseparable at this time from the groups which made up the Jewish diaspora. This view is presented by Rudolf Brändle and Ekkehard W Stegemann in chapter 5 of Judaism and Christianity in First-Century Rome. Karl P Donfried and Peter Richardson (eds) (Grand Rapids:Eerdmans, 1988).

[45] William L Lane, *Roman Christianity during the Formative Years from*

Nero to Nerva, in Karl P Donfried and Peter Richardson (eds), *Judaism and Christianity in First-Century Rome* (Grand Rapids: Eerdmans, 1988), p 213.

[46] See my discussion on the Jewish/Gentile make up of the Christian community in Rome at section 9.1 of this book.

[47] See for a full discussion of this issue see the following, L W Barnard, 'The early Roman Church, Judaism and Christianity' *Anglican Theological review*, 49, (1967). Karl P Donfrield and Peter Richardson (eds), *Judaism and Christianity in First-Century Rome* (Grand Rapids: Eerdmans, 1988). James S Jeffers, *Conflict at Rome Social order and hierarchy in Early Christianity* (Minneapolis: Fortress, 1991). J C Walters, *Ethnic Issues in Paul's Letter to the Romans* (Valley Forge, PA: Trinity Press International, 1993). William S Campbell, *Paul and the Creation of Christian Identity* (London/New York, T and T Clark, 2006), especially chapters 7 and 8.

[48] See K P Donfried and Peter Richardson (eds), *Judaism and Christianity in First-Century Rome* (Grand Rapids: Eerdmans, 1988),p120.

[49] Jews have subsequently returned to Rome under the reign of Nero (54 CE?) following their expulsion.

[50] This expulsion took place under the reign of Claudius (49 CE?). Cranfield in his commentary refers also to Acts 18:2 for incidental confirmation of this event. See C E B Cranfield, *The International Critical Commentary, Romans*, vol 2 (London/New York: T and T Clark, 1979), p783.

[51] Approximately a third of the text (Romans 9-11) is taken directly from 'Old Testament' quotations of which quotations from the prophet Isaiah predominate.

[52] Anthony J Guerra, *Romans and the apologetic tradition* (Cambridge: Cambridge University Press, 1995), p145.

[53] However, as Joseph Shulam states: "...in contrast to other midrashim he does not follow the strict order of any particular biblical text". See, Joseph Shulam, *A commentary on the Jewish Roots of Romans* (Baltimore: Lederer Books, 1997), p7.

[54] This is argued for by J Jervell, *The Letter to Jerusalem* in K P Donfried, (ed), 2nd ed *The Romans Debate* (Peabody, MA: Hendrickson, 1991), p53-64. In addition to the argument presented by Jervell other factors from Paul's missionary agenda have also been suggested as motivating the writing of this 'occasional' letter, for example Robert Jewett argues that gaining support for the Spanish mission is the rationale for the entire letter, Robert Jewett, *Romans A Commentary* (Minneapolis, Fortress, 2007) ,p723.

[55] Douglas Moo, *The Epistle to the Romans* (Grand Rapids: Eerdmans, 1996), p1.

[56] James Dunn, *Word Biblical Commentary, Romans 9-16* (Dallas: Word Books, 1988), p519.

Chapter 5

[1] Douglas Moo, *The Epistle to the Romans* (Grand Rapids: Eerdmans, 1996), p555.

[2] James Dunn, *Word Biblical Commentary, Romans 9-16* (Dallas: Word Books, 1988), p552.

[3] See Romans 8:39, in this text Paul has made the claim that nothing can in reality cut off the believer in Jesus from the love and destiny which is in Jesus.

[4] Moo points out in *The Epistle to the Romans* (Grand Rapids: Eerdmans, 1996), p559 a number of allusions to Moses within Romans 9-11 (9:14-18, 10:19 and 11:13-14) and sees that it is likely that Paul does come to see Moses to some extent, as his own model. Interestingly Dwight Pryor in his seminar teaching notes (distributed by the Centre for Judaic-Christian Studies) makes a powerful case that for Paul his main model from Jewish history is not Moses but the prophet Jeremiah.

[5] See 2 Corinthians 5:21.

[6] See Richard Bell, *Provoked to Jealousy* (Tubingen: Mohr/Siebeck, 1994), p173.

[7] Babylonian Talmud (London: Soncino Press, 1935) Tractate, Genesis Rabbah.

[8] The Torah (Proverbs 8:22), the Throne of God (Psalm 93:2), the Patriarchs (Hosea 9:10), Israel (Psalm 74:2), the Temple (Jeremiah 17:12) and the Messiah (Micah 5:2).

[9] Robert Jewett, *Romans A Commentary* (Minneapolis, Fortress, 2007), p557.

[10] James Dunn, *Word Biblical Commentary, Romans 9-16* (Dallas: Word Books, 1988), p523.

[11] Dwight Pryor, audio tape series entitled *'Paul—Jewish Apostle to the Roman World'*. Distributed by Centre for Judaic-Christian Studies, (2003), Website information- www.jcstudies.com.

[12] See Numbers 35:30, Deuteronomy 17:6, Matthew 18:16 and Hebrews 10:28.

[13] See Matthew 1:1. The Gospel of Matthew is often seen as a gospel account which has a particular Jewish flavour, hence the reference in the opening verse to arguably the two key covenantal characters in Israel's history, David and Abraham.

[14] In terms of the differing groups within the Roman congregation(s) there is much speculation by numerous commentators especially in the context of identifying the strong and the weak in Romans 14-15. Both, Paul Minear, *The Obedience of Faith* (London: SCM Press, 1971) and John Lodge, *Romans 9-11, A Reader-Response Analysis* (University of South Florida: Scholars Press, 1996) are particularly helpful in exploring the possible constituency and agendas of such groups.

[15] A fuller argument on the identity of 'Israel' will take place within the next chapter focusing in part on Romans 9:6.

[16] David Stern, *Jewish New Testament Commentary*, 6th edn (Clarksville: Jewish New Testament Publications, 1999), p386.

[17] James Dunn, *Word Biblical Commentary, Romans 9-16* (Dallas: Word Books, 1988), p526.

[18] Robert Jewett, *Romans A Commentary* (Minneapolis, Fortress, 2007), p562.

[19] John Ziesler, *Paul's Letter to the Romans* (London: SCM Press, 1989), p237.

[20] Ibid.

[21] Douglas Moo, *The Epistle to the Romans* (Grand Rapids: Eerdmans, 1996), p561.

[22] The other main line of argument suggests that what is being referred to here is the several layers of the one covenant with Moses. Rabbinic scholars outline three distinct stages within this covenant, Exodus 19:5-6, Deuteronomy 29-31 (at Moab) and Joshua 8:30-35 at Mount Gerizim and Ebal.

[23] See for example Romans 11:33-36, Ephesians 3:20-21 and 2 Thessalonians 2:16-17.

[24] See Robert Jewett p567-569, John Ziesler p238, David Stern p338, James Dunn p536 and Douglas Moo p566.

[25] Douglas Moo, *The Epistle to the Romans* (Grand Rapids: Eerdmans, 1996), p586.

[26] Ibid.

[27] David Stern, *Jewish New Testament commentary*, 6th edn (Clarksville: Jewish New Testament Publications, 1999), p388.

[28] Ibid.

[29] John Ziesler, *Paul's Letter to the Romans* (London: SCM Press, 1989), p239.

[30] James Dunn, *Word Biblical Commentary, Romans 9-16* (Dallas: Word Books, 1988), pp535-36.

[31] This is probably how the term *'proton'* is used in Rom 2:9, 2:10 and 3:2.

[32] See John Fieldsend, *Messianic Jews* (Crowborough: Monarch, 1993). This book contains a number of testimonies from Messianic Jewish believers in which their new faith in Jesus is seen to have resulted in a subsequent renewing, reaffirming or discovery of Jewish identity.

[33] See Tsvi Sadan, 'Keruv as guiding principle for proclamation of the Good News', (New York: *Borough Park Symposium Papers*, 2007).

[34] Walter Riggans, Ph.D. Thesis, *'Messianic Judaism and Jewish-Christian Relations: A case study in the field of religious identity'*, (University of Birmingham, 1991), p406.

[35] James Dunn, *Word Biblical Commentary, Romans 9-16* (Dallas: Word Books, 1988), p535.

[36] For an initial discussion see article by Susan Perlman, 'Coming Clean, Jewish or Christian?' See also article by Walter Riggans, 'The use of Jewish Symbols by Messianic Jews'. Articles in *Mishkan*, 19, (1993).

[37] See Dan Cohn-Sherbok, *Messianic Judaism* (London/New York: Cassell, 2000), pp169-171.

[38] Richard Harvey, 'Jesus the Messiah in Messianic Jewish Thought', *Mishkan*, 39, (2003), p13.

[39] Dwight Pryor, 'One God and Lord', *Mishkan*, 39, (2003), p53.

[40] Ibid., p54.

Chapter 6

[1] David Stern, *Jewish New Testament Commentary*, 6th edn (Clarksville: Jewish New Testament Publication, 1999), p389.

[2] Douglas Moo, *The Epistle to the Romans* (Grand Rapids: Eerdmans, 1996), pp568-69.

[3] For further study into this area see for example, D Bassinger (ed), *Predestination and Free Will* (Leicester: IVP, 1986).

[4] Anthony J Guerra, *Romans and the Apologetic Tradition* (Cambridge: Cambridge University Press: 1995), p148.

[5] Karl Barth, *Church Dogmatics, the Doctrine of God*, vol 2. Trans by G W Bromiley (Edinburgh: T and T Clark, 1957), pp25-26.

[6] Ibid., p259.

[7] Douglas Moo, *The Epistle to the Romans* (Grand Rapids: Eerdmans, 1996), p588.

[8] Dunn emphasises this point and while commenting on 9:7 states: "Israelites should not need reminding that the line of covenant promise is not the same as natural descent. They themselves would not claim that Ishmael (Abraham's son by Hagar) was within the covenant, despite his having been circumcised by Abraham (Gen17:23-27). So, clearly, the beneficiaries of the covenanted blessings (vv4-5), even on Jewish presuppositions, cannot be identified simply in terms of blood relationship and natural kinship". James Dunn, *Word Biblical Commentary, Romans 9-16* (Dallas: Word Book, 1988), p547.

[9] Robert Jewett, *Romans A Commentary* (Minneapolis: Fortress, 2007), p 575.

[10] In Romans chapter 2 Paul argues that Gentiles can show and have the positive response of Abraham. In contrast negatively Israel is not 'superior' to the Gentiles if they do not have the 'inner reality' of Abraham's qualities/ positive response to God.

[11] Jeremiah 18:6, Isaiah 29:16, 45:9 and 64:8.

[12] James Dunn, *Word Biblical Commentary, Romans 9-16* (Dallas: Word Books, 1988), p553.

[13] John Ziesler, *Paul's Letter to the Romans* (London: SCM Press, 1989), p241.

[14] David Stern, *Jewish New Testament Commentary*, 6th edn (Clarksville: Jewish New Testament Publications, 1999), p391.

[15] This majority who persist in rejecting and opposing the Gospel are seen as faced with God's judgment. See for example 1 Thessalonians 2:16. This judgment is both in the present but also has a future (eschatological) dimension.

[16] Maybe Peter also has this text in mind in 1 Peter 2:9-10?

[17] Joseph Shulam, *A Commentary on the Jewish Roots of Romans* (Baltimore: Lederer Books, 1997), p337.

[18] James Dunn, *Word Biblical Commentary, Romans 9-16* (Dallas; Word Books, 1988), p575.

[19] This line is argued for by Johannes Munck in his book, *Christ and Israel* (Minneapolis: Fortress Press, 1967).

[20] See for example Isaiah 49:22 in which the wider context is the restoration of Israel.

[21] See Romans 15:31, 2 Corinthians 8:1-5 and 9:13.

[22] John Lodge, *A Reader-Response Analysis* (University of South Florida: Scholars Press, 1996), p 97.

[23] John Ziesler, *Paul's letter to the Romans* (London: SCM Press, 1989), p239.

[24] A similar redefining could be seen to also be taking place within contemporary Rabbinic Judaism in terms of the "who is a Jew?" debate, with special reference to the issue of religious conversion/Israeli citizenship/identity.

[25] Ethnic Israel consists of all Jewish people (including Jewish believers in Jesus) through the line of Abraham/ Isaac.

[26] The church consists of all believers in Jesus both Jews and grafted in Gentiles

[27] Dispensational Theology is a method of interpreting history based on a complex deductive reading of prophetic biblical literature. It often divides history into seven eras and promotes a complete separation between the church and ethnic Israel. It is also wedded to a pre-millennial eschatology. Dispensation theology was initially developed by John Nelson Darby in the Nineteenth century. For a fuller exploration of Dispensational Theology, see Paul Richard Wilkinson, *For Zion's Sake* (Milton Keynes: Paternoster, 2007).

[28] My own hermeneutical principles outlined in this book, with its affirming of an inductive method of biblical application, lead me to reject Dispensational positions.

[29] James Dunn, *Word Biblical Commentary, Romans 9-16* (Dallas: Word Books, 1988), p539.

[30] Jewish believers in Jesus are fully part of both ethnic Israel and the church. These believers are to be identified as the remnant within Paul's theology outlined in Romans 9-11.

[31] David Stern, *Jewish New Testament Commentary*, 6th edn (Clarksville: Jewish New Testament Publications, 1999), p392.

[32] Harold Moore, 'A remnant chosen by grace', *Epworth Review*, 22, (1995), p98.

[33] James Dunn, 'The parting of the ways', *SCM Journal*, (1991), p248.

[34] It was in part on the basis of this Elijah remnant that Paul affirmed Jewish continuity both within the Christian community and ethnic Israel.

[35] This is the line of argument I will be developing within the development and promotion of Enlargement Theology.

Chapter 7

[1] See my specific text comments relating to 9:14 (for discussion on the nature of these questions/answers), within this thesis on p73.

[2] David Stern, *Jewish New Testament Commentary*, 6th edn (Clarksville: Jewish New Testament Publications, 1999), p393.

[3] Robert Jewett, *Romans A Commentary* (Minneapolis, Fortress,2007), p608.

[4] John A T Robinson, *Wrestling with Romans* (London: SCM Press, 1979), p110.

[5] John Ziesler, *Paul's Letter to the Romans* (London: SCM Press, 1989), p250.

[6] Ernst Käsemann, *Commentary on Romans*, 1st British edn. Trans by Geoffrey W Bromiley (London: SCM Press, 1980), p282.

[7] James Dunn, *Word Biblical Commentary Romans 9-16* (Dallas: Word Books, 1988), p581.

[8] Steve Motyer, *Israel in the plan of God* (Leicester: IVP, 1989), p88.

[9] Douglas Moo, *The Epistle to the Romans* (Grand Rapids: Eerdmans, 1996), p662.

[10] It is of interest to see how various commentators and translations use the lower case 'law' (R.S.V, N.I.V, R.E.B) while other use the capital case "Law". The CJB simply uses the term Torah consistently throughout Romans.

[11] C K Barrett, *From First Adam to Last* (London: A and C Black, 1962), p108.

[12] See my specific text comments relating to Romans 9:4 within this book at 5.3.

[13] David Stern, *Jewish New Testament Commentary*, 6th edn (Clarksville: Jewish New Testament Publications, 1999), p393.

[14] Joseph Shulam, *A Commentary on the Jewish Roots of Romans* (Baltimore: Lederer Books, 1997), pp338-339.

[15] John Ziesler, *Paul's Letter to the Romans* (London: SCM Press, 1989), p251.

[16] As argued by C K Barrett, *Essays on Paul* (London: SPCK, 1982), p144.

[17] Robert Jewett, *Romans A Commentary* (Minneapolis: Fortress, 2007), p 61.

[18] James Dunn, *Word Biblical Commentary, Romans 9-16* (Dallas: Word Books, 1988), p584.

[19] Acts 9:4-5, 22:7-8 and 26:9-16.

[20] 1 Corinthians 4:9-14.

[21] Romans 8:7-39.

[22] See chapter 6 of this book.

[23] Acts 22:3-4.

[24] 1 Corinthians 12:31, Acts 21:20 and 1 Peter 3:13.

[25] 2 Corinthians 12:20.

[26] Galatians 4:18.

[27] John Ziesler, *Paul's letter to the Romans* (London: SCM Press, 1989), p256.

[28] This is the preferred term for Jewett, Robert Jewett, *Romans A Commentary* (Minneapolis, Fortress, 2007), p619.

[29] In regard to Biblical references the Complete Jewish Bible which Stern uses as the key text uses Jewish terminology for example, MJ is Hebrews, 1 Ke is 1 Peter.

[30] David Stern, *Jewish New Testament Commentary*, 6th edn (Clarksville, Jewish New Testament Publications, 1999), p396.

[31] Anthony J Guerra, *Romans and the apologetic tradition* (Cambridge: Cambridge University Press, 1995), p151.

[32] W D Davies, *Torah in the Messianic Age* (Philadelphia: JLB Press, 1952).

[33] Joseph Shulam, *A Commentary on the Jewish Roots of Romans* (Baltimore: Lederer Books, 1997), p347.

[34] The Rabbinic term *'Kelal'* refers to the ultimate meaning or summary of the Torah.

[35] Karl Barth, *Church Dogmatics — The Doctrine of God*, vol 2. Trans by Geoffrey W Bromiley (Edinburgh: T and T Clark, 1957), p245.

[36] Good examples of this attempt to harmonise between the terminal and teleological interpretations are presented by V.P Furnish, *Theology and Ethics in Paul* (New York: Abingdon Press, 1968), pp161-163 and C K Barrett, *A Commentary on the Epistle to the Romans* (Philadelphia: A and C Black, 1957), pp 197-198.

[37] Matthew 5:17-20.

[38] Paul Minear, *The Obedience of Faith* (London: SCM Press, 1971), p77.

[39] Robert Badenas, *Christ the End of the Law* (Sheffield: JSOT Press, 1985), pp150-151.

[40] Acts 21:17-26.

[41] For a full discussion on this point see David Stern, *Jewish New Testament*

Commentary, 6th edn (Clarksville: Jewish New Testament Publications, 1999), pp397-400.

[42] Robert Jewett, *The Cambridge Companion to St Paul* (Cambridge: Cambridge University Press, 2003), p101.

[43] John Ziesler, *Paul's letter to the Romans* (London: SCM Press, 1989), p261.

[44] Robert Jewett, *Romans A Commentary* (Minneapolis, Fortress, 2007), p630.

[45] John Lodge, *Romans 9-11 A Reader-Response Analysis* (University of South Florida: Scholars Press, 1996), p120.

[46] Acts 16:3, 18:18 and 21:20-26.

[47] The debate about the precise implication of claiming that Jesus is 'Lord' is a major debate. Does such a statement explicitly affirm the deity of Jesus? Is it the same as saying Jesus is Yahweh/Adonai? See the quote from David Stern in my comments on 10:9. Also for a fuller discussion see the *Mishkan Journal*, 19, (2003), which contains three key articles on the issues around the divinity of Jesus by Richard Harvey, John Fischer and Dwight Pryor.

[48] Dan Cohn-Sherbok, *Messianic Judaism* (London/New York: Cassell, 2000) refers on p176 to David Stern's work *Messianic Jewish Manifesto* (Clarksville: Jewish New Testament Publications,1997) and helpfully outlines five Messianic Jewish approaches to keeping Torah . Also for a full analysis of Torah in theory and practice from a Messianic Jewish perspective see Richard Harvey, *'Mapping Messianic Jewish Theology'*, Ph.D. University of Wales, Lampeter, 2007) especially chapters 4 and 5.

[49] Harald Hegstad, 'The development of a Messianic Jewish Theology', *Mishkan*, 25, (1996), p69.

[50] See the teaching in Ephesians 2:11-22 and 4:1-6.

[51] An example of such a God fearing/righteous Gentile is Cornelius (Acts 10)

[52] In terms of punitive Replacement Theology such a view is not accepted. It was often deemed necessary for a Jew to renounce their Jewish identity and have it replaced by a 'new Christian identity'.

[53] Interestingly many Christian commentators have despite the teaching in 14:10, been sure that the weak refers to those Jewish believers who still show signs of Torah observance especially in terms of food laws. Clearly the text itself makes no such identification of who are the weak and who are the strong. Perhaps in terms of best pastoral practice we all need to realise that each individual Christian is probably able to identify with both groups in part at certain times and in certain areas of faith and practice.

Chapter 8

[1] John Ziesler, *Paul's letter to the Romans* (London: SCM, 1989), p264.

[2] Another example of such Pauline transferring and applying would be Philippians 2:10.

[3] David Stern, *Jewish New Testament Commentary*, 6th edn. (Clarksville: Jewish New Testament Publications, 1999), p402.

[4] Richard Bell, *The Irrevocable call of God* (Tubingen: Mohr Siebeck, 2005), p44.

[5] Karl Barth, *Church Dogmatics, The Doctrine of God*, vol 2. Trans by Geoffrey W.Bromiley (Edinburgh: T and T Clark, 1957), p252.

[6] Robert Jewett, *Romans A Commentary* (Minneapolis, Fortress, 2007),p 637.

[7] James Dunn, *Word Biblical Commentary, Romans 9-16* (Dallas: Word Books, 1988), p628.

[8] This sense of a large team of sent messengers all sharing the good news of Jesus as opportunities arose may have particular resonance for the congregation(s) in Rome. It is probable that the gospel 'took root' in Rome through a range of messengers, probably Jewish believers in Jesus, who took up residence in Rome or Jewish people originally from Rome who heard the gospel through contact with Jewish believers while on pilgrimage to and from Jerusalem (Acts 2:10) or in other ways. There is no indication of a focused apostolic mission directed to Rome before Paul's contact with an already established (before 48 CE—Acts 1:2) if somewhat fragmented and perhaps immature congregation(s).

[9] Joseph Shulam, *A Commentary on the Jewish Roots of Romans* (Baltimore: Lederer Books, 1997), p354.

[10] Joseph Shulam, *A commentary on the Jewish Roots of Romans* (Baltimore: Lederer Books, 1997), p356.

[11] Leslie Newbigin, *Christian Witness in a Plural Society* (London: British Council of Churches, 1977), p23.

[12] Many from the Messianic Jewish movement may suggest it would be more accurate to state that the 'Christian position affirms that of the Messianic Jewish movement'.

[13] One example of this is that for some Jewish people 'Christian evangelism' appears to be an expression of anti-Semitism. However, such charges of anti-Semitism can not stand if the evangelistic work is pioneered by people who seek to honour, maintain and strengthen their own Jewish identity.

[14] Blu Greenberg, *Mission, Witness and Proselytism* (University Press of America: 1990), p229.

[15] Susannah Heschel quoted in *A Mutual Witness*. C Williamson (ed), (London: Chalice Press, 1992), p45.

[16] Walter Riggans, *Yeshua Ben David* (Crowborough: Monarch, 1995), p11.

[17] It is worth noting that while Stan Telchin is a Messianic Jewish believer he is in many ways a strong critic of many aspects of the wider Messianic Jewish movement. See for example his recent book, *Messianic Judaism is not Christianity* (Grand Rapids: Chosen Books, 2004).

[18] Stan Telchin, *Abandoned* (London: Marshall Pickering, 1997), p175.

Chapter 9

[1] For example I have addressed the issue of Replacement Theology in comments made in relation to 9:1-5, 9:6, 9:32 and 10:14-21.

[2] Law (Rom 11:8 /Deut 29:4), prophets (Rom 11:8/Isaiah 29:10) and the writings (Rom 11:9-10/Psalm 69:22-23).

[3] John Ziesler, *Paul's letter to the Romans* (London: SCM Press, 1989), p269.

[4] James Dunn, *Word Biblical Commentary, Romans 9-16* (Dallas: Word Books, 1988), p645.

[5] Such a view presents Paul with the polar opposite problem than he was faced with earlier in his dealings with the church in Galatia caused by the predominance of Jewish (Messianic Jews?) Judaizers. However, in Galatia, Paul had the distinct advantage in writing to a community which he had established. In terms of the dating of Galatians and the circumstances of Paul's apostolic mission, I on balance would affirm the earlier South Galatian hypothesis rather than the later North Galatian hypothesis. For a fuller discussion on this hypothesis debate see Donald Guthrie, *New Testament Introduction, The Pauline Epistles* (London: Tyndale Press, 1961).

[6] John Ziesler, *Paul's letter to the Romans* (London: SCM Press, 1989), p26.

[7] James Dunn, *Word Biblical Commentary, Romans 9-16* (Dallas: Word Books, 1988), p644.

[8] Karl P. Donfried and P.Richardson (eds), *Judaism and Christianity in First- Century Rome* (Grand Rapids: Eerdmans, 1998), p122.

[9] The exact nature of this expulsion edict and the effects this had on relationships between non- messianic Jews, messianic Jews and Gentile believers in Jesus is helpfully discussed in *Judaism and Christianity in First Century Rome*, Karl P Donfrield and P Richardson (eds), (Grand Rapids: Eerdmans, 1998), see especially chapters 4, 5 and 8.

[10] Richard Hays, *Echoes of Scripture in Paul* (New Haven: Yale University Press, 1989), p67.

[11] See Romans 11:15 and 11:26. Paul also refers to his Jewish identity in a very positive way in 2 Corinthians 11:22 and Galatians 2:15. See also Paul's testimonies recorded by Luke (Acts 22:3-21, 23:1-8 and 26:1-29.)

[12] David Stern, *Jewish New Testament Commentary*, 6th edn (Clarksville: Jewish New Testament Publications, 1999), p404.

[13] Ibid.

[14] Robert Jewett, *Romans A Commentary* (Minneapolis, Fortress, 2007), p 653-654.

[15] 1 Samuel 9.

[16] Both John Ziesler, *Paul's letter to the Romans* (London: SCM Press, 1989), p270 and Douglas Moo, *Epistle to the Romans* (Grand Rapids: Eerdmans, 1996), pp676-677 suggest that Paul sees clear historical parallels between Elijah and himself (does Paul see himself as the Elijah of this 'eschatological age?') both in terms of faithful remnants and in terms of spiritual confrontation — Elijah's spiritual confrontation on Mount Carmel and Paul's ongoing and future confrontation with key Jewish leaders in Jerusalem and elsewhere.

[17] The focus on Abraham can have a spiritual focus as in Galatians 3:4 but here in Rom 11:1 the emphasis is primarily upon the promise of physical/ethnic descent.

[18] Acts 22:3, 23:6, 26:5, Galatians 1:13-14, 2 Corinthians 11:22 and Romans 9:4.

[19] James Dunn, *Word Biblical Commentary, Romans 9-16* (Dallas: Word Books, 1988), p644.

[20] John Ziesler, *Paul's letter to the Romans* (London: SCM Press, 1989), p269.

[21] James Dunn, *Word Biblical Commentary, Romans 9-16* (Dallas: Word Books, 1988), p637.

[22] The number 7000 can not be deduced from the Elijah story in 1 Kings. Clearly the number seven (and multiples of seven) has some symbolic significance pointing to themes of completeness and perfection. Such completion and perfection may well underpin the term 'all Israel' which Paul later uses in 11:26.

[23] The emphasis on grace with it's fourfold use in verses 5-6, seems to exclude any narrow or limited understanding of the breadth of response within Israel (and beyond).

[24] Richard Bell, *Israel and the irrevocable Call of God* (Tubingen: Mohr Siebeck, 2005), p273.

[25] Ben Witherington, *Paul's Narrative Thought World* (Louisville: Westminster/John Knox Press, 1994), pp67-68.

[26] David Stern, *Jewish New Testament Commentary*, 6th edn (Clarksville: Jewish New Testament Publications, 1999), p405.

[27] As used in the New International Version.

[28] David Stern, *Jewish New Testament Commentary*, 6th edn (Clarksville: Jewish New Testament Publications, 1999), p406.

[29] With this term there may be for Paul an intended citation to the heart of stone (Ezekiel 36:26) with the promise of Israel's future restoration and renewal linked with the outpouring of God's Spirit and the removal of the hardness that covers the heart.

[30] See W Sanday and A Headlam, *The Epistle to the Romans* (Edinburgh: T and T Clark, 1902), p315.

[31] See Paul's teaching in 1 Corinthians 10.

[32] While I believe Stern is right in general terms in commenting on the 'table' issue, I think it would be fair to say that this line of reasoning has come about not just from interpreting the text, but it also has connections with some of the pressing pastoral tensions of shared (Messianic and Non Messianic) Jewish community life. Such 'pastoral tensions' Stern and many of his contemporary Messianic Jewish friends would be personally aware of.

[33] David Stern, *Jewish New Testament Commentary*, 6th edn (Clarksville: Jewish New Testament Publications, 1999), p406.

[34] Babylonian Talmud (London: Sonico Press, 1936), Talmud (Tractate Pirkei Avot 5.19). It is stated 'Whoever possesses these three things, he is of the disciples of Abraham our father . . . : a good eye, a humble spirit and a lowly soul'. Although the Talmud was compiled later (edited around 200 CE) than Paul's time, it seems reasonable to suggest at the very least that there is a striking similarity between some of Paul's teaching and some of the Talmud. This points to the view that Paul (and other Rabbinic students/teachers) would be familiar with much of the oral law of Jewish tradition which later went through a process of containing, selecting and codifying within the Talmud.

[35] Baruch Maoz, 'Jewish-Christian Paradigms in Israel', *Mishkan*, 29, (1998), pp18-19.

Chapter 10

[1] Paul Minear, *The Obedience of Faith* (London: SCM Press, 1971), pp79-80.

[2] Ibid.

[3] This pattern of teaching is also found elsewhere in Romans, see for example 2:17.

[4] 11:17-24 is the only section in Romans 9-11 that Paul draws largely from a metaphor from the natural world rather than a biblical text.

[5] Robert Jewell, *Romans A Commentary* (Minneapolis: Fortress, 2007),p 693.

[6] Babylonian Talmud (London: Soncino Press, 1936) Tractate, Menahot 53 b, Kodashim. Also cited by Joseph Shulam, *A Commentary on the Jewish Roots of Romans* (Baltimore: Lederer Books, 1997), p373.

[7] Ernst Käsemann, *Commentary on Romans*,1st British edn. Trans by Geoffrey W Bromiley (London: SCM Press, 1980), p304.

[8] John Lodge, *Romans 9-11, A Reader-Response Analysis* (University of South Florida: Scholars Press, 1996), p193.

[9] David Stern, *Jewish New Testament Commentary*, 6th edn (Clarksville: Jewish New Testament Publications, 1999), p406.

[10] The term 'how much more' has echoes with the teaching of Jesus recorded in Luke 11:13. In Luke 11 Jesus is teaching about prayer and the goodness of the Father in giving good gifts (the fullness of the Holy Spirit) to his children, while Paul here is focusing on the Father's goodness to his children (Israel) again which will involve the outpouring of God's gifts/blessings. While it is impossible to know if Paul was aware of the wording in Luke 11:13 (this raises a range of issues about the source material/dating of Luke's Gospel etc) it appears that Paul is 'in step' with the same sense of expectation as Jesus was in regard of the purposes of God as worked out within the emerging Kingdom of God fuelled by the out pouring of the Holy Spirit.

[11] In terms of 'to make Israel envious' (v12 and v14) it is not exactly clear what Paul has in mind. It seems probable that Paul is hoping that the transformation of Gentiles away from living 'pagan lives' to living 'holy lives' may stimulate Jewish interest in the power of the gospel. Equally it may have connections with the hope outlined in Isaiah 2:2f, namely that in the final generation Gentiles would come to Zion in service and worship. Maybe, Paul believed that his fellow Jews would see this happening now through the mission of the largely Gentile church and through such actions as the collection/offering he was to bring from largely Gentile believers to Jerusalem. This collection/offering was clearly of great significance for Paul as he refers to it in every letter written during his third missionary journey and in referring to it is clear that this collection/ offering has for Paul 'spiritual ramifications' as well as simply being a pragmatic act of charity.

[12] Every single Jew or every single Jew of a specific generation, or simply the majority of Jews?

[13] John Lodge, *Romans 9-11, A Reader-Response Analysis* (University of South Florida: Scholars Press, 1996), p170.

[14] Timothy Butlin, *'A Prophet in search of a Prophecy'*, (M.Theol dissertation, University of Wales, 2005), pp57-58.

[15] In Acts 18:6-7 for example Paul clearly, for a time following Jewish opposition, focuses his mission work upon Gentiles. However, this is only for a limited period for later Paul is once again involved in active mission to the Jewish people, as shown in Acts 18:19 and 19:8 . At times of oppositions as in Corinth (Acts 18:6) it seems wise to Paul to move away from those who refuse to listen. This is in keeping with the tradition of the Jewish prophets (Ezekiel 18:16-19). It seems to me to be shallow and false to argue on the basis of Acts 18:6 that Paul no longer saw the importance of Jewish mission.

[16] James Dunn, *Word Biblical Commentary, Romans 9-16* (Dallas: Word Books, 1988), p669.

[17] For a good overview of the main lines of argument see the following, Douglas Moo, *The Epistle to the Romans* (Grand Rapids: Eerdmans,

1996), pp694-696. David Stern, *Jewish New Testament Commentary*, 6th edn (Clarksville: Jewish New Testament Publications, 1999), pp 411-412. John Ziesler, *Paul's Letter to the Romans* (London: SCM Press, 1989), p276.

[18] David Stern, *Jewish New Testament Commentary*, 6th edn (Clarksville: Jewish New Testament Publications, 1999), p411.

[19] Douglas Moo, *The Epistle to the Romans* (Grand Rapids: Eerdmans, 1996), p694.

[20] This preference is to do in part with the eschatological/apocalyptic context of these verses and reminds us of the eschatological context for Paul's evangelistic ministry and soteriological understandings.

[21] David Stern, *Jewish New Testament Commentary*, 6th edn (Clarksville: Jewish New Testament Publications, 1999), p412.

[22] Joseph Shulam, *A Commentary on the Jewish Roots of Romans* (Baltimore: Lederer Books, 1997), p371.

[23] In regard to the use of these metaphors, see James Dunn, *Word Biblical Commentary, Romans 9-16*. (Dallas: Word Books, 1988), p672. Dunn makes the point that these metaphors are 'complimentary rather than synonymous'.

[24] David Stern, *Jewish New Testament Commentary*, 6th edn (Clarksville: Jewish New Testament Publication, 1999), p413.

[25] John Ziesler, *Paul's Letter to the Romans* (London: SCM Press, 1989), p277.

[26] David Stern, *Jewish New Testament Commentary*, 6th edn (Clarksville: Jewish New Testament Publications,1999), p413 suggests that the identification by the early Church Fathers gained currency within the early church with it's growing Replacement Theology because "of it's tendency to want to deprive the Jews of their place as God's people, the root and firstfruits of faith".

[27] Karl Barth, *Church Dogmatics, the Doctrine of God*, vol 2. Trans by Geoffrey W Bromiley (Edinburgh: T and T Clark, 1957), p286.

[28] Within this honouring of the Gentiles there is a sense that the olive shoots which have been and will be grafted in help to reinvigorate the host tree.

[29] See my specific text comments on 11:26 in this book on p160ff.

[30] William S Campbell, *Paul and the Creation of Christian Identity* (London/New York,T and T Clark, 2006), p105.

[31] See Romans 3:27 and the teaching in Rom 12-15 which emphasises key qualities and attitudes such as humility and sober judgment (12:3), honouring one another (12:10), submission (13:1), acceptance (14:1,:10,:13, :22 and 15:7) and unity (15:5) All such activities and attitudes rule out any sense of boasting or arrogance.

[32] The term kindness is more than just an emotion of God. It connects with God's fundamental purposes—Dwight Pryor in his teaching tapes (Published by Centre for Judaic-Christian Studies — www.jcstudies.com)

uses the term 'covenantal faithfulness' in place of 'kindness'.

[33] James Dunn, *Word Biblical Commentary, Romans 9-16* (Dallas: Word Books, 1988), p674.

[34] Ibid., p675.

[35] John Lodge, *Romans 9-11: A Reader-Response Analysis* (University of South Florida: Scholars Press, 1996), pp189-190.

[36] Romans 12:4-6 and Eph 2:11-3:6.

[37] See Acts 15 and 1 Peter 2:4-10.

[38] Daniel Boyarin promotes a radical contemporary Jewish Rabbinic position so he may well not be representative of many within contemporary Rabbinic Judaism. However, his argument which I outline here is one which I believe is shared (with some nuances) by many contemporary Rabbinic Jews and I chose to refer to it as I think the argument helpfully focuses in on key issues dealing with the identity of 'God's people.'

[39] See Daniel Boyarin, *A Radical Jew* (University of California Press, 1994), pp201-206.

[40] The issue of the allegorization of Israel and the Jew is a theme which Boyarin develops subsequently in *A Radical Jew*. See pp209-14 with reference both to the dialogue between Justin Martyr and Trypho and later in the writings of Bultmann, Käsemann and Hamerton-Kelly.

[41] Boyarin refers to the position he sees in John's Gospel where he understands God has rejected the Jews tout court.

[42] Daniel Boyarin, A Radical Jew (University of California Press, 1994), p203.

[43] Boyarin affirms E P Sanders understanding is right in one sense that the only flaw Paul finds in Jews is that they are not Christian. However, Boyarin contrasts himself with E P Sanders understanding in as much as Boyarin sees that not being a Christian is far more than 'an arbitrary, Christological or purely formalistic disqualification'. Daniel Boyarin, *A Radical Jew* (University of California Press: 1994), p206.

[44] Ibid.

[45] Daniel Boyarin, *A Radical Jew* (University of California Press, 1994), p203.

[46] Ibid.

[47] Ibid., p204.

[48] Ibid., p203.

[49] This 'positive view' of Jewish religious life often finds expression through what can best be described by the umbrella term as "Jewish roots teaching". This teaching seeks to honour and draw out insights from Jewish faith and life and to apply such insights into the wider life of the church. Such insights would include developing a Hebraic mindset rather than a Greek dominated mindset, the celebration of biblical feasts, the valuing of Sabbath, Jewish liturgy/music etc. The pursuit of

Jewish roots teaching clearly raises issue around what is culturally and contextually appropriate. For further study into Jewish roots teaching, see the following: Chuck and Karen Cohen, *Roots of our Faith.* (Jerusalem: CFI Publishing, 2002), David Stern, *Restoring the Jewishness of the Gospel* (Clarksville: Jewish New Testament Publications, 1998) and Marvin Wilson, *Our Father Abraham* (Grand Rapids: Eerdmans, 1989).
[50] Daniel Boyarin, *A Radical Jew* (University of California Press, 1994), p205.

Chapter 11

[1] For the church in Rome the first step in this redemptive plan for the world is to fully open themselves up to the Spanish mission. See Robert Jewett, *Romans A Commentary* (Minneapolis: Fortress, 2007), p 723.

[2] John Ziesler, *Paul's Letter to the Romans* (London: SCM Press, 1989), p283.

[3] Rowan Williams, *Archbishop of Canterbury CEFACS lecture* delivered 3.11.2004.

[4] The term appears 20 times, once more in Romans (16:25). For some additional examples see 1 Corinthians 4:1, Ephesians 3:3, Colossians 1:26 and 2 Thessalonians 2:7.

[5] Karl Barth, *The Epistle to the Romans*, 6th edn. Trans by Edwyn Hoskyns (Oxford: Oxford University Press,1933), p413.

[6] C E B Cranfield, *The International Critical Commentary, Romans*, vol 2 (London T and T Clark: 2004 reprint), p573.

[7] John Ziesler, *Paul's letter to the Romans* (London: SCM Press, 1989) p283.

[8] James Dunn, *Word Biblical Commentary, Romans 9-16* (Dallas: Word Books, 1988), pp 690-691.

[9] Rom 10:9-13.

[10] David Stern, *Jewish New Testament Commentary*, 6th edn (Clarksville: Jewish New Testament Publications, 1999), p418.

[11] Dan Juster, *Jewish Roots* (Shippensburg: Destiny Image, 1995), p103.

[12] In this scenario there is the teaching that is in the forefront of much Messianic Jewish thinking and Christian Zionism that the restoration of the State of Israel creates a new spiritual climate which will hasten the redemptive purposes of God towards 'all Israel'. For a flavour of this teaching, see Hal Lindsay, *The Late Great Planet Earth* (London: Lakeland, 1970) and Lance Lambert, *The Battle for Israel* (Eastbourne: Kingsway, 1975). Most of this type of teaching would, in terms of an eschatological framework see the nearness of the return of Christ within a pre-Millennium and largely (but probably not exclusively) dispensationalist framework.

[13] It is difficult to speculate on how this could have worked out, but perhaps

the most obvious way this may have worked out in the ministry of Paul is helpfully outlined by Dan Juster who states: "What if instead of a minority, the majority of Jews had accepted ? . . . Imagine the pressure for the Judaizing viewpoint from three to five million Jews "all zealous for the law" (Acts 21). This would have had a huge barrier to the Gospel among the gentiles who were not called to be a part of the nation Israel. Now we see the sense of Paul's words; but once the purpose of hardening has been accomplished, "how much more will their full inclusion mean". Jewish rejection also caused an intensified effort in preaching to non-Jews". Dan Juster, *Jewish Roots* (Shippensburg: Destiny Image, 1995), p101.

[14] Pieter W Van der Horst, 'A short note on the meaning of kai houtos' *Journal of Biblical Literature*, No.3 (2000), pp 521-525.

[15] James Dunn, *Word Biblical Commentary, Romans 9-16* (Dallas: Word Books, 1988), p681.

[16] David Stern, *Jewish New Testament Commentary*, 6th edn (Clarksville: Jewish New Testament Publications, 1999), p418.

[17] David Stern, *Jewish New Testament Commentary*, 6th edn (Clarksville: Jewish New Testament Publications, 1999), p421.

[18] William S Campbell, *Paul and the Creation of Christian Identity* (London/New York, T and T Clark, 2006), p 123.

[19] This is the view of Robert Jewett. See *Romans A Commentary* (Minneapolis: Fortress Press, 2007), p702.

[20] The Babylonian Talmud (London: Soncino Press, 1935) Tractate Sanhedrin, Nezekin 10.

[21] David Stern, *Jewish New Testament Commentary*, 6th edn (Clarksville: Jewish New Testament Publications,1999), pp.421-423.

[22] C E B Cranfield, *The International Critical Commentary, Romans* vol 2 (London: T and T Clark 1979 (2004 reprint), pp576-577.

[23] James Dunn, *Word Biblical Commentary, Romans 9-16* (Dallas: Word Books, 1998), pp681-683.

[24] Douglas Moo, *The Epistle to the Romans* (Grand Rapids: Eerdmans, 1996), pp 720-721. However, Moo also shows some support for the second position based in part of Paul's use of Israel in Rom 9:6 and the fact that the issue in 11:26 is not focusing on the fact that all Israel will be saved but on the manner in which Israel will be saved.

[25] John Ziesler, *Paul's letter to the Romans* (London: SCM Press, 1989), p285. However, Ziesler refuses to be drawn between the third and fourth position and states; "All we can say is that the argument requires that historical Israel as a whole will come in".

[26] James Boice, *Romans 9-11* (Grand Rapids: Baker Books, 1993), pp1375-1389.

[27] Robert Jewett, *Romans A Commentary* (Minneapolis, Fortress Press, 2007), p704.

28 David Stern is not drawn in his commentary to speculate about the

timing of this salvation apart from saying the time is now. It would appear that Stern would favour the position taken by Dwight Pryor (see his teaching audio tapes — 'Paul-Jewish Apostle to the Roman World,' Produced by The Centre for Judaic-Christian Studies) who argues that Paul expected to see the saving of all Israel (National entity) within his own ministry period. For Paul the deliverer has already come to Zion and is now going from Zion in the apostolic mission of the church. On balance Pryor sees reference to 'the deliverer will come' not as a reference to the Parousia but to the ongoing mission of the church which Paul is spearheading. Firstly with his planned mission with the church in Rome and then on to Spain. Pryor would see that Paul is not focussing on a future event for the future is already here for Paul. Pryor speaks of "the holy now" hence the present tense of 11:5 and 11:31. On a pastoral and hermeneutical note one obvious issue with Pryor's position is that if Paul had this expectation clearly it was not fulfilled. If so was he mistaken? If yes then can Paul be relied upon in other matters? As far as I know Pryor does not deal with this concern yet clearly he has a very high view of the perspicuity, authority and reliability of scripture.

[29] C E B Cranfield, *The International Critical Commentary, Romans*, vol 2 (London: T and T Clark 2004 Reprint), p577.

[30] K Stendahl, *Paul among Jew and Gentiles* (London: SCM Press, 1977).

[31] John Ziesler, *Paul's letter to the Romans* (London: SCM Press, 1989), p285.

[32] For a fuller exploration of this eschatological framework see two very different approaches. Stephen Sizer, *Christian Zionism* (Leicester: IVP, 2004), pp183-205, and Arnold G Fruchtenbaum, *Israelology* (Tustin: Ariel Ministries,1996), pp766-819.

[33] James Dunn, *Word Biblical Commentary, Romans 9-16* (Dallas: Word Books, 1998), p692.

[34] Karl Barth, *The Epistle to the Romans* 6th edn, trans by Edwyn Hoskyns (Oxford: Oxford University Press, 1993 (1968 Reprint 24), p417.

[35] See Rom 11:34-35.

[36] This engaging with imperfection and incompletion is not something which is easy to accept in emerging religious communities and certainly it not something which systematic theologians relish. This point is made by William S Campbell, *Paul and the Creation of Christian Identity* (London/New York, T and T Clark, 2006), p172.

[37] John Ziesler, *Paul's letter to the Romans* (London: SCM Press, 1989), p288.

[38] Ernst Käsemann, *Commentary on Romans*. 1st British edition. Trans by Geoffrey W Bromiley (London: SCM Press, 1980), p320.

[39] Perhaps outlined as a song or for some other form of liturgical response? Note also the concluding amen which would invite a congregation response and/or a response from Paul's readers/listeners.

[40] It has been suggested that Paul may have used or adapted a hymn from the synagogue. Douglas Moo draws attention to the understanding that wisdom concepts are seen in verses 34 and 35 and traces of a Hellenistic Jewish tradition in verse 36. See Douglas Moo, *The Epistle to the Romans* (Grand Rapids: Eerdmans, 1996), p740.

[41] There is a general consensus that Paul is citing Job 41:3, however the textual differences are not insignificant and therefore some caution is prudent. See Robert Jewett, *Romans A Commentary* (Minneapolis. Fortress, 2007), p 720.

[42] Steve Motyer, *Israel in the plan of God* (Leicester: IVP, 1989), p162.

[43] David Stern, *Jewish New Testament Commentary*, 6th edn (Clarksville: Jewish New Testament Publications, 1999), p423.

[44] Stephen Sizer, *Christian Zionism* (Leicester: IVP, 2004), p200.

[45] See the quote from James Dunn in chapter 4 above.

[46] See the discussion on Romans 11:26, pp160ff.

[47] See the discussion on Romans 9:4 in chapter 5 above, and 11:25 in this at 11.2 above.

[48] This is the line of argument presented by David Stern in his interpretation of Israel in Rom 9:4

[49] See Rom 9:6.

[50] For a fuller discussion on this see David Stern, *Jewish New Testament Commentary*, 6th edn (Clarksville: Jewish New Testament Publications, 1999), pp574-575.

[51] See for example Romans 10:12, Ephesians 4:5, Philippians 2:9-11 and Colossians 1:15-20.

[52] See above, including 5.3, 7.3, 11.3, 9.3.

[53] See the paper by Michael Rydelnik entitled 'The Jewish People and Salvation', presented at the Messianic Jewish Leaders, Borough Park Symposium, 2007.

[54] See 5.3.

[55] See discussion at 10.3.

[56] See for example Paul's teaching in Galatians 3.

[57] In terms of naming this community, the term εκκλησιαι is, in the vast majority of translations, simply rendered as church. Yet as stated in the very beginning of this thesis (p1) the issue of terminology within Jewish-Christian relations is of extreme importance as issues of identity are being explored, tested and defined. For example, within the Complete Jewish Bible translation the term church is not used but rather congregation or (Messianic) community is used. For some within Messianic Judaism the term church has an explicit Gentile feel, so the term is avoided and terms such as synagogue or perhaps more 'neutral terms' such as fellowship, assembly or community are used. I personally find no problem with using the term church as long as it is clear that the term church includes both

Jew and Gentile in Christ but often in Messianic Jewish circles I prefer to use the term Body of Christ/Messiah. It may also be of interest that in Romans the term 'εκκλησιαι' does not appear apart from the greetings in chapter 16:5 and :16.

[58] The New International Version of the text has 77 question marks within the text.

[59] The precise identification of the weak and the strong is open to debate. Often the weak in traditional Christian thinking is seen as the Torah observing Jewish believers in Jesus, while M.D Nanos, *The Mystery of Romans* (Minneapolis: Fortress Press, 1986), identifies the weak as non-believing Jews, while A Andrew Das, *Paul and the Jews* (Peabody: Hendrickson, 2003) argues for identifying the weak as non-Torah observant Gentile Christians. I think in general this view of Das would be the prevailing view within Messianic Jewish interpretation but not within the wider church community.

Chapter 12

[1] As stated earlier in this book I have presented the case for Enlargement Theology in contrast with two significant theological approaches namely Replacement Theology and Two-Covenant Theology. However, I am aware that many Christians do not perceive themselves as belonging to either of these main groupings. As this book now considers a model for encounter and engagement I am not advocating that the only alternative to either Replacement Theology or Two Covenant Theology is my presentation of Enlargement Theology for I know there are other approaches and nuanced positions especially as one reflects upon complex and controversial issues such as, religious identity, evangelistic mission to Jewish people and Israel and the land. However in choosing to present the case for Enlargement Theology in contrast to Replacement Theology and Two Covenant Theology I would argue that a fundamental and coherent framework is being established which will help holders of a range of theological approaches to reflect upon and refine their own varied and nuanced positions.

[2] For further study into the development of Messianic Jewish Theology, see the following, Arnold Fruchtenbaum, 'The Quest for a Messianic Theology', *Mishkan*, 2, (1985),1-16. Russell Resnik, *The Root and the Branches* (Albuquerque: Adat Yeshua, 1997). David Stern, *Restoring the Jewishness of the Gospel* (Clarksville: Jewish New Testament Publications, 1988). Daniel Juster, *Growing to Maturity* (Albuquerque: UMJC, 1982). Kai Kjaer-Hansen (ed), *Jewish Identity and Faith in Jesus* (Jerusalem: Caspari Center, 1996). Mark Kinzer, *Post-Missionary Messianic Judaism* (London/New York: Brazos Press, 2005). Dan Cohn-Sherbok, *Messianic Judaism* (London/New York: Cassell, 2000). Richard

Harvey, Ph.D. thesis, 'Mapping Messianic Jewish Theology', (Lampeter: University of Wales, 2007).

[3] This faithfulness to the Bible is taken to mean following a broad evangelical hermeneutic, yet one which seeks to uphold and draw from the Hebraic contours of the New Testament and the backdrop of First century Jewish faith and life. See Arnold Fruchentbaum, 'The Quest for a Messianic Theology', *Mishkan*, 2, (1985), pp1-17 and *Mishkan* 3, (1985), pp67-68. Also refer back to my hermeneutical values and methodology in exploring Romans 9-11, in chapter 4 above.

[4] See the comments on Rom 9:14- 29 by John Lodge, *Romans 9-11, A Reader-Response Analysis* (University of South Florida: Scholars Press, 1996), p84.

[5] Key prophets in this context would include Zechariah (14:1-11) Malachi (Ch 4) Ezekiel (Ch 36) and Jeremiah (31:31-34).

[6] In terms of Messianic Jewish thinking, the return of Jesus is often linked to a pre-Millennial framework. While there is a vast range of views and much speculation about the return of Jesus in Christian Theology, what is always clearly taught is that the return of Jesus is exactly what is said, namely the return of Jesus. This is the return of the same Jesus who was crucified, resurrected and ascended. Nowhere in Christian Theology is credence given to the view expounded in some Rabbinic Jewish circles of two different and chronologically separate Messiahs. For a Messianic Jewish perspective on 'two Messiahs', see Dan Juster, *Jewish Roots* (Shippensburg: Destiny Image Publishers, 1995), pp178-179.

[7] I understand that many people drawn to Enlargement Theology may well also hold to a pre-Millennial eschatological timetable (see note 6). Yet such a view is not explicit to my understanding and promotion of Enlargement Theology. This reluctance to be drawn into a particular eschatological doctrinal position for Enlargement Theology is partly because Enlargement Theology is not attempting to be a complete systematic theology but rather is hoping to be seen as an 'umbrella term' under which many can gather in order to focus creatively on the church's relationship with Israel, Jewish people and the emerging Messianic Jewish movement.

[8] A good biblical picture of this faithfulness is from the prophet Hosea, who uses the image of God's love being like that of a parent to a child. This love, as Hosea states, may well be frustrated by ignorance or disobedience of the child (Israel) yet the parental love holds fast, even when (perhaps especially when) such love is not acknowledged by the child (Hosea 11:1-4). This love however does not, as Hosea makes clear (Hosea 12:1-13:16), condone Israel's sin, so judgment will come but such judgment is to bring about ultimately Israel's restoration, not replacement or destruction (Hosea 14).

[9] See for discussion on the use of Israel as a symbol of church, Mark

Reasoner, *Romans in full circle* (Kentucky: John Knox Press, 2005), p127.

[10] N T Wright, *The Climax of the Covenant* (Edinburgh: T and T Clark, 1991), p250.

[11] This is in disagreement with E P Sanders who sees that the restoration of Israel is still a future event. Seeing the restoration of Israel as a future event is the position of Enlargement Theology and in most readings of Messianic Jewish Theology. A part of this future restoration may be glimpsed in the restoring of Israel as a State. Yet full restoration for Enlargement Theology waits for the eschatological event of the deliverer coming from Zion (Romans 11:26).

[12] See the discussion relating to both the legitimacy and the importance of evangelistic mission activity amongst Jewish people, at 12.4 below.

[13] This insight about differing contexts is one made powerfully by supporters of Two Covenant Theology. See Franz Rosenzweig, *The Star of Redemption* (London: Routledge and Kegan Paul, 1971). For the supporters of Two Covenant Theology, such differing contexts lead in part to the understanding that there must be different entry criteria for Jews and Gentiles into two differing (yet related) covenants. Such understandings are refuted by holders of Enlargement Theology.

[14] See texts such as 1 Corinthians 12:2 and 1 Thessalonians 1:9. However, this linking of Gentiles with paganism needs to be qualified through the understanding that some Gentiles followed faithfully the Noahide laws and some were seen as God fearers and some became full Jewish proselytes.

[15] Romans 11:17-24.

[16] This view of the ethnicity of Israel needs to be seen with the caveat that historic Israel was enriched by non-Jews becoming part of Israel. For example, as shown in the story of the Moab Ruth.

[17] I am happy to use the term church to describe this community and I do so elsewhere in this Thesis yet I am aware, as with so many issues within the Messianic Jewish/Rabbinic Jewish/Christian encounters, terminology is used in a manipulative way and terminology is therefore strongly disputed. So at this stage of introducing core convictions of Enlargement Theology I prefer to use a somewhat open-ended term, namely 'Communities of Jewish and Gentile believers in Jesus'. For some within the contemporary Messianic Jewish movement and those within the Rabbinic community the term church can simply mean Gentile Christians. To avoid this false assumption, David Stern, throughout his New Testament translation, uses the term 'messianic community' or 'congregation' rather than the term 'church'.

[18] Romans 11:25-26 and :36.

[19] Revelation 21:12 and :24.

[20] William S Campbell, *Paul and the Creation of Christian Identity* (London/New York, T and T Clark, 2006), pp138-139.

[21] John Kelly, Ph.D. thesis, 'Gotteslehre and Israellehre in the theology of Jurgen Moltmann' (University of Sheffield, 1995), p58.

[22] John Kelly, Ph.D. thesis, 'Gotteslehre and Israellehre in the theology of Jurgen Moltmann'. (University of Sheffield, 1995), p324.

[23] See above 12.1A

[24] See Alex Jacob, 'Root and Branch? Exploring relationship models between the Messianic Jewish Movement and the wider Church community,' *Olive Press Quarterly*, 6, (2007).

[25] David Stern, *Jewish New Testament Commentary*, 6th edn (Clarksville: Jewish New Testament Publications, 1999), p415.

[26] Ibid., p416.

[27] Karl Barth, *Church Dogmatics, the Doctrine of God*, vol 2. Trans by Geoffrey W Bromiley (Edinburgh: T and T Clark, 1957), p200.

[28] This conversation took place in August 1966 in Basel and is recorded by Michael Wyschogrod in *Abraham's Promise: Judaism and Christian Relations*. R. Kendall Soulen (ed), (Grand Rapids: Eerdmans, 2004), p211.

[29] George Hunsinger (ed), *For the sake of the World* (Grand Rapids: Eerdmans 2004), p117.

[30] These dispensations are not from Barth's reasoning as Christian dispensational theology upholds, namely that dispensations are separated in time with one dispensation succeeding/replacing the other.

[31] Karl Barth, *Church Dogmatics, the Doctrine of God*, vol 2. Trans by Geoffrey W Bromiley (Edinburgh: T and T Clark, 1957), p200.

[32] Ibid., p271.

[33] Karl Barth, *Against the Stream*. Trans by Geoffrey W Bromiley (New York: Philosophical Library Press, 1954), p200.

[34] I am aware for example, that for some from a multi-faith /pluralist agenda may take my metaphor as affirming their argument of different religions having the same 'source', flowing within different tributaries and finally coming together in one multi-faceted point of completion. This line of argument is an abuse of my intention within the exploration of Enlargement Theology. For a useful exploration of the multi-faith agenda see, Peter Sammons, *The Empty Promise of Godism* (Saffron Walden: Glory to Glory Publications, 2009).

[35] I found Douglas Moo helpful here in regard to his understanding that the church not Israel is now the locus of God's work in the world. Douglas Moo, *The Epistle to the Romans* (Grand Rapids: Eerdmans, 1998), p709.

[36] Peter von der Osten-Sacken, *Christian-Jewish Dialogue* (Philadelphia: Fortress Press, 1986).

[37] Ibid., p105.

[38] It seems that at one point this was the expectation of Peter von der Osten-Sacken. See *Christian-Jewish Dialogue* (Philadelphia: Fortress Press, 1986), p72.

[39] Peter von der Osten-Sacken, *Christian-Jewish Dialogue* (Philadelphia: Fortress Press, 1986), p17 and p75.

[40] Ibid., p73.

[41] Peter van der Osten-Sacken, *Christian-Jewish Dialogue* (Philadelphia: Fortress Press, 1986), p72.

[42] See N T Wright, *The Climax of the Covenant* (Edinburgh: T and T Clark, 1991), pp 234-238.

[43] Anthony Guerra, *Romans and the apologetic tradition* (Cambridge: Cambridge University Press, 1995), p156.

[44] In the very early period there was some opposition to mission beyond the Jewish community. It is not until Acts 10 that the first baptism of a non-Jew takes place. The implication of this leads to the council of Jerusalem (Acts 15) and beyond into the wider predominantly Gentile mission context.

[45] Richard Bell, *Provoked to Jealousy* (Tubingen: Mohr Siebeck, 1994), p356.

[46] See Richard Bell, *The Irrevocable call of God* (Tubingen: Mohr Siebeck, 2005), pp376-386.

[47] See *The New Strong's Exhaustive Concordance of the Bible* (Nashville: Thomas Nelson Publishers, 1995), pp807-817. In some of these occasions the promise is linked to spiritual restoration, some may have been partly or completely fulfilled in the period of return under Cyrus (Nehemiah/Ezra) but most are not in this context. Some of the promises are conditional but most are not. Some may be interpreted allegorically but a literal interpretation seems in the vast number of occasions the most appropriate hermeneutical method.

[48] 1 Corinthians 3:16, 2 Corinthians 6:16, Hebrews 7:24 and Romans 15:16.

[49] There is a vast range of literature exploring the Israel-Palestine conflict, It is beyond the scope of this thesis to review this material but the following works I have found to provide a good introduction: Benny Morris, *One State, Two States* (New Haven: Yale University Press, 2009). Gary M Burge, *Whose Land? Whose Promise?* (Exeter, Paternoster Press, 2003). Colin Chapman, *Whose Promised Land* (Oxford, Lion, 1992).

[50] Within Enlargement Theology these three understandings fit together within what I am promoting as a coherent mission approach. I would understand that this approach is a correct development of Paul's covenantal teaching summed up in Romans 15:8. This promise of the land is never revoked from this teaching. However, other theological approaches would not want to link these three understandings together. For example, one approach may want to uphold the importance of evangelistic mission to Jewish people while not upholding the significance of the land. This view is strongly advocated by Stephen Sizer. See Stephen Sizer, *Zion's Christian Soldiers* (Liecester: IVP, 2007), pp95-96.Clearly there are

numerous variations of approach drawing from Replacement Theology, Two Covenant Theology and other theological resources within the field of Jewish-Christian relations. This issue of the land and the understanding of Messianic Jewish identity are probably the initial areas of divergence.

Chapter 13

[1] See the following; James Charlesworth (ed), *Jews and Christians* (New York: Crossroads, 1990). Jacob Neusner, *Jews and Christians* (London: SCM Press, 1991). Jacob Neusner, *Telling Tales* (Louisville: Westminster/John Knox Press, 1993). A James Rudin and Marvin Wilson (eds), *A Time to Speak* (Grand Rapids: Eerdmans, 1987). Gerald Sigal, *The Jew and the Christian Missionary* (New York: Ktav publishing, 1981). Marcus Braybrooke, *A Time to Meet* (London: SCM Press, 1990). Marcus Braybrooke and Tony Bayfield (eds), *Dialogue with a Difference* (London: SCM Press, 1992). Samuel Silver, *Exploring Judaism to Jews and Christians* (New York: Acro Publishing, 1973). Helga Croner and L Klenicki (eds)., *Issues in the Jewish-Christian Dialogue* (New York: Paulist Press, 1979). L Klenicki and P .Neuhaus, *Believing Today* (Grand Rapids: Eerdmans, 1989). Geoffrey Wigoder, *Jewish-Christian Relations since the Second World War* (Manchester: Manchester University Press, 1988).

[2] D. Dawe and A.Fule (eds), *Christians and Jews Together* (Louisville: Presbyterian Publishing House, 1991).

[3] Carl Braaten and Robert Jenson (eds), *Jews and Christians: People of God* (Grand Rapids/Cambridge: Eerdmans, 2003).

[4] Don Finto, *Your People Shall be My People* (Ventura: Regal Books, 2001).

[5] Peter Von der Osten-Sacken, *Christian-Jewish Dialogue* (Philadelphia: Fortress Press, 1986).

[6] See Carl Kinbor, 'Missing factors in Jewish Christian dialogue', *Princeton Theological Review*, (1980).

[7] See the following five articles in the Journal of Ecumenical Studies. Robert Hann, 'The undivided Way', 14, (1977). Hans Küng and Pinchas Lapide, 'Is Jesus a bond or a Barrier?' 14, (1977). Isaac Rottenberg, 'Jewish-Christian Dialogue', 29, (1992). Isaac Rottenberg, 'Thank you, Rabbi Neusner but No thank you', 30, (1993). Francine Samuelson, 'Messianic Judaism, Church, Denomination, Sect or Cult?' 3, (2000).

[8] See the article by Jacob Jocz, 'The Jewish-Christian Dialogue: A Theological Assessment', and the article by Oskar Skarsaune, 'The Jewish-Christian Dialogue in Ancient and Modern Times: A survey of recent literature', articles in *Mishkan*, 3, (1985).

[9] Wolfhart Pannenberg in *Jews and Christians People of God*. Carl Braaten and Robert Jenson (eds), (Grand Rapids/Cambridge: Eerdmans, 2003), p.185.

[10] Walter Riggans, 'Messianic Judaism and Jewish-Christian Relations: A case study in the field of Religious identity'. Ph.D. thesis (University of Birmingham, 1991), p406.

[11] This insistence by some within the Jewish community not to engage with Messianic Jews within the wider process of Jewish-Christian relations raises a significant dilemma for many Christians who want to honour and affirm the role of Messianic Jews. By accepting the terms of engagement proposed, this will inevitably result in the undermining the value and integrity of Messianic Jews within the wider Christian community. However insisting on their inclusion may well result in the collapse of dialogue and fellowship with the majority of Jewish groups at the present time.

[12] Mitch Glaser, 'Authentic dialogue between Messianic and Non-Messianic Jews', *Mishkan*, 36, (2002).

[13] Ibid., p91.

[14] Carol Harris-Shapiro, *Messianic Judaism: A Rabbi's Journey through Religious Change in America* (Boston: Beacon Press, 1999).

[15] Daniel Cohn-Sherbok, *Messianic Judaism* (London/New York: Cassell, 2000).

[16] Ibid., p213.

[17] David Novak, *Jewish-Christian Dialogue* (Oxford: Oxford University Press, 1989), p22.

[18] This issue of identity and recognising key differences is carefully explored by the following Rabbi Jonathan Sacks, *The dignity of difference* (London: Continuum Press, 2003). William S Campbell, *Paul and the Creation of Christian Identity* (London/NewYork, T and T Clark, 2006). Kai Kjaer-Hansen (ed), *Jewish Identity and Faith in Jesus* (Jerusalem: Caspari Center for Biblical and Jewish Studies, 1996).

[19] Hans Ucko, *Common Roots—New Horizons* (Geneva: WCC Publications, 1994), pp9-10.

[20] The New Testament material which I have focused on has been Romans 9-11, yet this new perspective from Messianic Jewish insights is not simply limited to one segment of the biblical text but has significance in other areas. For example, gaining insight into 'the Jewishness of Jesus' and the subsequent interpretation and application of the gospel narratives and wider aspects of NT texts, including the NT use (or abuse?) of OT texts.

[21] For example, areas relating to Jewish identity such as keeping the Sabbath, keeping Kashrut and general support for and identification with Israel. All these areas have much which could stimulate engagement within contemporary Jewish-Christian relations.

[22] The classic paradigm sees the parting of Christianity and Rabbinic Judaism as a clear-cut division, probably almost completed by the early second century. However some scholars challenge this understanding, see for example, A Becker and A Reed (eds), *The ways that never parted*

(Tubingen, Mohr Siebeck, 2003). See also the initial historical and theological overview of Jewish-Christian relations in chapter 1 above.

[23] Oskar Skarsaune and Reidar Hvalvik, *Jewish Believers in Jesus* (Massachusetts: Hendrickson Publishers, 2007) p8.

[24] Romans 11:26.

[25] Romans 11:32-36.

Bibliography

Austin-Sparks Stephen 'The Way of Life', *Kesher*, 16, (2003), 'The People and the Land of Israel, Retained or Replaced?' (M.Th. thesis, Spurgeon's College, 2006).

Badenas Robert *Christ the End of the Law* (Sheffield: ISOT Press, 1985).

Balfour Glenn 'Is John's Gospel Anti-Semitic?' *Tyndale Bulletin*, 48, (1997).

Barkley J *So all Israel shall be saved* (Barking: Messianic Testimony, 1971).

Barnard L W 'The Early Roman Church, Judaism and Jewish-Christianity' *Anglican Theological Review*, 49, (1967).

Barrett C K *The Epistle to the Romans* (London: A and C Black, 1957). — *From First Adam to Last* (London: A and C Black, 1962). — *Essays on Paul* (London: SPCK, 1982).

Barth Karl *The Epistle to the Romans*, 6th edn trans. by Edwyn C Hoskyns (Oxford: Oxford University Press, 1933).

— *Against the Stream*, trans. by Geoffrey W Bromiley (New York: Philosophical Library Press, 1954).

— *Church Dogmatics, the Doctrine of God*, vol 2 trans. by Geoffrey W Bromiley (Edinburgh: T and T Clark, 1957).

Barth M 'The People of God', *Journal for the Study of the New Testament* (1983).

Baum Gregory *The Jews and the Gospel* (London: Bloomsbury Publishing, 1961).

Baumann H. Arnulf 'The Two Ways/Two Covenants Theory', *Mishkan*, 11, (1980).

Basinger David (ed), *Predestination and Free Will* (Leicester: IVP, 1988).

Becker A and Reed A (eds), *The ways that never parted* (Tubingen: Mohr Siebeck, 2003).

Beker J C *Heirs of Paul* (Minneapolis: Fortress, 1991).

Bell Richard *Provoked to Jealousy* (Tubingen: Mohr Siebeck, 1994). — *The Irrevocable Call of God* (Tubingen: Mohr Siebeck, 2005).

Berger D 'Jewish-Christian Relations: a Jewish perspective', *Journal of Ecumenical Studies*, 21, (1983).

251

Berger D and Wyschograd M *Jews and Jewish Christianity* (New York: Seabury Press, 1978).

Berkhof Louis *Systematic Theology* (London: Banner of Truth, 1966).

Bockmuehl Markus *Jewish Law in Gentile Churches* (Edinburgh: T and T Clark, 2000).

Boccaccini Gabrielle *Middle Judaism* (Minneapolis: Fortress Press, 1991).

Boice M James *Romans 9–11* (Grand Rapids: Baker Books, 1993).

Benhayim Menachem 'Jewish Survival and its significance for the Church', *Mishkan*, 4, (1986).

—'Between Church and Synagogue', *Tishrei*, 2, (1994).

Bowler G Maurice 'Rosenzweig on Judaism and Christianity', *Mishkan*, 11, (1989).

Boyarin Daniel *A Radical Jew* (University of California Press, 1994).

—*Dying for God* (Stanford: Stanford University Press, 1999).

—*Border Lines* (Philadelphia: University of Pennsylvania Press, 2004).

Braaten C and Jenson D (eds), *Jews and Christians: People of God* (Grand Rapids/Cambridge: Eerdmans, 2003).

Braybrooke Marcus *A Time to Meet* (London: SCM Press, 1990).

—*Children of One God* (London: SCM Press, 1991).

Braybrooke M and Bayfield T (eds), *Dialogue with a Difference* (London: SCM Press, 1992).

Brown L Michael 'Messianic Judaism and Jewish Jesus Research', *Mishkan*, 33 (2000).

Bruce F F *The Epistle to the Romans* (London: Tyndale Press, 1963).

—*Apostle of the Heart Set Free* (Exeter: Paternoster Press, 1984).

Buber Martin *Two Types of Faith* (London: Macmillan, 1951). — *Pointing the Way* (London: Harper, 1963).

—*Israel and the World* (New York: Schocken, 1963).

Burge Gary M *Whose Land? Whose Promise?* (Exeter: Paternoster Press, 2003).

Butlin Timothy 'A Prophet in search of a Prophecy', (M.Theol, University of Wales, 2005).

Campbell William S *Paul and the Creation of Christian Identity* (London/New York: T and T Clark, 2006).

Carson D O'Brien P and Seifrid M (eds), *Justification and Variegated Nomism* (Tubingen: Mohr Siebeck, 2004).

Chapman Colin *Whose Promised Land?* (Oxford: Lion, 1992).

—'One Land, Two Peoples-How many States?' *Mishkan*, 26, (1997).

Charlesworth H James (ed), *Jews and Christians* (New York: Crossroads Publishing, 1990).

Cohen Arthur Alan *The Natural and Supernatural Jew* (New York: Pantheon Books, 1962).

—*Tremendum* (New York, Crossroad Publishing, 1988).

Cohen M and Croner H (eds), *Christian Mission-Jewish Mission* (New York: Paulist Press, 1982).

Cohn-Sherbok Dan 'Don Cupitt and Judaism', *Theology*, 726, (1985).

—*Messianic Judaism* (London/New York: Cassell, 2000).

Conybeare F C *Dialogue of Athanasius and Zacchaeus and Timothy and Aquila* (London/Oxford: Society of Biblical Literature, 1898).

Cooper H and Morrison P *A Sense of Belonging* (London: Weidenfeld and Nicolson, 1991).

Cracknell Kenneth *Towards a New Relationship* (London: Epworth, 1986).

Cranfield C E B *The International Critical Commentary, Romans*, vol 2 (London/New York: T and T Clark, 1975).

— *Romans—A shorter commentary* (Edinburgh: T and T Clark, 1985.

Crombie Kelvin *For the Love of Zion* (London: Hodder and Stoughton, 1991).

—'Early Christian Zionists', *Mishkan*, 26, (1997).

— *Restoring Israel* (Jerusalem: Nicolayson's Ltd, 2008).

Croner Helga *Stepping Stones to Further Jewish-Christian Relations* (London/New York: Stimulus Books, 1977).

Croner H and Klenicki L (eds), *Issues in the Jewish-Christian Dialogue* (New York: Paulist Press, 1979).

Danielou J *The Theology of Jewish Christianity* (London: Darton, Longman and Todd, 1964).

Das A Andrew *Paul and the Jews* (Peabody: Hendrickson, 2003).

Davies A *The Gospel and the Land* (University of California Press, 1974).

—*Anti-Semitism and the Foundations of Christianity* (New York: Paulist Press, 1979).

Davies W D *Paul and Rabbinic Judaism* (London: SPCK, 1948). — *Torah in the Messianic Age* (Philadelphia: JLB Press, 1952).

Dawe D and Fule A (eds), *Christians and Jews Together* (Louisville: Presbyterian Publishing House, 1991).

Dixon Murray *Israel, Land of God's Promise* (Lancaster: Sovereign World, 1988).

Dodd C H *The Meaning of Paul for Today* (London: Collins, 1958).

Donfrield P Karl and Richardson Peter (eds), *Judaism and Christianity in First-Century Rome* (Grand Rapids: Eerdmans, 1998).

Dorff E 'The Covenant', *Anglican Theological Review*, 64, (1982).

Downey Amy Karen *Paul's Conundrum* (Oregon: Wipf and Stock, 2011).

Drane J *Paul: Libertine or Legalist* (London: SPCK, 1975).

Dunn D G James *Christianity in the Making* (Vol 2) – *Beginning from Jerusalem* (Cambridge: Eerdmans, 2009).

— *Word Biblical Commentary – Romans 9 – 16* (Dallas: Word Books, 1998).

— *The Parting of the Ways* (London: SCM Press, 1991).

— (ed) *The Cambridge Companion to St Paul* (Cambridge: Cambridge University Press, 2003).

Eckardt A Roy *Elder and Younger Brothers* (New York: Charles Scribner's and Sons, 1967).

Efroymson D Fisher E and Klencki L (eds), *Within Context* (Minnesota: Liturgical Press, 1993).

Elgvin Torleif 'The Theology of Messianic Jewish Worship', *Mishkan*, 29, (1998).

— 'The Church and Israel – Dialogue and Witness', *Mishkan*, 36, (2002).

Feher S *Passing over Easter* (Walnut Creek: Altamira Press, 1998).

Fieldsend John *Messianic Jews* (Tunbridge Wells: Monarch, 1993).

Finto D *Your People shall be My People* (Ventura, California: Regal Books, 2001).

Fischer John 'Yeshua: The Deity Debate', *Mishkan*, 39, (2003).

Flanery H Edward *The Anguish of the Jews* (New York: Paulist Press, 1985).

Ford David 'A Messiah for the Third Millennium', *Modern Theology*, 16, (2000).

Fruchtenbaum G Arnold 'The Quest for a Messianic Theology', *Mishkan*, 2, (1985).

— *Israelology* (Tustin: Ariel Ministries, 1996).

— 'The use of the Siddur by Messianic Jews', *Mishkan*, 25, 1996).

Fry Helen *Christian–Jewish Dialogue* (Exeter: University of Exeter, 1996).

Furnish V P *Theology and Ethics in Paul* (New York: Abingdon Press, 1968).

Glaser Mitch 'Critique of the Two Covenant Theory', *Mishkan*, 11, (1989).

— 'Authentic dialogue between Messianic and Non-Messianic Jews', *Mishkan*, 11, (2006).

Glatzer N *Franz Rosenzweig – His life and Thought* (New York: Schocken, 1961).

—*Great Twentieth Century Jewish Philosophers* (New York: Schocken, 1985).

Goble P 'Messianic Judaism: A Biblical Apologetic with a view to Liturgical Reform', (Ph.D. thesis, Fuller Theological Seminary, 1975).

—*Everything you need to know to grow a Messianic Yeshiva* (South Pasadena, CA: William Carey Library, 1981).

Goldingay John *Models for Interpretation of Scripture* (Grand Rapids: Eerdmans, 1995).

Greenberg Blu *Mission, Witness and Proselytism* (University Press of America, 1990).

Guerra J Anthony *Romans and the Apologetic Tradition* (Cambridge: Cambridge University Press, 1995).

Gundry N Stanley and Goldberg Louis (eds), *How Jewish is Christianity?* (Grand Rapids: Zondervan, 2003).

Guthrie Donald *New Testament Introduction: The Pauline Epistles* (London: Tyndale Press, 1961).

Guy H A *The Acts of the Apostles* (London, Macmillan, 1952).

Haley W John *Alleged Discrepancies of the Bible* (Grand Rapids: Baker Books, 1977).

Hann R 'The Undivided Way', *Journal of Ecumenical Studies*, 14, (1977).

Harris-Shapiro C *Messianic Judaism: A Rabbi's Journey through Religious Change in America* (Boston: Beacon Press, 1999).

Harvey Richard 'Jesus the Messiah in Messianic Thought', *Mishkan*, 39, (2003).

—'Mapping Messianic Jewish Theology', (Ph.D. thesis, University of Wales, 2007).

—*Mapping Messianic Jewish Theology— A Constructive Approach* (Milton Keynes: Paternoster Press, 2009).

Hays B Richard *Echoes of Scripture in the letters of Paul* (Yale University Press, 1989).

Hegstad Harald 'The Development of a Messianic Jewish Theology', *Mishkan*, 25, (1996).

Hender Don *The Nation of Israel* (Bournemouth: Pearl Publishing, 2001).

Hendriksen W *New Testament Commentary*, Romans (Edinburgh: Banner of Truth, 1981).

Hilton Michael *The Christian Effect on Jewish Life* (London: SCM Press, 1994).

Hocken Peter *The Glory and the Shame* (Guildford: Eagle Press, 1994).

— *The Marranos – A History in Need of Healing, Towards Jerusalem 2*, booklet series No.3, (2006).

Holgate David and Starr Rachel *Biblical Hermeneutics* (London: SCM Press, 2006).

Holwerda E David *Jesus and Israel: One Covenant or Two?* (Grand Rapids: Eerdmans, 1995).

Horrell David *An Introduction to the Study of Paul* (London/New York: Continuum, 2000).

Hulse Erroll *The Restoration of Israel* (Worthing: H Walter Press, 1968).

Hunsinger George (ed) *For the sake of the World* (Grand Rapids: Eerdmans, 2004).

Issac Jules *Jesus and Israel* (New York: Rinehart and Winston, 1971).

Jacob Alex 'Root and Branch?' Exploring Relationship Models between the Messianic Jewish Movement and the Wider Church community', *Olive Press Quarterly*, 6 (2007).

— A Promise Keeping God. Exploring the Covenants, Israel and the Church, *Olive Press Quarterly*, 7 (2010).

Jocz Jacob *The Jewish People and Jesus Christ* (London: SPCK, 1949).

— *The Jewish People and Jesus Christ after Auschwitz* (Grand Rapids: Baker Books, 1981).

— 'The Jewish-Christian Dialogue: A Theological Assessment', *Mishkan*, 3, (1985).

Jeffers James S *Conflict at Rome: Social Order and Hierarchy in Early Christianity* (Minneapolis: Fortress, 1991).

Jewett Robert *The Cambridge Companion to St Paul* (Cambridge: Cambridge University Press, 2003).

Romans – A Commentary (Minneapolis: Fortress, 2006).

Juster Dan *Growing to Maturity* (Albuquerque: UMJC Press, 1982).

— *Jewish Roots* (Rockville: Davar Publishing, 1986).

Kaiser Walter *Towards an Old Testament Theology* (Grand Rapids: Baker Books, 1978).

Kasdan B *God's Appointed Customs* (Baltimore: Lederer Publications, 1996).

Käsemann Ernst *Commentary on Romans*, 1st British edn, trans by Geoffrey W Bromiley (London: SCM Press, 1980).

Kelly John 'Gotteslehre and Israellehre in the Theology of Jurgen Moltmann', (Ph.D. thesis, University of Sheffield, 1995).

Kinbor C 'Missing factors in Jewish Christian Dialogue', *Princeton Theological Review*, (1980).

Kinzer S Mark *The Nature of Messianic Judaism* (Pasadena: Hashivenu Archives, 2001).

— *Post-Missionary Messianic Judaism* (Grand Rapids: Baker Academic, Brazos Press, 2005).

Kjaer-Hansen K (ed), *Jewish Identity and Faith in Jesus* (Jerusalem: Caspari Centre for Biblical and Jewish Studies,1996).

Klenicki L and Neuhaus P *Believing Today* (Grand Rapids: Eerdmans, 1989).

Krentz E *The Historical-Critical Method* (Philadelphia: Fortress Press, 1975).

Küng H and Lapide P 'Is Jesus a bond or a barrier?' *Jewish Christian Dialogue*, 14, (1977).

Lalleman Hetty *Celebrating the Law?* (Milton Keynes: Paternoster Press, 2004).

Lapide P and Stuhlmacher P *Paul, Rabbi and Apostle* (Minneapolis: Augsburg Publishing House, 1984).

LaTourette K *A History of Christianity* (London: Eyre and Spottiswoode, 1964).

Lee B *The Galilean Jewishness of Jesus* (New York: Stimulus/Paulist Press, 1988).

Lindsay M *Barth, Israel and Jesus* (Aldershot: Ashgate, 2007).

Lipson I *The Greatest Commandment* (Clarksville: Lederer Books, 2007).

Loden Lisa 'The development of Songs and Music within the Messianic Jewish Community', *Mishkan*, 29, (1998).

Lodge J *Romans 9–11, A Reader-Response Analysis* (University of South Florida: Scholars Press, 1996).

Longenecker N Richard *The Christology of Early Jewish Christianity* (Grand Rapids: Eerdmans, 1975).

— *Paul: The Apostle of Liberty* (Grand Rapids: Eerdmans, 1976).

Lundin Roger Thiselton C Anthony and Walhout Clarence *The Responsibility of Hermeneutics* (Grand Rapids: Eerdmans, 1985).

McKnight S *A New Vision for Israel* (Grand Rapids: Eerdmans, 1999).

Merton Thomas *A Vow of Conversation* (New York: Farrer, Straus and Giroux, 1988).

Miller D 'Messianic Judaism and the Theology of the Land', *Mishkan*, 26, (1997).

Minear Paul *The Obedience of Faith* (London: SCM Press, 1971).

Moaz Baruch 'Jewish-Christian Paradigms in Israel', *Mishkan*, 29, (1998).

— *Judaism is not Jewish* (Ross-shire: Christian Focus Publications, 2003).

Moo Douglas *The Epistle to the Romans* (Grand Rapids: Eerdmans, 1996).

Moore H 'A Remnant Chosen by Grace', *Epworth Review*, 22, (1985)

Moore James 'The Passion of the Christ—A Protestant Perspective', *Shofar*, 23, (2005).

Morris Benny *One State, Two States* (New Haven: Yale University Press, 2009).

Morris L *The Epistle to the Romans* (Leicester: IVP, 1988).

Motyer Steve *Israel in the Plan of God* (Leicester: IVP, 1989).

—*Your Father the Devil* (Exeter: Paternoster Press, 1997).

Munck Johannes *Christ and Israel* (Minneapolis: Fortress Press, 1956).

Nanos M D *The Mystery of Romans* (Minneapolis: Fortress Press, 1996).

Nerel Gershon 'Creeds among Jewish Believers in Yeshua', *Mishkan*, 34, (2001).

Neusner Jacob *Judaism in the matrix of Christianity* (Philadelphia: Fortress Press, 1986).

—*Telling Tales* (Louisville: Westminster/John Knox Press, 1993).

—*Jews and Christians: The Myth of a Common Tradition* (Binghamton: Global Academic Publishing, 2001).

Newbigin Lesslie *Truth to Tell* (London: SPCK, 1991).

—*Christian Witness in a Plural Society* (London: British Council of Churches, 1997).

Novak David *Jewish-Christian Dialogue* (Oxford: Oxford University Press, 1989).

—*The Election of Israel* (Cambridge: Cambridge University Press, 1995).

—*Talking with Christians* (Grand Rapids: Eerdmans, 2005).

Oeming Manfred *Contemporary Biblical Hermeneutics*, trans by Joachim Vette (Aldershot: Ashgate Publishing, 2006).

Osborne R Grant *The Hermeneutical Spiral* (Downers Grove: IVP Academic, 2006).

Pannenberg Wolfhart *Systematic Theology*, vol 3 (Grand Rapids: Eerdmans, 1998).

Parkes James *A History of the Jewish People* (London: Pelican, 1964).

Pawson David *Defending Christian Zionism* (Terra Nova, 2008).

— *Israel in the New Testament* (Terra Nova, 2010).

Piper J *Let the Nations be Glad* (Grand Rapids: Baker Books, 1993).

Ponsonby Simon *And The Lamb Wins* (Colorado Springs: David Cook Press, 2008).

Pryor Dwight 'One God and Lord', *Mishkan*, 39, (2003).

Rashkover Randi *Revelation and Theopolitics: Barth, Rosenzweig and the politics of Praise* (London: T and T Clark, 2005).

Rausch David *Messianic Judaism* (New York/Toronto: Edward Mellon Press, 1982).

Reason G 'Competing Trends in Messianic Judaism', *Kesher*, 17, (2004).

Reasoner Mark *The Strong and the Weak in Romans 14:1−15:13 in Context* (Cambridge: Cambridge University Press, 1999).

—*Romans in Full Circle* (Kentucky: John Knox Press, 2005).

Reith G *Justin Martyr -Dialogue with Trypho* (Edinburgh: Ante-Nicene Christian Library, 1897).

Resnik Russell *The Root and the Branches* (Albuquerque: Adat Yeshua, 1997).

—'Defining Messianic Judaism', *Kesher*, 16, (2003).

Reuther R *Faith and Fratricide* (New York: Seabury Press, 1974).

Riggans, Walter. 'Messianic Judaism and Jewish-Christian Relations: A case study in the field of religious identity', (Ph.D. thesis, University of Birmingham, 1991).

—'Image and Reality', *Mishkan*, 19, (1993).

—*Yeshua Ben David* (Crowborough: Monarch, 1995).

Robinson J A T *Wrestling with Romans* (London: SCM Press, 1979).

Robinson Richard 'My Yiddishe Paul', *Mishkan*, 20, (1994).

Rosen Ceil and Rosen Moishe *Christ in the Passover* (Chicago: Moody Press, 1978).

Rosenzweig Franz *The Star of Redemption* (London: Routledge and Kegan Paul, 1971) [first published in Frankfurt, 1921].

Rottenberg Isaac 'Thank You Rabbi Neusner, but No Thank You', *Christian-Jewish Dialogue*, 30, (1993).

Rowland Christopher *Christian Origins* (London: SPCK, 1985).

Rudin A J and Wilson M (eds), *A Time to Speak* (Grand Rapids: Eerdmans, 1987).

Rudolph David 'Yeshua and the Dietary Laws', *Kesher*, 16, (2003).

Sacks Jonathan *Crisis and Covenant* (Manchester: Manchester University Press, 1992).

—*Faith in the Future* (London: Darton, Longman and Todd, 1995).

—*The Dignity of Difference* (London: Continuum Press, 2002).

Sadan Tzvi 'The Place of the Siddur in the Messianic Community', *Mishkan*, 25, (1996).

Sammons Peter *The Empty Promise of Godism* (Saffron Walden: Glory to Glory Publications, 2009).

Samuelson F 'Messianic Judaism, Church, Denomination, Sect or Cult?', *Jewish-Christian Dialogue*, 37, (2000).

Sanday W and Headlam A *The Epistle to the Romans* (Edinburgh: T and T Clark, 1907).

Sanders E P *Paul and Palestinian Judaism* (London: SCM Press, 1977).

—*Paul, the Law and the Jewish People* (Philadelphia: Fortress Press 1983).

—*Jesus and Judaism* (London: SCM Press, 1985).

—*Jewish Law from Jesus to the Mishnah* (London; SCM Press, 1990).

—*Paul* (Oxford: Oxford University Press, 1991).

Santala Risto *Paul, The Man and The Teacher* (Jerusalem: Keren Ahvah Meshihit, 1995).

Saperstein Marc *Moments of Crisis in Jewish-Christian Relations* (London: SCM Press, 1989).

Schoeps Hans Joachim *The Jewish-Christian Argument* (London: Faber, 1963).

Schonfield H *The History of Jewish Christianity* (London: Duckworth, 1936).

Schreckenberg H *The Jews in Christian Art* (London: SCM Press, 1996).

Schwarzchild S 'Rosenzweig on Judaism and Christianity', *Journal of Conservative Judaism*, (1956).

Segal Alan *Rebecca's Children* (Harvard University Press, 1986).

—*Paul the Convert* (Yale University Press, 1990).

Sigal G *The Jew and the Christian Missionary* (New York: Ktav Publishing, 1981).

Silver S *Exploring Judaism to Jews and Christians* (New York: Acro Publishing, 1973).

Shanks H (ed), *Christianity and Rabbinic Judaism* (London: SPCK, 1993).

Shulam Joseph with Hilary LeCornu *A Commentary on the Jewish Roots of Romans* (Baltimore: Lederer Books, 1997).

Simon Marcel *Verus Israel* (London: Littman Press, 1996).

Sizer Stephen *Christian Zionism* (Leicester: IVP, 2004).

—*Zion's Christian Soldiers?* (Leicester: IVP, 2007).

Skarsaune Oskar 'The Jewish-Christian Dialogue in Ancient and Modern Times: A survey of recent literature', *Mishkan*, 3, (1985).

—'Jewish Believers in Jesus', *Mishkan*, 35, (2001).

Skarsaune Oskar and Hvalvik Reidar (eds), *Jewish Believers in Jesus—The Early Centuries* (Massachusetts: Hendrickson Publishers, 2007).

Snell Adrian *City of Peace* (Crowborough: Monarch, 1996).

Snodgrass Klyne *Between Two Truths* (Grand Rapids: Zondervan, 1990).

Soulen R Kendall *The God of Israel and Christian Theology* (Minneapolis: Fortress Press, 1996).

—(ed), *Abraham's Promise: Jewish and Christian Relations* (Grand Rapids: Eerdmans, 2004).

Stendahl K *Paul among Jew and Gentile* (London: SCM Press, 1977).

Stern H David *Messianic Jewish Manifesto* (Clarksville: Jewish New Testament Publications, 1997).

—*The Complete Jewish Bible* (Clarksville/Jerusalem: Jewish New Testament Publications, 1998).

—*Jewish New Testament Commentary*, 6th edn (Clarksville: Jewish New Testament Publications, 1999).

Stott R W John *The Message of Acts* (Leicester: IVP, 1990).

Tate W Randolph *Biblical Interpretation*, 3rd edn (Peabody: Hendrickson, 2008).

Taubes Jacob 'Argument and Doctrine', *Jewish Publications Society Journal*, (1970).

Telchin Stan *Abandoned* (London: Marshall Pickering, 1997).

—*Messianic Judaism is not Christianity* (Grand Rapids: Baker/ Chosen Books, 2004).

Torrance W David (ed), *The Witness of the Jews to God* (Edinburgh: Handsel Press, 1982).

—'Two Covenant Theology', *Mishkan*, 11, (1989).

Torrance F Thomas *The Mediation of Christ* (Colorado Springs: Helmers and Howard, 1992).

Ucko Hans *Common Roots, New Horizons* (Geneva: WCC Publications, 1994).

Urbach C 'Issues for clarification in the self-defining statement', *Kesher*, 16, (2003).

Van Bruan P *Discerning the Way* (New York: Seabury Press, 1980).

—*A Christian Theology of the People of Israel* (New York: Seabury Press, 1983).

—*A Theology of the Jewish Christian Reality* (San Francisco: Harper and Row, 1988).

Van der Horst Pieter *Hellenism–Judaism–Christianity*, 2nd edn (Leuven:Peeters Press, 1998).

—'A short note on the meaning of *kai houtos*', *Journal of Biblical Literature*, No.3 (2000).

Van Landingham C *Judgment and Justification in Early Judaism and the Apostle Paul* (Peabody: Hendrickson, 2006).

Vermes Geza *Jesus the Jew* (London: SCM Press, 1994).

Vermes P *Buber* (London: Weidenfeld and Nicolson, 1988).

Von der Osten-Sacken Peter *Christian-Jewish Dialogue* (Philadelphia: Fortress Press, 1986).

Vos Geerhardus *Biblical Theology* (Edinburgh: Banner of Truth, 1975).

Walker P W L (ed), *Jerusalem Past and Present in the Purposes of God* (Carlisle: Paternoster, 1994).

Walters J C *Ethnic Issues in Paul's Letter to the Romans* (Valley Forge, PA: Trinity Press International, 1993).

Westerholm S *Israel's Law and the Church's Faith* (Grand Rapids: Eerdmans, 1988).

— *Perspectives Old and New on Paul* (Grand Rapids: Eerdmans, 2004).

White David *Replacement Theology* (London: Christian Friends of Israel Communications, 1997).

Wigoder G *Jewish-Christian Relations since the Second World War* (Manchester: Manchester University Press, 1988).

Wilken L Robert *The Land Called Holy* (New York: Yale University Press, 1992).

Wilkinson Richard Paul *For Zion's Sake* (Milton Keynes: Paternoster, 2007).

Williams D 'The Sabbath-Mark of Distinction', *Themelios*, 14, (1989).

Williamson C (ed), *A Mutual Witness* (London: Chalice, 1992).

Wilson R Marvin *Our Father Abraham* (Grand Rapids: Eerdmans, 1989).

Withington Ben *Paul's Narrative Thought World* (Louisville: Westminster/John Knox Press, 1994).

Wright N T *The Climax of the Covenant* (Edinburgh: T and T Clark, 1991).

— *The New Testament and the People of God* (Minneapolis: Fortress, 1992).

— *The Resurrection of the Son of God* (London: SPCK, 2003).

Wyschogrod Michael *The Body of Faith* (Northvale: Jason Aronson, 1996).

Young H Brad *Jesus the Jewish Theologian* (Peabody: Hendrickson, 1995).

Younghughes B *Christian Jewish Heritage* (East Wittering: Angel Press, 1988).

Ziesler John *Paul's Letter to the Romans* (London: SCM Press, 1989).

Main biblical text used was the New International Version (London, Sydney and Auckland: Hodder and Stoughton, 1973). See full acknowledgement on copyright page.

The following journals and conference papers were also used as resource and research materials:

1) Themelios. Published by the Religious and Theological Studies Fellowship. Leicester. UK.

2) Mishkan. Published by the United Christian Council in Israel. Jerusalem, Israel.

3) Tishrei. Published by Dr Clifford Denton, Swansea, UK.

4) Kesher. Published by the Union of Messianic Jewish Congregations, Albuquerque, USA.

5) Journal of Ecumenical Studies. Published by Temple University, Philadelphia, USA.

6) Princeton Theological Review. Published by the Theological Students Fellowship, Princeton, USA.

7) Journal of Jewish Studies. Published by the Oxford Centre for Hebrew and Jewish Studies, Oxford, UK.

8) Journal of Biblical Literature. Published by the Society of Biblical Literature, Atlanta, USA.

9) Evangelical Review of Theology. Published by Paternoster Press, Carlisle, UK.

10) Olive Press Quarterly. Published by The Church's Ministry among Jewish People (CMJ), Eagle Lodge, Farnsfield, UK.

11) Tyndale Bulletin. Published by Tyndale House, Cambridge, UK.

12) Shofar: An interdisciplinary Journal of Jewish Studies. Published by Purdue University Press, USA.

13) Journal of Conservative Judaism Published by the Jewish Theological Seminary, New York, USA.

14) Theology. Published by SPCK, London, UK.

15) Lausanne Consultation on Jewish Evangelism Bulletin. Published by LCJE, Lystrup, Denmark.

16) Conference papers from the United Messianic Jewish Congregations, annual conference. San Antonia, USA, 2005.

17) Conference papers from the LCJE International Conference. Lake Balaton, Hungary, 2007.

18) Conference papers from the Messianic Jewish Leaders Borough Park Symposium. New York, USA, 2007. (www.Boroughparksymposim).